THE FLEET
THAT HAD TO DIE

RICHARD HOUGH

Birlinn

This edition published in 2000 by
Birlinn Limited
8 Canongate Venture
5 New Street
Edinburgh
EH8 8BH

www.birlinn.co.uk

ISBN 1 84158 044 9

British Library Cataloguing-in-Publication Data
A catalogue record for this book is available
from the British Library

Printed and bound by
Cox and Wyman Ltd, Reading

CONTENTS

ACKNOWLEDGEMENTS

I am grateful to the Admiralty for the use of their library, and for giving me access to the Royal Navy's Attachés' Reports on the Battle of Tsu-Shima, to the Papers captured from the Russians by the Japanese, the Fleet Orders, etc., of Admiral Rozhestvensky, and pages from the Diary of an officer of the battleship *Sisoy Veliky*.

Acknowledgements are also due to Messrs. John Murray for allowing me to quote from Vladimir Semenoff's *Rasplata: The Reckoning* and *The Battle of Tsu-Shima*, to Messrs. Hodder and Stoughton for allowing me to quote from Nicholas Klado's *The Battle of the Sea of Japan*, and to Messrs. George Allen and Unwin for the use of extracts from *Tsu-Shima* by A. Novikoff-Priboy. Several of the illustrations first appeared in *The Illustrated London News* and are reproduced by permission of the Proprietors.

FOREWORD TO THE 1975 EDITION

Since the first publication of this book seventeen years ago, a number of books on Admiral Rozhestvensky's fateful voyage and closely related subjects have been written, and a list of the most important is listed below.

As to the Russian Navy and the influence of sea power in the world seventy years after the Battle of Tsu-Shima, one might repeat the old cliché, *plus ça change, plus c'est la même chose*. In spite of nuclear fission, intercontinental ballistic missiles, and a host of equally diabolical weaponry, the most determined major military power in the world has invested most strongly in its navy.

From the brave, bedraggled fleet that Rozhestvensky sailed half round the world in 1905, the Soviet Navy today has become the most powerful in the world, and controls bases in every ocean – more than Rozhestvensky could have believed possible as he searched hungrily along the coasts of Africa and Asia for somewhere to rest, refit and replenish his bunkers.

The fleet that had to die in 1905 has indeed risen Phoenix-like from the flames of Tsu-Shima.

Richard Hough, May, 1975

ILLUSTRATIONS

This is the story of a fleet and the admiral who sailed it on one of the most heroic voyages in the history of the sea. The fleet was a collection of forty-two mainly old and all badly-equipped men-of-war; the admiral a frustrated and irascible aristocrat who placed duty to his country and his Emperor above all else.

It is the story of an 18,000-mile Odyssey, a tragi-comedy with a cast of 12,000 sailors, whose spirits and courage rose and fell like the tides of the oceans on which they sailed. For the man who led them, the voyage was a ceaseless struggle against the incompetence and perfidy of his subordinates, the corruption of his superiors, the antagonism and mockery of the world; culminating in the greatest sea battle of modern times. Yet even in the worst moments of agony and despair, neither the admiral nor his fleet could escape the twists of ironical farce which beset them on their voyage to meet the enemy at Tsu-Shima – the Island of the Donkey's Ears.

This book is not primarily concerned with history, though it is a true story set in one of the most wretchedly useless wars ever fought. It is a book about men and ships: men taken from their homes and caught ludicrously unprepared for the rigours of a great journey and a great battle; and ships which should never have gone to sea.

R.H.
November 1957

INTRODUCTION TO THE
BIRLINN EDITION

As the nineteenth century neared its end, the Russian Empire seemed to be reaching one of its cherished goals – a warm weather port on the Pacific. Over the dying Manchu Empire, the great powers fought and squabbled for the spoils, and in that race Russia was at the forefront. She knew she could safely ignore the backward and degenerate Orientals of China and Japan, a Japan that only recently had opened up to the west after the visit of Commander Perry, and, despite rapid change, still seemed sunk in medieval anachronism. She had already seized Sakhalin from Japan and it was the growing Japanese fear of Russia that led Japan into conflict with China in Korea.

In 1891, to show her commitment to the east, the Siberian Railway Project began, involving a huge commitment of Russian resources towards her eastern empire. 1894 saw a Japanese victory over China, drawing her yet further into the morass of Korea. For the first time Russia saw that it was Japan that stood in her way. Mobilising Germany and France, the Russians forced Japanese withdrawal from their war gains – including the strategically crucial Port Arthur. Utterly humiliated, the Japanese invested the indemnity extracted from China as a face-saver for their territorial withdrawal in a modern battlefleet. In 1897 the Russians leased Port Arthur from China, consolidating their position with another new railway through Manchuria, and precipitating a scramble for territory which led to the Boxer Rebellion and the famous Siege of Peking in 1900. British concern over growing Russian power led to an agreement with Japan. The scene was now set.

On 8 April 1902 a Russian agreement with China promised withdrawal from Manchuria. First, the Russians ignored their own treaty, and then forced a series of

completely unwarranted further demands down the throats
of the enfeebled Chinese. Domestic unrest in Korea further
strengthened Russia's hand, and growing troop strength
and commercial deals made it apparent to the Japanese
that Russia had no intention of honouring its treaty
commitments. To a Japan which depended on trade with
China and Korea, its very existence was being threatened:

'We do not want war for it would cost us so much, and
we have nothing to gain even if we win; but by keeping
peace too long we may lose even our national existence.'

In a desperate attempt to resolve the situation the
Japanese effectively offered the Russians a free hand in
Manchuria in exchange for a free hand for themselves
in Korea. There was to be no answer. The Japanese
withdrew their ambassador. Even the notoriously arrogant
and incompetent Russian administration began to suspect
that the Japanese might genuinely mean what they said.
However, the Far East Viceroy, Admiral Alexeiev, assured
them that it was merely bluff. It was just the first of many
miscalculations that the admiral was to make.

On 8 February 1904, Vice-Admiral Oscar Victorovich
Stark, Commander of the Russian Far Eastern Fleet at
Port Arthur, was preparing for a party. As the champagne
flowed on shore, the seven great battleships of the fleet
lay at anchor in the roadsteads outside the harbour. It was
11.50 p.m. when the first torpedoes struck. The *Pallada*
quickly turned turtle, the *Retvizan* was heavily holed
and the *Tsarevitch* crippled. The next morning the main
Japanese battlefleet steamed up to a fleet in chaos and
began bombarding the Russian ships before drawing off as
the return fire became increasingly effective. But, although
the Russian fleet was not destroyed, it was now under an
increasingly effective blockade. Admiral Togo had achieved
his main aim – control of the seas so that the Japanese
armies could be safely transported across to the Korean
coast.

On 8 March Vice-Admiral Makaroff arrived to take over from the unfortunate Stark, and on 12 March came the announcement of the appointment of General Kuropatkin as Land Commander. With the appointment of these two able men, the Russians at last seemed to have woken up to the gravity of the crises. On 10 March Makaroff reacted swiftly and decisively to a Japanese demonstration outside Port Arthur. At the same time the Russians were able to return the *Retvizan* and *Tsarevitch* to active duty. Morale soared and at last the tide seemed to be turning. But, on 13 April, disaster struck the Russians. Turning Makaroff's aggression against him, the Japanese drew him out of harbour over a minefield at high tide. As the rest of the Japanese fleet closed in, Makaroff ordered his battleships back under the cover of the guns of Port Arthur. But this time the tide had dropped exposing the minefield. At 9.43 a.m. the first explosion ripped through the *Petropavlovsk*, Makaroff's flagship, then a second and a third. In one minute, she, her crew, and Russia's finest admiral had disappeared beneath the waves. The Japanese stood quietly on their decks, removing their caps to honour the Russian dead. Six hundred and thirty-five men went down, and with them morale and hope for the Russian fleet. In St. Petersburg the news stirred the growing revolutionary clamour beginning to engulf the Tsarist regime. But the Japanese too were not immune to losses. On 15 May one third of their first line battle fleet – the battleships *Hatsuse* and *Yashima* – sank from Russian mines. It was a comment on the state of Russian morale that no advantage was taken of the catastrophe.

On land, events moved apace: Russian reinforcements were pouring east along the unfinished Transiberian railway and the Japanese had to move fast before the build-up became overwhelming. Kuropatkin knew that the first battle could be decisive. He was one of the few Russians who did not share contempt for the 'yellow monkeys':

'It is very important that they should not gain the consciousness of victory in the opening combat when they will be superior in numbers. This would still further raise their spirits.'

On 1 May 1904 the Russian army was massively defeated on the Yalu River. Although Russian losses only amounted to 2,700 men (two and a half times Japanese losses), a European army had been defeated by an Oriental one, America and Britain began to finance the Japanese war effort, and the bankruptcy of Russian military doctrine had been fully reveal-ad. *The Times* remarked:

'The echoes of the battle will reverberate afar and distant is the day when the story will weary in the telling, among the races of the unforgiving East.'

More immediately, the Russian armies had been split from Port Arthur and forced north into Manchuria. The ensuing months saw a melancholic litany of Russian defeat – Nanshan, Telissu, the approaches to Liaoyang. The purpose and energy on the Japanese side contrasted with the confusion and chaos on the Russian – withdraw until strength was built up (Kuropatkin's favoured view), counterattack (Alexieff's – not a little influenced by the profitable little business side lines that he had built up in the east). Political dictates overwhelmed military realities resulting usually in the wrong choices being made to be executed by commanders who did not believe in them. When one notes that ability was usually only incidental in the appointment of these commanders then all the ingredients for disaster are in place.

On 3 September the next blow against Russian arms fell at the crucial town of Liaoyang. Kuropatkin's behaviour demonstrated all too clearly that he was now mentally broken and overwhelmed, defeated before the battle had even begun. A British military observer, General Sir Ian Hamilton, records:

Such a mad jumble of arms and accoutrements mingled with the bodies of those who so lately bore them, arrested, cut short, in the fury of their assault, and now, for all their terrible menacing attitudes so very, very quiet. How silent, how ghastly; how lonely seemed this charnel house where I, a solitary European, beheld rank upon rank of brave Russians mown down by the embattled ranks of Asia.

By mid June 1904 General Nogi had begun to push against the outer defences of Port Arthur. On 10 August Admiral Witgeft reluctantly determined to follow his orders and take the fleet to Vladivostok. The Battle of Round Island that followed saw the Russians exchanging blow for blow with the Japanese fleet while still breaking loose towards the open sea and Vladivostok. It was then that chance once again took a hand. A 12-inch shell struck the conning tower of the *Tsarevitch* killing Witgeft instantly and throwing the battle line into complete confusion. The Russian fleet turned and fled back to port. It next put to sea as captives of a triumphant Japan. The ensuing months saw the siege steadily tighten round the port. On 5 December 203 Metre Hill fell. Overlooking Port Arthur and the captive fleet its fall spelt doom for the Russian defenders. On 2 January 1905, to the sounds of explosions as the Russians blew their ships and defences up, Port Arthur surrendered. One hundred thousand men had fallen in the course of the siege and many thousands more were captured.

On 20 October an indecisive battle halted a Russian counter-offensive at Sha Ho. It was the largest battle of the war so far, with almost 80,000 casualties, and it sealed the fate of Alexieff as Viceroy. Recalled to St. Petersburg, he vanished from the scene and, free from his malign influence, Kuropatkin was left free to plan his next move. It was to result in the largest battle in human history – the Battle of Mukden. The enormous strength of Russia was now gathering day by day. Kuropatkin was in command of over 300,000 men, with more arriving all the time. The Japanese, on the other hand, could commit a maximum of 250,000 men, including the army from Port Arthur, and were at the very limits of their resources, both of manpower and money. They faced the paradoxical position of winning virtually every engagement yet losing the war. 10 March 1905 saw yet another overwhelming Russian defeat. One hundred thousand Russian troops were killed, captured or simply vanished. While Japan had not managed to utterly destroy the armies ranged against her, they were now mesmerised by the Russian's endless defeat. Kuropatkin was relieved from command and the land campaign petered to a close. *The Times* stated:

> The crowning victory of Mukden was won, first and foremost because the statesmen of Japan had the spirit and the backbone to declare war at their own hour; it was won because Japan was united in the attainment of national aims and shrank from no sacrifice to secure it; because the moral forces within the nation doubled and trebled material strength; because all was prepared, weighed, studied, known; because the shortcomings of the enemy, which were many, were recognised and profited by; because a general staff, framed on the best existing model, was able to direct all forces to a common end; because each soldier and seaman knew and understood the part he had to play, and played it wholeheartedly for his country regardless of his own unimportant fate; and last but not least because the offensive in naval war was the beginning and middle and end of national strategy.

It was into this scene that Rear Admiral Zinovi Petrovich Rozhdestvenski, and the Russian Imperial Baltic fleet were about to sail . . .

Hugh Andrew
July 2000

CHAPTER ONE

The Promotion of the Captain

THE Emperor was due to arrive at ten o'clock, and with
Prussian precision the handsome white-painted yacht
Hohenzollern steamed slowly into Reval roadstead, escorted
by two men-of-war, dead on time. Accompanying the Ger-
man ships were a Russian cruiser and the royal yacht
Shtandart, as immaculately turned-out as their German
guests, and carrying the host, His Excellency Tsar
Nicholas II, his aged uncle Grand Admiral the Duke Alexis
Alexandrovitch, and a massed contingent of senior officers
of the Admiralty.

In silence the six ships steamed past the lines of anchored
Russian ironclads, slowed and dropped anchor for the
climax of the carefully prepared royal reception. The ten
thousand sailors manning their dressed ships from stem to
stern watched for a sign of movement on the *Hohenzollern*;
then with the the passing of the hushed interval that royalty
must observe, distant figures, sparkling with emblems and
decorations, epaulettes and gilded tricornes, were seen
emerging onto the deck of the yacht and descending the
gang-ladder in careful procession. In the wide expanse of
Reval harbour the gentle throb of the imperial pinnace's
engine was the only sound, and its slow progression from
one royal yacht across the water to the other the only
movement.

Kaiser Wilhelm II marched onto the decorated *Shtandart*
at the head of his entourage and made his way step by
stately step up to the bridge, where the consummation came
at last as the German and Russian Emperors clasped hands.

Simultaneously the signal guns pounded out the thirty-one-gun salute, the shots echoing across the bay and filling the harbour with an ever-thickening cloud of black smoke. A weird static naval battle might have been in progress, with every ship paralysed, like floundered tanks in Flanders' mud.

There was little wind and the smoke took time to clear; it was still dispersing, rising slowly above the Isle of Nargen, when the bands began. Above the cheering of the sailors 'Deutschland Uber Alles' was played on the Russian battleships, followed by the Russian national anthem on the German cruisers. By mid-day, the sky had cleared, the sun was shining brightly, and the music was gaily martial. The Tsar and the Kaiser went below for luncheon.

In the afternoon there was to be a three-hour display of gunnery, under the supervision of Captain Zinovi Petrovitch Rohestvensky, who sat at luncheon in the *Shtandart's* wardroom between his Chief of Staff, Commander Clapier de Colongue, and an admiral of the German Navy. He ate and drank well, consuming the seven courses and numerous glasses of wine with obvious relish, talking courteously in hesitant German to the guest, and showing no signs of the weight of the responsibility he was carrying.

July 24th, 1902, was the most important day in the career of Captain Rozhestvensky. Peacetime promotion in the Tsar's navy was slow and dependent on more than competence and an excellent record. If he was ever to clamber into the hierarchy of elderly admirals who gathered around Grand Admiral Alexis Alexandrovitch in the Admiralty at St. Petersburg, some spectacular achievement was called for. The afternoon's gunnery display, the centre-piece of the review designed to demonstrate to the Kaiser and his staff the efficiency of the Imperial Navy, was the great opportunity Rozhestvensky had been waiting for.

For weeks this fiery, irascible officer had been putting the Baltic Fleet's gunners through a severe course of training, forcing them to a higher standard of speed and precision than they had ever reached before. For 'Boyavin' (the lord) Rozhestvensky was fifty-three years old, and time was running out. The quality of Russian naval gunnery had shaped Rozhestvensky's career. The eyes of his gunlayers, the accuracy of rangefinders and sights, the quality of rifling and shells, above all the results of his ruthless training methods, had brought him promotion and the decorations he wore at the Tsar's table at luncheon on the *Shtandart*. Rozhestvensky had invested his life in the high-explosive projectile; and his last years were to resemble the trajectory of a twelve-inch naval shell as it curves towards its point of detonation.

Guns were Rozhestvensky's passion as a boy, and when he entered the Marine Corps as a seventeen-year-old cadet he specialized in the gunnery branch. At the Artillery Academy he passed his examinations with special distinction, and four years later, as a full lieutenant, he was using live ammunition against the Turks. The Turkish war revealed his reckless bravery and skill as a gunnery officer, but it was not only Rozhestvensky's complete disregard for the enemy's gunfire that might have ended his career, for the stupidity of his captain nearly brought them both before a court-martial.

The *Vesta*, in which Rozhestvensky served as second-in-command, was a small armed steamer that had been doing well against Turkish shipping until it chanced on an enemy ironclad many times its size and power. Captain Baranoff, acting with neither discretion nor valour, turned his ship about, made off at full speed, and later reported that he had sunk the battleship. Fame and decorations followed, and the *Vesta* became a legend in the Black Sea Fleet. But her gunnery officer was left in a state of acute embarrassment and uncertainty. For months Rozhestvensky nursed his guilty secret, and only when the war was over and the Turkish Admiral Hobart Pasha had revealed the falsity of the Russian version of the engagement in a letter to the newspaper *Novoe Vremya*, did he have to face the first great crisis of his career.

It was a delicate position, demanding tact and diplomacy, qualities which Rozhestvensky did not even recognize. Without consulting Baranoff, he wrote a letter to the paper confirming Hobart Pasha's claim, attempting to justify neither Baranoff nor himself. By a miracle the bull got through the china shop unscathed: Baranoff was sacked; Rozhestvensky survived the crisis and was actually promoted.

The reorganization of the gunnery branch of the Bulgarian Navy, an odd and, one would imagine, a thankless task, occupied him for a short time, and in 1885 he was appointed Naval Attaché in London. He did not care much either for London or the British, but acquired a grudging respect for the Royal Navy's gunnery, which was unquestionably the best in the world, and appears himself to have been liked and respected. He was tall, good-looking, well-mannered, and well-bred. That he was obviously efficient and knew his job was less important. He was a captain by 1894 and commanded Admiral Alexieff's flagship in the Far East during the war between China and Japan, seeing there ample evidence of Japan's strength and purpose at sea, before returning to St. Petersburg as Commander of the Baltic Fleet's gunnery practice squadron.

If this was not quite demotion, it was certainly not the promotion he had expected, and the inner councils of the St. Petersburg Admiralty seemed as distant as ever. It was not Rozhestvensky's highly-strung temperament, nor his irritability, and certainly not the occasional tyrannous treatment he meted out to his men that was holding him back. Nor would he have reached as far as this had he not been an aristocrat. Rozhestvensky's trouble was that he had no relatives in the right place to help him, and it was almost impossible to break into the inner clique of the

Higher Naval Board without the assistance either of log-rolling or of some spectacular achievement.

Luncheon was over by three o'clock. The officers of the Baltic Fleet changed into more business-like service dress, the Kaiser into the uniform of a Russian Admiral, Tsar Nicholas into that of an Admiral of the German Navy. Everybody on the *Shtandart* was getting on well after the prolonged banquet, and was looking forward to Rozhestvensky's afternoon performance. The two Emperors, Prince Henry Frederick, Grand Admiral Alexis, von Tirpitz, the German Minister of Marine, and their assembled staffs and suites left the yacht and proceeded to sea on the bridge of the cruiser *Minin*. In the centre of the group, appearing calm and completely self-confident, stood Rozhestvensky, a fine, erect figure, apart from his Chief of Staff the only officer below admiral's rank present. This was his show.

The selected battleships, cruisers and torpedo-boats opened their well-rehearsed manœuvres, timing their fire perfectly, first at fixed targets on Carlos Island, and then, at the end of the three-hour demonstration, on targets towed at speed by torpedo-boats. The shooting was steady, regular and astonishingly accurate. Rozhestvensky gave no sign of his satisfaction, occasionally issuing orders to increase the rate of fire. Only once was there any evidence of the strain and responsibility he was bearing. A torpedo-boat lost station momentarily, and he turned, shouted impatiently at Clapier de Colongue, throwing his arms wide and sending his binoculars sailing overboard. His Chief of Staff at once passed him his own pair; it was not the first time this had happened.

As the targets crumpled one after the other, the Kaiser did not attempt to conceal his admiration; this was efficient even by German standards. 'I wish I had such splendid admirals as your Captain Rozhestvensky in my fleet,' was his comment to the Tsar, pointedly within hearing of von Tirpitz. That autumn Rozhestvensky was promoted Chief of Naval Staff with the rank of Rear-Admiral, and appointed aide-de-camp to the Tsar.

'If only we could fight now, Sire,' the Tsar had regretfully responded to Kaiser Wilhelm II's words of commendation at the conclusion of Rozhestvensky's gunnery display. Two years later the Russian appetite for battle had been satiated in a series of defeats in the Far East; her armies had been driven back across Korea, her navy humiliated.

Russian power had been challenged by the precocious nationalism of a state that was barely fifty years old, and against everyone's predictions, had come off very badly. The Sino-Japanese war had demonstrated Japan's astonishing grasp of modern warfare, and the Treaty of Shimonoseki in 1895 had left her with treaty rights in Southern Manchuria, the Liao-Tung Peninsula, and the important harbour of Port Arthur.

To the Japanese, Port Arthur was more than a key base and the most northerly ice-free port on the mainland of Asia. Taken by bloody banzai storm at prodigious cost, it was a symbol of the Japanese soldiers' bravery and the nation's new independence. Port Arthur was Japan's Yorktown; but within two years Russian pressure, reinforced by Germany and France, had forced her out, and by 1897 it was firmly in Russian hands. Russia's conception of a balance of power in the Far East did not countenance the upsetting influence of this youthful country, and she shut her ears to the lusty, aggressive sounds from across the Yellow Sea. Both Manchuria and Korea were rich in natural resources, and it was intolerable that any country but Russia should develop them. But Japanese complaints and pressure became so strong that some empty gesture was finally called for, and in April 1902 Russia reached an agreement with China for the evacuation of Manchuria by stages. The promise meant nothing, Japanese protests were ignored, and Russia embarked on a policy of deliberate provocation. Admiral Alexieff was responsible for effecting this policy. As Far-Eastern viceroy and supreme commander, this pompous, stupid and short-sighted nobleman regarded the Japanese as insignificant vermin who must be destroyed; and he had no doubt that the process of extermination would be swift.

If Russia could rely on the backing of Germany, Japan had her defensive alliance with Britain, and the moral support of the United States. Not that the Mikado and his military and naval chiefs felt the need for encouragement and sympathy. Japan had already developed that condition of boundless self-confidence which was to persist right up to the Battle of Midway forty years later. All she wanted was a little time, to train her new army and order warships from European and American yards. Her diplomats provided this, and when the time came to strike, they worked together with the military leaders with the same wily, minutely-timed close co-ordination that they employed in November and December 1941.

There is an astonishing similarity between the Port Arthur attack in 1904 and that on Pearl Harbour. Relations between Japan and Russia had been in a state of high tension for a long time, but neither Russia nor the rest of the world was aware that a crisis point had been reached when Admiral Togo, lurking at the naval base of Sasebo with his powerful and highly trained fleet, was informed secretly on the night of the 5th of February that relations would be broken off in St. Petersburg on the next afternoon. Togo at once ordered all commanders to his flagship, the *Mikasa*.

When the officers filed quietly into their C.-in-C.'s cabin, they knew a decision for war had been reached. On a table in the centre of the cabin, resting on an unlacquered ceremonial tray, lay an unsheathed sambo, the short sword used by the Samurai in the past for the rite of seppuku. In a tense atmosphere, Togo pronounced the solemn words of confirmation, 'We sail tomorrow, and our enemy flies the Russian flag.' The Mikado's command to vanquish the Tsar's fleet followed, and then the conference got down to business. Togo had had his orders weeks ago, and the plan had been worked out to the last detail. The supremely efficient Japanese spy organization knew not only the precise disposition of the Russian squadrons at Vladivostock and Port Arthur, but were able to report to Tokio every change of berth of every vessel. Togo possessed as clear a picture of Port Arthur harbour and roadstead as if reconnaissance planes had just returned with high-level photographs.

The briefing was precise and business-like and few questions were necessary. As the commanders returned to their ships, a sense of excitement spread through the fleet, which reached a climax when the destroyer and torpedo-boat flotillas cleared the harbour through rising mist at dawn. At Pearl Harbour, 350 planes from six aircraft carriers formed the spearhead of the attack; for his first quick stab against an equally unprepared enemy, Admiral Togo was relying on the new Whitehead torpedo, and at half-past ten on the evening of the 8th of February, the low, sleek little boats went in.

'Show yourselves worthy of the confidence I place in you,' Togo had told his destroyer and torpedo-boat commanders; and they did. The lights of the town were glowing innocently, the battleships and cruisers, lit from stem to stern, were at anchor in a neat row outside the harbour. The shore batteries were unmanned, nearly all the officers were in the town. The ships' only defence was their few manned light guns, and their torpedo nets. But by the simple ruse of using Russian signals, the Japanese were at a range of a few hundred yards before they were recognized, and their first attack was delivered without any opposition.

Within a few hectic minutes, two of Russia's best battle-ships and a cruiser were crippled by nine torpedoes carry-ing a special net-cutting device; and the next day, in a long-range bombardment, Togo severely damaged four more ships. For the price of six lives, he had reversed the balance of naval power in the East as effectively as Yama-moto was to reverse it in 1941, and had gained a moral advantage for his fleet far more profound than his succes-sor ever achieved over the United States.

For the next fifteen months, Togo followed a cautious policy of containment. He was not often given the choice of accepting or refusing battle, for the Russians seldom emerged from the safety of their bases. When he met them at sea, he was content to disengage as soon as he had caused sufficient damage to the enemy to ensure continued moral supremacy, and because the Russians were usually fleeing, this was not difficult. At Chemulpo, at the battles of August 10th and August 14th, 1904, and in numerous minor engagements, Togo succeeded in further whittling down the power of Russia's Far Eastern fleet, and also in killing several of her admirals. It was a policy that demanded skill, patience and the severest disciplinary con-trol over his eager commanders. But it was the right policy. The continuance of the war in Manchuria and Korea, and Japan's very life, depended on her navy; it was her most precious possession, and while she continued to com-mand the seas, it was folly to risk it.

Japan had no sizeable shipyards to replace lost vessels, no reserves to draw on, and every ship was committed to the struggle. But in the Baltic, Russia possessed an idle fleet of more than a hundred ships, and fitting out in her dockyards were four powerful battleships of the most modern type, the backbone of a new fleet numerically equal to anything Togo could muster, and when combined with Russia's Port Arthur and Vladivostock squadrons, crushingly superior. In May 1904, Japan had suffered a

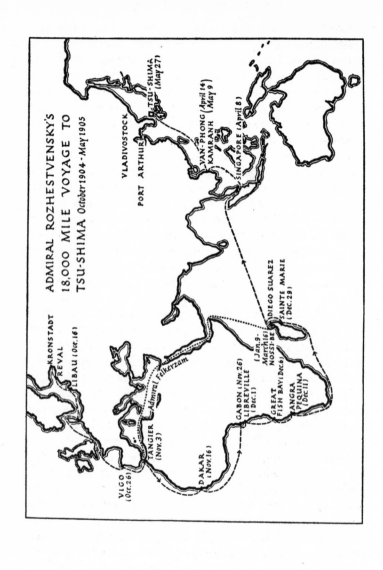

ADMIRAL ROZHESTVENSKY'S
18,000 MILE VOYAGE TO
TSU-SHIMA October 1904 - May 1905

KRONSTADT
REVAL
LIBAU (Oct. 16)

VIGO
(Oct. 26)

TANGIER
(Nov. 3)

Admiral Felkerzam

DAKAR
(Nov. 16)

GABON (Nov. 26)
LIBREVILLE
(Dec. 11)

GREAT
FISH BAY (Dec. 6)

ANGRA
PEQUINA
(Dec. 11)

NOSSI-BE
(Jan. 9 -
March 16)

DIEGO SUAREZ
SAINTE MARIE
(Dec. 29)

VLADIVOSTOCK

PORT ARTHUR

TSU-SHIMA
(May 27)

VAN-PHONG (April 14)
KAMRANH (May 9)

SINGAPORE (April 8)

catastrophe that could have cost her the war, a double misfortune that her C.-in-C., with his fleet almost constantly at sea, had feared above anything else. On one day the battleships *Hatsuse* and *Yashima* were both sunk by mines while on blockade duty, and Japan found her first line of attack reduced by a third. It was now more than ever vital that the army should capture Port Arthur, destroy the powerful squadron there before the arrival of reinforcements, and deprive Russia of her most powerful naval base in the Far East. Togo knew that only the delayed completion of the four great battleships had prevented the armada from sailing at the outbreak of hostilities, and at Sasebo he and his staff followed anxiously the reports of the progress of their fitting-out.

By October the whole world knew that the four ironclads were at the Baltic base of Libau, ready to sail, and speculation about their size and power began to grow.

The *Kniaz Suvoroff* was to be the flagship of the Second Pacific Squadron, which was to raise the siege of Port Arthur, avenge the humiliations Alexieff had suffered, and 'wipe the infidels off the face of the earth' as Tsar Nicholas had commanded. Her identical and equally powerful sister ships were the *Borodino*, *Alexander III* and *Oryol*. As originally laid down, the *Suvoroff* was to have been of 13,500 tons, but in course of construction her displacement had been increased to well over 15,000 tons. She was an imposing looking vessel, with twin smokestacks close together amidships, separating the superstructures with their delicate fire control mechanisms, rangefinders and searchlight platforms. On the fore deck and aft was the main armament, heavily protected turrets each carrying two great twelve-inch guns capable of hurling over ten miles, by a nitro-cellulose propellant, a high-explosive shell weighing a third of a ton. Incorporated in the bow was her sharp-pointed ram, still retained by all ironclads at the turn of the century for the *coup de grâce* in a close action. Abaft the fore superstructure, amidships and below the mizzen mast in pairs on each beam were the twelve forty-five calibre six-inch guns. Twelve- and six-pounder weapons, on battery deck, on bridge wings and platforms, in combination with the new electric searchlights, provided the defensive armament against the battleship's greatest enemy, the torpedo-boat. Strips of ten-inch Harveyed steel, each weighing as much as a destroyer, protected the ship's waterline, and there was four-inch armour on the decks, fourteen-inch on the vital barbettes, and heavy steel canopies on conning-tower and lower fighting position.

The *Suvoroff's* 16,300 horsepower engines gave her a top speed of over eighteen knots. Her hull from stem to stern, her towering superstructures, her masts and boats, all were painted black; only the tall twin funnels amidships, of brilliant lemon yellow black-banded at the top, contrasted with the dour purposefulness of the rest of the ship.

Her name was heavily embossed in gold letters at bows and stern: *Kniaz Suvoroff*, after that great eighteenth-century Russian fighter and patriot who had quelled insurrections and fought ruthlessly against Frenchmen, Turks and Cossacks. It was a name rich in bloody tradition; and in the epic voyage that lay ahead of her, she was to carry the flag of Admiral Zinovy Petrovitch Rozhestvensky.

CHAPTER TWO

Preparations for Departure

I T was not until June 1904, with the war in the Far East
four months old, that the decision to dispatch naval reinforcements was reached in St. Petersburg. Everyone had
confidently expected hostilities to be over within weeks;
instead, the German-trained Japanese troops had advanced
with astonishing rapidity into Korea, and by April 20th
were along the banks of the Yalu.

Japan had timed the land campaign nicely. On the
morning after the Port Arthur attack, Togo's cruisers had
escorted the first seven battalions of infantry across the
narrow strip of sea, and the Mikado's eager, devoted army
began their assault against an enemy whose front extended
over nine hundred miles of rough, mountainous country,
frozen hard in the winter and deep in mud in the rainy
season. Russian reinforcements had to travel over six
thousand miles of the jerry-built Trans-Siberian railway,
and because the permanent way round Lake Baikal was not
even completed, and ice prohibited the use of ships, a
hundred-mile route-march further delayed them.

If Kuropatkin, the Russian C.-in-C., had been allowed to
form his own policy and use his natural initiative, he might
have survived the sharp, widely-scattered Japanese attacks.
But neither Alexieff nor the army council in St. Petersburg
would countenance a strategic withdrawal or a shortening
of the front to permit a concentration of the defences. No
soldier of the Tsar was to give ground before a half-
civilized heathen. Consequently, minor units were wiped
up one after the other, fighting a clumsy, unimaginative,

stubborn defence, and lacking the leadership and initiative to counter-attack.

By May 14th Port Arthur was cut off from the outside world, and the Japanese began the assault on the town with a series of bloody suicide attacks. At sea, Togo patrolled up and down like a tiger hovering over its victim and making spasmodic stabs with its paws. For Russia the relief of Port Arthur and the reinforcement of the Pacific Fleet had suddenly become terribly urgent.

On June 20th the Tsar convened and presided over a meeting of the Higher Naval Board, represented by that decaying, ineffectual old nobleman, the Grand Admiral Alexis, the Minister of Marine, Admiral Avellan, Admirals Niloff, Wirenius and Dibassof, the Chief of Defence in the Baltic, Admiral Birilioff—a jolly, wily wag who was regarded by many as the Russian Navy's most proficient administrator—and Admiral Rozhestvensky. The Tsar, Alexis and Birilioff had between them already selected their Commander-in-Chief: Rozhestvensky had had experience in action in Black Sea and Eastern waters, his determination and powers of organization were a by-word in the Admiralty, he was known to be a severe disciplinarian, he was the most experienced gunnery officer in the navy —and the Tsar had taken a fancy to him.

Rozhestvensky was a glutton for responsibility. Any new burden to be carried in the name of the Tsar, the Empire and the Navy was eagerly received onto those broad shoulders. To Rozhestvensky, efficient completion of a duty—any duty, regardless of size and possible consequences—was almost a passion, and he accepted with fervour the greatest commission his country had to offer.

For three months Rozhestvensky devoted himself wholly to the task of preparing the armada, working with a passionate intensity, sustained by his great physical strength and his 'nerves of hardened steel'. Eighteen hours a day was normal; sometimes he went for three nights without sleep, issuing directives, organizing the victualling, the supplies of ammunition of all calibres, the torpedoes and mines, the personnel. Making use of his intimate know-ledge of the elaborate and graft-ridden stores and pur-chasing departments of his service, he slashed angrily through thick webs of red tape; he sacked and promoted, demanded, was refused, and obtained in record time, count-less essentials for his ships. He became a one-man power station, and the most unpopular officer in St. Petersburg.

In simple terms, it was his task to prepare a fleet of over forty vessels, with auxiliaries, supply, repair and hos-pital ships; to transport this fleet over a distance of eighteen thousand miles; and after linking up with the besieged but potentially powerful squadron at Port Arthur, to destroy the enemy. It was a commission without prece-dent, a prodigious undertaking even with a well-equipped fleet manned by experienced officers and men, provided with regular supply bases and a secure anchorage at its destination. To anyone but Rozhestvensky it would have seemed utterly impossible.

'We shall sail on July 15th,' Rozhestvensky announced at an interview he gave to the St. Petersburg correspon-dent of the *Petit Parisien*. For the Far East of course? 'Final directives have not been issued,' the Admiral told him cagily. 'But of course that is a long voyage taking many weeks, and there will be nothing for me to do in the Far East by September. The Japanese will have capitulated long before then.'

By the end of September, in spite of announcements in every European paper that the Second Pacific Squadron had sailed, Rozhestvensky was ordering that those of his ships that were ready (and many of them were not) must carry out a prolonged course of manœuvres and target practice in the Baltic; while off Korea, the Imperial Navy had lost two more battleships, several cruisers and two successive Commanders-in-Chief in action.

In the summer of 1904, when news of Rozhestvensky's departure was daily expected, and frequently prematurely announced, many naval statisticians and correspondents were busy adding up the fire power, tonnage, speed, protection and seaworthiness of the respective fleets. Statistics showed that with the all-important twelve-inch and ten-inch guns, the Russians were likely to have a clear superiority, that there was little disparity between the respective secondary armaments; and, of course, Togo, whose battleship had been constantly at sea, in action and sometimes damaged, had nothing to match against the *Suvoroff* and her sister ships.

As usual, simple arithmetic did not mean a thing. In its organization and administration the Russian Admiralty was ponderous, bureaucratic and inefficient, a giant, rusting, Heath Robinson affair oiled by bribery. The ships were built in Russian naval yards in a haphazard, leisurely manner, often taking five or six years to fit out after launching, to designs based loosely on British practice, and fitted with guns and armour that were already outdated. The sailors, recruited in peacetime largely from the peasant class and limited to six months' sea-going training a year because of ice in the Baltic, possessed none of the mechanical aptitude of the British, American, German or French bluejackets; and since the departure of sail, science had become as important as seamanship. No amount of fierce and sometimes cruel discipline could make up for their lack of fighting tradition. At Victoria's Diamond Jubilee review the British tar found his Russian opposite 'odorous, rough, coarse, but a happy lot'. These seamen were mostly out in the Far East at the start of the war; in their place, to man the old ships taken out of storage and the new ones fitting out, Rozhestvensky had to depend largely on low-caste conscripts and reservists, or transferred merchant seamen without naval experience. 'One half have to be taught everything,' a gunnery lieutenant on the *Suvoroff* complained before they sailed, 'because they know nothing, the other half because they have forgotten everything; but if they do remember anything, then it is obsolete.'

Not until it was too late was it discovered that a substantial proportion of each half were revolutionaries, 'slackers and dangerous elements' whose chief interest was to ensure that the great expedition was a debacle. 'If we gained a victory over the Japanese', one of them wrote, 'we should hinder the revolution, which was the only hope of the country.' To a lesser degree a Marxist element was also evident in the wardrooms, as the paymaster steward of the *Oryol* recounted in his reference to the crippled engineer officer Vasilieff ('my main thought was that the navy might become a leading factor in the struggle against autocracy'), the owner of a large library of subversive literature which was lent out freely to the bluejackets.

It was Vasilieff's ship which was almost destroyed by fire when she was on the stocks and almost sank when she was launched. In dock her hawsers somehow parted and the rivet holes opened up simultaneously so that she settled on her side at thirty degrees. On her trials scrap steel found its way into her cylinders, and she succeeded in grounding when she was ready at last to leave Kronstadt.

Rozhestvensky's men had no illusions about their ships. 'Our wiseacres pretend that by multiplication of the guns, shells, personnel, the speed, etc., a battle coefficient of the squadron is obtained which is not much lower than Togo's,' commented the *Suvoroff's* navigating officer to one of the Admiral's Staff as they were clearing harbour. 'But this is simply nothing but a fraud—an infamous fraud.'

Never before, in the whole annals of naval warfare, had a Commander-in-Chief sailed forth on such a long, such a dangerous and difficult mission with such an ill-assorted selection of vessels. On paper the new battleships could have been formidable. What was not generally known was that during their long and chequered period of construction, their designers had been prevailed upon to add more and more weight above the waterline in the form of officers' accommodation and comforts, which were taken seriously in the Russian Navy, and additional armoured protection. To a Russian designer, perfection was only achieved by afterthought. With the *Suvoroff* class this resulted in an alarming top-heaviness which meant that the lower secondary armament could not be used in any sort of a sea, and that all but two feet of the main belt of armour plate was submerged when they were normally loaded. This affected not only their speed, but also their stability, and the danger of their capsizing was so grave that Rozhestvensky received a signal a few days after he had left ordering him to strip unnecessary weight from decks and superstructure, even to the extent of avoiding hoisting all but essential signals from the yards. Bunting was to be regarded as *de trop*.

At Queen Victoria's Jubilee review, Russian officers had seen the new electric firing mechanism adopted by the Royal Navy, and every first-class navy but the Russian then used telescopic sights. But seven years later, even the *Suvoroff* and her sister ships sailed fitted with the uncertain and non-instantaneous lanyard method of firing, and *en route* dockyard workers were still cutting holes in their turrets for telescopic sights. To the gun crews, it seemed, these were objects of curiosity only, until the enemy was met, for practice ammunition was not to be carried.

To support the backbone of the ironclads in the line of battle, Rozhestvensky had three older, slower and less heavily armed and armoured battleships. The *Oslyabya*, named after a gallant monk who had distinguished himself fighting in armour over his habit in the Battle of the Don in 1380, was the least ineffective, and was to fly the flag of the commander of the second division. Some strange whim of the design staff had resulted in her carrying ten-inch main armament, reinforced by a vast number of smaller weapons scattered in ports along her towering sides.

With the *Oslyabya* in the second division were two very slow old ironclads of around 10,000 tons each, armed with obsolete guns, the *Sisoy Veliky* and *Navarin*. The *Sisoy* could barely manage twelve knots under favourable conditions; the *Navarin*, which was never intended for anything more serious than coastal defence work, looked rather like the *Monitor*, which had fought the *Merrimac* so indecisively forty years before, and sported no less than four funnels in pairs side by side amidships. But these were not Rozhestvensky's oldest ships. The design of the armoured cruiser *Dmitri Donskoy* dated back to the 'seventies, and she had in fact originally been commissioned as an armoured frigate, rigged for sails, and had only recently been modernized. Funnels seemed out of place on her high, flat maindeck, and her engines gave her a speed only a little above ten knots. The *Svetlana*, 'half cruiser, half yacht, a caprice of our luckless naval designers', was good for her twenty knots, but for little else; and the only vessels which could be formed into a homogeneous fighting unit (though they never were) were the modern, fast cruisers *Oleg*, *Aurora*, *Zhemchug* and *Izumrud*, and the nine minute torpedo-boat destroyers of 350 tons each, which were to roll and pitch their way half round the world.

If the Admiralty had had its way, more ancient, rusting old tubs, which had not been to sea for a dozen years, would have been inflicted on Rozhestvensky; only after the strongest pressure would the Higher Naval Board agree that he should leave them behind.

Supporting the battle fleet was a host of auxiliary craft— transports, armed merchantmen, a water condensing vessel, tugboats and a hospital ship—among which was the *Kamchatka*, a sort of floating workshop carrying jigs, lathes and spare equipment of all kinds. The *Kamchatka* was to acquire distinction as the squadron buffoon, her captain having a predilection for making hilarious misjudgements and for always being in the wrong place at the wrong time.

In all there were forty-two ships in Rozhestvensky's armada, and towering above his many other problems of organization and preparation was that of providing coal for them. At their most economical cruising speed the ships would consume over three thousand tons daily; at full speed this would increase to ten thousand tons. Even in harbour, heating, lighting, the auxiliaries, etc., would consume over five hundred tons. Coal was the ultimate problem. For months this dirty, black mineral was to govern the Admiral's thoughts, calculations and strategy. Coal haunted him on the voyage from the time he awoke to the sight of yellow funnels forever belching great trails into the morning sky and received the regular consumption and bunker reports from his ships, to the time he left the bridge—usually long after nightfall—when darkness hid the black cloud that marked their progress. Coal and coaling were twin nightmarish figures that made the feeding of ten thousand men seem a simple matter of logistics.

Until the arrival of oil-burning engines, coal was the governing factor in the policy and disposition of every navy in the world. Coal was heavy, extravagant and space-consuming. For nations like Britain, with widely scattered interests to protect, the only answer was to build up numerous coaling stations all over the world, and this she had done with much care and labour.

But Russia was without a single base along the entire length of Rozhestvensky's route. The battleship *Asahi* had consumed 5,700 tons of good Cardiff coal on her voyage out from her British yard to Japan in 1902, and British-built armoured-cruisers had eaten up an average of 4,000 tons each. Where was the 500,000 tons Rozhestvensky would need to come from? And how was it to be supplied?

This was what he and his Staff, and the Admiralty authorities in St. Petersburg, had to resolve in the weeks before they sailed.

Neutral ports, by international law, were almost certain to be closed to them; they would get no change out of the British, who were devoted to the cause of the Mikado; useful German bases hardly existed on the squadron's route; only their friends, the French, might possibly show a trace of sympathy, but they would be susceptible to the tides of battle in the Far East. 'The immense distance', wrote *Novoe Vremya*, 'must be traversed without any assistance in face of the markedly unfriendly attitude of neutral powers. Couldn't the Dutch government cede us one of the many islands off Sunda or Molucca archipelago?' was their *cri de cœur*. It was equally likely that Togo would turn tail and fly at the sight of Rozhestvensky's fleet.

There was only one solution, which in itself raised so many monumental complications that foreign naval authorities ruled it out as impractical, and that was to acquire another equally large fleet of colliers and coal at sea. Coaling at sea, an exhausting operation even in a flat calm, had been resorted to by most navies in emergencies or under exceptional circumstances. But to coal forty ships, perhaps thirty or forty times, in unpredictable weather outside the three-mile limit! Sage old salts in the British Admiralty shook their heads in disbelief. The man was mad—but then what could you expect from those wild Russians?

For it was soon common knowledge that St. Petersburg had entered into a contract with the German Hamburg-Amerika line to supply the entire armada from some sixty colliers from Libau in the Baltic to Port Arthur in the Yellow Sea. Rozhestvensky was to insinuate his way into neutral ports as and when he could; when this was impossible, the coal was to be shipped, sack by sack, ton by ton, from colliers to warships hove-to on the ocean, and to be

deposited from Russian sailors' backs into the bunkers—
five hundred thousand tons of it.

Towards the end of August 1904, Rozhestvensky had
succeeded in gathering together sufficient warships, new
and refitted, to board the *Kniaz Suvoroff* in Kronstadt roadstead and formally assume command of the Second Pacific
Squadron. 'Safe voyage and success against the enemy',
Admiral Birilioff at once signalled. The C.-in-C. gratefully
acknowledged the farewell message, though it was some
seven weeks premature, and went to sea to shake down
his crews, practise some of the more elementary manœuvres
and carry out target practice with the six-inch and twelve-
pounder weapons.

The results of this brief little cruise were not encouraging. 'We did not make a single strike', reported one of the
gunnery officers frankly, a regular who had taken part in
Rozhestvensky's triumphant display before the Tsar and
the Kaiser two years before, and the *Suvoroff's* navigating
officer was in equal despair. 'Moving in close formations,
keeping station—let us hope we shall learn all this during
our long voyage', he tried to console himself. 'But battle
exercises, execution of different tactical plans—that is a
matter of years of preparation.' There were just two weeks
of intensive drill that included night firing, mine-laying
and torpedo-firing, interrupted by frequent engine-room
breakdowns, while one by one as they were pronounced
ready for active service, the light cruisers, the armoured
cruisers, the destroyers and the old ironclads joined up
with the squadron.

Off Reval in the early hours at the beginning of September, Rozhestvensky sprang a surprise alarm. His order
number 69 the following morning tells the story. 'Today
at 2 a.m. I instructed the officer-of-the-watch to issue the
signal for defence against a torpedo attack. Eight minutes
afterwards there was no sign of anyone taking up his

station. All officers and men were sound asleep. And when at last a few hands of the watch did appear, what did they do? Nothing. It seemed that they did not know where to go, nor was there a single searchlight ready for use.'

One hundred orders were posted during those last weeks, and few of them were less discouraging than number 69. But the squadron's departure could be delayed no longer, and back at Kronstadt the ships anchored and began to take on supplies. For day after day the harbour was alive with lighters and pinnaces and small boats of all kinds, while the warships' holds and magazines swallowed the vast stores of salt meat barrels and biscuit boxes, dried vegetables (for the sailors' staple soup diet), tins of butter, salt and preserves, hundreds of crates of vodka and champagne for the officers, ammunition from rifle bullets to twelve-inch shells, torpedoes and mines and engine-room spares.

On a hazy, still afternoon, with the harbour cleared at last of the launch-loads of wives and children and relatives, anchors were weighed, and the four *Suvoroff* class battleships were towed out to the roadstead by eight tugs. They were so heavily overloaded that their lower decks were almost awash, and they had assumed the rakish appearance of coastal monitors. The flagship, the *Borodino* and the *Alexander III* survived the dangerous shoals and were soon proceeding under their own steam into the Gulf of Finland.

The *Oryol*, which was drawing nearly twenty-nine feet and had neglected to take soundings, was less fortunate, and the great vessel came to rest on a sandbank. The incident spoilt the majesty of the fleet's departure, and greatly embarrassed the ironclad's commander, Captain Yung. Admiral Birilioff, still in full dress uniform, hastened to the spot in a steam pinnace and took over the salvage operations personally, directing the tugs in one direction and then in another, while the entire ship's complement of nine hundred men ran with shouts of mixed mockery and enthusiasm to and fro across the main deck in an attempt to rock her 16,000 tons off the mud. 'Take care, lads,' they shouted to one another. 'We may capsize the old tub if we don't look out!'

The next morning she was still there, and only twenty-four hours later had three dredgers cleared a deep enough passage for the ironclad. The *Oryol* hastened off in pursuit of her sister ships.

The official send-off was to take place at Reval, where the men-of-war and their attendants foregathered at the end of the first week in October. The nation had been whipped up into a state of great enthusiasm for the fleet that was to reverse their misfortunes in battle, and Rozhestvensky had become a national hero weeks before he sailed on his first command. To the Tsar and many of his subjects, his mission was regarded as a religious expedition, its leader as a crusader armed with the cross in one hand, a sword in the other.

'The Empress', ran Fleet Bulletin No. 32, 'has given official intimation that she intends to present ships which have a chapel with a chalice of her own workmanship. This is because their Most Gracious Majesties know that in their inmost hearts all men of the fleet, both high and low, are but awaiting the time when they may effectually do their duty to God and to our country.' And 'Holy Water is to be sprinkled by priests as a blessing on guns and decks before the enemy is engaged', was an instruction included among the Fleet Orders.

The Second Pacific Squadron was the panacea for the destruction of Eastern infidelism and the raising of Russia's fallen morale, and its departure was to be honoured with a full ceremonial review by the Tsar and Tsarina. On the 7th of October the sprucing-up work began. 'A fury of cleaning and polishing took possession of the ship', wrote Novikoff-Priboy. 'Again and again we washed the gang-

ways with soap and water; we scrubbed the bridges;
touched up the paint; scoured the brasswork. Engines and
stokeholes were not forgotten, though it was most unlikely
that the visitors' exalted feet would tread the narrow
ladders giving access to the bowls of the ironclad. . . .
Cleanliness became a mania.'

The morning of the 9th was cool and blustery, with sharp
squally showers and sun patches following each other in
succession across the harbour, and the wind flecking white
the wave-tops and flicking the pennants and bunting on
every ship with sharp cracks.

At nine o'clock Admiral Zinovy Petrovitch Rozhestvensky, in full dress uniform, decorated with the Crosses
of St. George and St. Vladimir, the scarlet ribbon of the
Order of St. Anne and the silver cords of a Staff Officer,
stood on the chilly arrival platform at the Baltic Railway
Station and watched the Royal Train draw in and grind to
a halt.

At attention by Rozhestvensky's side stood his second-
in-command, Admiral von Felkerzam, short, obese, beard-
less and with a tiny mouth 'as round as the opening of a
thimble'; and the commander of the cruiser division,
Admiral Enkvist, whose flowing white beard, the most
luxuriant in the Imperial Navy, was his great pride. Both
appeared dwarfed—even comically dwarfed—beside their
C.-in-C.

As he stepped down from his carriage onto the carpet,
the Tsarina at his side, the Tsar could hardly fail to be
impressed by the bearing, air of distinction and rock-like
authority of his Commander-in-Chief, if not by his subordinates. The comparison with his mother's brother-in-law,
the King of England, the senior by seven years, would not
have occurred to Nicholas, but the tall Admiral with the
piercing black eyes, prominent, straight nose and neat
pepper-and-salt beard suggested a more stalwart, decisive
and erect Edward VII taking the salute at a Spithead re-

view. Rozhestvensky was a figure to restore confidence in his service, to avenge the humiliations in Asia, and to bring to their knees his country's enemies who were disputing Russian aspirations in the Far East. Uncle Alexis had chosen well.

After a brief conversation, the distinguished party, now joined by Grand Admiral Alexis, Admiral Avellan, the Minister of Marine, Admiral Birilioff and the other members of the Higher Naval Board, left for the harbour. Among them, on unusually familiar terms with these senior officers, was a certain Captain Nicholas Klado, a gregarious, sharp-faced, sharp-witted member of Rozhestvensky's Staff, whose intrigues were to influence the whole course of the fleet's voyage.

There was a brief conference in the lavishly decorated wardroom of the *Suvoroff*, at which Alexis explained to his nephew some of the intricacies of the vast organization required to gather together and prepare for sea a fleet of this size for an eighteen-thousand-mile journey to destroy his Majesty's enemies, successfully justified the six-months' delay in its departure, and finally emphasized its overwhelming superiority over Togo's waiting armada. Nicholas listened, entranced by Alexis's panegyric. The outcome of this Holy War meant more to this quiet, ineffectual and undemonstrative Emperor than was sometimes evident.

After luncheon on the flagship, the bands struck up and the sky cleared and the scene was as gay and memorable as on Kaiser Wilhelm's visit two years before. The Tsar had been anxious for the review to be a family affair, but the Tsarina decided it was still too cold for her and her baby, so Nicholas alone, with his suite and the bevy of admirals led by Alexis and Rozhestvensky, descended to the imperial pinnace in the early afternoon for his review of the ironclads.

Seven times in turn the Tsar boarded his great ships,

greeted by shouts of 'Long Live Your Imperial Majesty' from the sailors, in their new blue jumpers and black trousers, lining the rails. After receiving the officers, he climbed to the forebridge of each vessel and made his speech, 'telling us to take vengeance on the insolent Japanese who had troubled the peace of Holy Russia; and to maintain the glory of the Russian Navy'. As the cheering died he wished them 'a victorious campaign and a happy return to your native land'.

It was a glorious day, and only once, briefly, in the evening was the spell broken. The Tsar had by then returned to St. Petersburg, and it was left to the Admiralty, headed by Grand Admiral Alexis, formally to entertain the officers at a banquet. Speech after speech accompanied the champagne and brought forth rounds of applause. The note of realism was struck by Captain Bukhvostoff of the *Alexander III.* 'You have all wished us a lucky journey,' he began, 'and have expressed the conviction that with our brave sailors we will smash the Japanese. We thank you for your good intentions, but they only show that you do not know why we are going to sea. But we know why we are going to sea. We also know that Russia is not a sea power and that the public funds spent on ship construction have been wasted. You wish us victory, but there will be no victory. . . .' Bukhvostoff had a reputation for speaking his mind, and in spite of the wine that had been drunk, there was as much sincere conviction in his final pledge: 'But we will know how to die, and we shall never surrender.'

Thirty-six hours later Rozhestvensky gave orders for the Second Pacific Squadron to sail.

CHAPTER THREE

The Admiral Blunders

THE squadron made a last call at Libau to coal and to take on further supplies. Its final departure was not propitious. At 4 p.m. the *Suvoroff* steamed slowly out between the harbour moleheads at the head of the fleet, and almost at once struck bottom, her navigating officer, like the *Oryol's* two weeks before, having misjudged the tide and the draft of his ship.

'This is an infernal harbour,' stormed Rozhestvensky, who had only just sent a furious signal to the *Sisoy Veliky*, which had lost its anchor somewhere and was still searching for it. Since leaving Reval, the C.-in-C. had had frequent recourse to his favourite gesture of reprimand, the firing of blank charges at offending vessels, and once he had sent live ammunition across the bows of a ship which had three times ignored a signal. Two days before, one of the destroyers had rammed and holed herself against the *Oslyabya* while closing to pass her a message; twice the *Oryol* had been in trouble again, in the engine room and her steering compartment. It was a miserable afternoon, 'Low grey clouds; half fog, half icy drizzle; dark faces, hands buried in overcoat pockets; heads drawn well into turned-up collars, into which streams of cold water were trickling steadily; general nervousness and irritability . . .'

The next day, the 17th of October, the weather improved, and as the squadron proceeded in cruising formation out of the Baltic, spirits rose. From the bridge of the *Suvoroff* Rozhestvensky surveyed his armada for the first time with something like pride, and even felt a flicker of confidence in their future. Watching this formidable array of power steaming that morning in reasonably disciplined formation a few miles off the flat coastland, he found it easy to dismiss the shortcomings of his ships and his crews and to forget the fearful difficulties that lay ahead.

Standing, as always, at Rozhestvensky's side, his Chief of Staff Clapier de Colongue was more cheerful and less harassed now that at last the false starts were over and they were on their way. Like all good Chiefs of Staff, this punctilious, smartly turned-out officer—of aristocratic French birth—was susceptible to the moods of his Admiral. Every day, and for the best part of every night, for seven months, the tall, fair, willowy figure was to be seen up on the *Suvoroff's* bridge, mostly beside and always within earshot of his chief, sharing the boredom and the hectic vagaries of the fleet's passage to the other side of the world, a certain reflection of Rozhestvensky's temper, an echo of his commands, his reprimands and rare commendations. Always charming, always civil, no matter how bullied he was, poor de Colongue was nevertheless to become the fleet's most unloved officer and one of the most tragic minor characters in naval history. But October 17th was a carefree day for de Colongue, perhaps the only happy one of the voyage.

Later that morning, the cruiser *Heimdal, en route* to England with the King of Denmark aboard, and a division of torpedo-boats, were sighted. Courtesy salutes were exchanged, and then the squadron anchored without incident off the coast of Langeland. The first three Hamburg-Amerika colliers were there according to schedule, as another good omen, and even the coaling went off without a hitch. That night there was a slight fog, and the sea got up, but still the first and second divisions of ironclads maintained well-spaced formation, and Rozhestvensky dropped anchor close to the Fakkjeberg light to take on

fresh bread and meat in the morning and to await the
arrival of pilots and the rest of the squadron.

Ahead of them lay the dangerous waters of the Great
Belt and the Skaw, but it was not the navigational hazards
of these channels that at this point gave the Russians concern; it was the Japanese. Togo and the fleet they were to
destroy might still be eighteen thousand miles away, but
Rozhestvensky and his commanders were in no doubt that
the Danish and Norwegian coasts, and even the North Sea,
were the operating grounds of enemy spies and saboteurs.
For the past months, reports of torpedo-boats disguised
as trawlers lurking in fiords, of submerged submarines, of
destroyers fitting out hastily in British yards while their
Japanese crews stood by, of armed merchantmen hovering
in the German Bight, all awaiting the departure of the
Russian fleet, had been arriving at St. Petersburg in a
steady stream.

That Japan had built up what amounted to a suicide
detachment in northern Europe was common knowledge in
Russia, and even Rozhestvensky's brief manœuvres from
Kronstadt had been attended by frequent alarms and diversions that were not in the training programme. By the
time the squadron sailed, the European press was beginning to show serious interest in this threatened interven-
tion which might have dangerous repercussions, and even
the British Admiralty and the French and German Minis-
tries of Marine were making sceptical inquiries. Five days
before the ships arrived off Gulstav, Admiral Wirenius told
a correspondent of the *Echo de Paris* that the Skaw was 'particularly favourable for an attack, owing to its narrowness
which obliges the fleet to proceed in Indian file. We know
that officers of the Japanese fleet have left for Europe. We
have to fear an attack by means of mines thrown along the
route of the squadron.'

The Russians had not been idle. Weeks before, a Captain Hartling had been dispatched to Copenhagen by the

Admiralty to set up a counter-espionage agency, and by the time Rozhestvensky was sailing towards the Danish islands, carefully briefed spotters were at their posts, ready to telegraph news of any suspicious vessels in the fleet's path.

No one was in greater debt to Captain Hartling and the Russian consular agents in Norway, Germany and Denmark, who had set off the trail of false rumour that eventually became an enormous self-fabricated hoax, than Admiral Togo. In fact not a single spy or agent or vessel of any kind had been sent to this area by the Japanese, who possessed neither the means nor the experience for such a dangerous operation as the Russians feared. Yet within a few days of their departure, Rozhestvensky's fleet, already low enough in morale, was reduced first to a state of acute nervousness and finally to a panic that brought Russia within an ace of war in Europe and made her the laughing-stock of the world. Second only to the opening shot which had killed Admiral Witthoft at the Battle of the Yellow Sea, it was Togo's greatest piece of good fortune of the war.

Anxious to prove their worth, Captain Hartling's agents became ever more assiduous as the fleet approached, and reports of suspicious vessels hove-to in isolated creeks poured in to the Admiralty and were passed on to the *Suvoroff*. Watches were doubled and the men stood by their guns night and day, while at night searchlights swept the water continuously around every ship. 'No vessel of any sort whatever must be allowed to get in amongst the fleet,' ran an order from the flagship, and any merchant-man or fishing vessel that approached was promptly signalled off, its departure hastened on more than one occasion by shots.

Aware of the disastrous loss of fighting strength, to say nothing of prestige, which would be caused by the sinking of one of his new battleships, Rozhestvensky determined to take no chances, and after the fleet had coaled on the 18th of October, he ordered the narrow channel leading to the entrance to the Great Belt to be swept for mines at dawn.

It was a tall order, for there were neither minesweepers nor sweeping gear in the fleet, and the mechanics on the *Kamchatka* were up all night adapting and fitting fifty grapnels to a length of cable. At first light the tug *Roland* and the ice-breaker *Yermak* set off with their makeshift sweep, an oddly-matched pair, since one was twice the power and size of the other. Not surprisingly, when the *Yermak* made a turn, the *Roland* on the outer circumference could not keep up, and the sweep parted. Two or three more attempts were made before Rozhestvensky became exasperated. 'The passage is to be considered as swept,' he signalled irritably at seven o'clock, and ordered anchors to be weighed. They passed safely through the danger zone, only the *Oryol* having renewed trouble with her steering gear, which Captain Yung in his report to his C.-in-C. ascribed to sabotage. She caught up with her division later in the day, still yawing dramatically, before they anchored just south-west of the Skaw itself.

The reports awaiting them were more numerous and alarming than ever, telling of trawlers in the North Sea fishing grounds armed with torpedo tubes, and of floating mines by the score. Security precautions were redoubled, and coal was taken on from waiting colliers in an atmosphere of acute anxiety. Two fishermen, commissioned by the local Russian consular agent to carry a message to the flagship, were given a hostile reception and their boat was driven off. When it was collected by a destroyer later and delivered to the *Suvoroff's* bridge, it turned out to be a telegram for Rozhestvensky from the Tsar, informing him that His Imperial Majesty had been graciously pleased to promote him to the rank of Vice-Admiral. 'We cannot but be moved to tears when we read in this telegram of the supreme solicitude of Their Majesties', Rozhestvensky informed the fleet the following morning. 'But I do not wish thoughtlessly to appropriate this kind consideration all to myself,' he added generously, 'but to share it equally with my officers and men. Heaven above will surely bless all those who are about to undertake this difficult journey on behalf of our country.'

Later that night, a clear night with a full moon transforming the calm sea into a darkened mirror, Rozhestvensky was seized with a sudden fear that a crisis demanding immediate action was upon him. At dusk unidentified torpedo-boats had been reported leaving from secret bases in Norway, and then under the light of that brilliant moon, which picked out clearly the shadows of the anchored ironclads, cruisers and colliers and made conditions perfect for a surprise enemy attack, balloons were reported.

The signal was flashed first from the *Navarin*, and then other look-outs picked up the two silvery shapes high up in the sky moving slowly from south-west to north-east. There could be no doubt of it: these were enemy reconnaissance spotters identifying the fleet and reporting its position to the waiting flotillas. It was the final straw, blown on a westerly wind, to the sailors a supernatural omen of disaster, to Rozhestvensky and his staff confirmation that the wily Japanese were as usual one step ahead of them.

Perhaps those balloons were as intangible as today's flying saucers, for they were never traced nor seen again, but it was a measure of the tremendous fear and awe which the Japanese had inspired after nine months of war that without further delay Rozhestvensky broke off the coaling operations and ordered an immediate departure. It was also the first occasion in naval warfare (and years before the first heavier-than-air flight in Europe) when the action of a fleet was influenced by air power. Later that night a red glow suddenly shot up on the port horizon, flickered, rose again and finally died. So the enemy must have struck at last!

There was no lessening of the tension the following morning when the fleet, safely through the Skaw, steamed into the North-Sea in a thick fog. Each vessel advanced cautiously in its solitary detached world, feeling its way forward over an oily swell with the sirens shrieking all around, 'trying to outdo one another in the loudness of their stentorian halloos, uttering shrieks of agony as if to announce some terrible misfortune'. To the many raw crew members who had never before seen a dense fog at sea, it seemed like a weird prolongation of the nightmare.

At noon the wind got up and the fog quickly cleared, revealing only the first and second divisions of battleships widely scattered in loose formation. Enkvist's cruisers with the auxiliaries were far ahead, searching out the enemy, and the fleet was now divided into two parts. Only the *Kamchatka* was lost, somewhere ahead of the flagship after an engine breakdown during the night. And it was this ship that at last reported making contact with the elusive foe, who had seemed always to be just beyond the horizon.

'Chased by torpedo-boats,' she wirelessed succinctly at dusk, and after a pause announced that she was firing on them.

'How many?' the *Suvoroff* demanded. 'From which side?'

'About eight. From all directions.'

'Have they discharged any torpedoes?' signalled the *Suvoroff*.

There was a short interval when the radio-operator's quick dash on to deck for a glance over the rails could be pictured, then: 'We haven't seen any.'

The *Kamchatka* later appeared anxious to locate her flagship and repeatedly asked her to expose her search-lights. But Rozhestvensky, prepared for every Japanese trick, refused to disclose his position. It wouldn't have been the first time that the Japanese had sent out false signals on Russian wavelengths. 'Change your course,' came the cautious reply. 'Indicate your position and we will send further instructions.'

'Fear messages will be intercepted.' It seemed like a deadlock. There was a long silence, then the *Suvoroff* tried again.

'The Admiral wishes to know whether torpedo-boats still in sight.'

The *Kamchatka* was still afloat. 'We cannot see any,' she replied promptly.

It seemed curious that the Japanese should reveal themselves and single out the old *Kamchatka*, which looked like any merchantman, when the first and second divisions of ironclads, unprotected by their cruisers, would so soon be passing. 'Somebody's making a fool of us,' one of the *Suvoroff's* officers remarked as he came off watch. All the wardroom was conscious of the sense of unreality and impending disaster in the air, and the officers were talking in low, urgent tones. Vladimir Semenoff, a supernumery on Rozhestvensky's staff, retired to his cabin. Beside his bunk was a photograph of Admiral Makaroff, his old commander in the Far East, whom he had so admired and whose death in action he still mourned. The choppy seas had splashed through the porthole, smearing the photograph's red-stained frame across his hero's face and breast. Semenoff picked it up in concern. 'That is a bad omen!' he said to himself.

Ninety minutes later the bugle calls for action stations were sounding, and the acute tension of the past hours found release in a sudden outburst of sound and movement as nine hundred men in each ship ran shouting along the iron decks and gangways to their posts amid the rumbling of drums, the rattle of ammunition carriers in their hoists and the roar of the twelve-inch shells' hand-trucks on their rails, the deep threatening boom of the range and order transmitter gongs—and then the sudden fierce crack as the six-inch guns opened fire, their recoil sending a shudder along the length of the great vessels.

Wild scenes occurred on every ironclad, and there were shouts on all sides of, 'Where are they?' 'Dozens of them —over there, look!' 'It's a full-scale attack.' 'Those aren't torpedo-boats, they're cruisers!'—and as the *Borodino* opened up with a heavy gun, 'That was a torpedo exploding!' 'We're hit! we're hit!' 'Some seized lifebelts,' Novkoff-Priboy recounted, 'others running to their hammocks took out the cork mattresses. Some crossed themselves, while others mouthed curses. . . .'

A steward on another battleship later told Edgar Wallace of the *Daily Mail*, 'A midshipman rushed into the mess room and exclaimed in most excited tones, "The Japanese are attacking us." All the officers immediately rushed on deck. Some little time afterwards a sailor came down to me and said that Lieutenant — wanted me to bring up on deck two glasses of brandy. Just as I reached the upper deck I heard shooting.' Variations of the scene that met him on deck were reproduced on every ironclad in the two divisions. 'All the sailors were lying on their faces and the officers were all under cover and were talking at the tops of their voices. Midshipman R—— was waving a drawn sword, crying out "The Japanese!" I took the brandy to the lieutenant who told me I was to remain on deck as I might be wanted. . . .'

It had all begun on the bridge of the *Suvoroff*, from which two flares had suddenly been sighted ahead. Searchlights were at once swung in their direction, the emergency 'Engage enemy' signal was flashed, and the sea and sky about the ironclads became a dazzling criss-cross kaleidoscope of white beams that flitted and darted, paused to probe a wave and flashed up again to the base of the clouds. One light's hesitancy brought forth a hail of shell and machine-gun fire from every ship that could bring a gun to bear. The enemy appeared to be on every side.

It was some time before the errant searchlights chanced on their real target—the group of little vessels, with a larger one among them—and concentrated their beams on it. The boats were barely half a mile away, gossamer white in the blinding light, like scattered toys surprised in the night. On every ship the gun barrels swung round and a withering fire opened up at a rate the gunners had never approached before.

Soon the ammunition for some of the twelve-pounders was running low and the trolleys with fresh supplies were not arriving. Amidst all the disorder on the *Oryol* a midshipman ran from the after bridge onto the main deck waving an empty shell case. 'They've fired away my shells,' he was crying in anguish. 'Give me more ammunition!'

Strikes were already being made; three of the boats had been hit, and one was listing heavily; the tide of battle was running with the Russians. Then suddenly from the west, fresh batteries of searchlights sprung up, sweeping over the ironclads and blinding the gunners. Between the beams muzzle-flashes were observed and shells whined overhead and sent up fountains of sea-water beside the *Suvoroff*.

Again the cry of 'Cruisers!' The Japanese were bringing up reinforcements, they had met with the main fleet. . . . The great turrets swung round, and as the range-finders called out the distance the twelve-inch guns slowly rose and one by one opened fire.

The Gamecock Fleet of little hundred-ton, single-screw trawlers, each with a crew of eight or nine, left Hull on the 19th of October, and reached its fishing ground on the Dogger Bank 220 miles east by north of Spurn Head on the evening of the 21st. The sun had just set; there was a slight haze, and a moderate sea which rocked the boats about but would not interfere with the fishing, when the smacksman on the *Ruff* gave the order to shoot trawls. Standing by for the catch in the morning was the fleet's steam carrier, the *Magpie*.

By midnight several merchantmen had approached and steered clear, warned off by the boats' Duplex fishing signals and their red, white and green lanterns. The Dogger Bank was always thick with trawlers, and there were over a hundred out from East Coast ports that night.

Shortly after twelve o'clock, the lights of several ships were seen to the north-east steering in loose line-ahead formation. They could only be warships—probably Admiral Lord Charles Beresford's Channel Fleet returning from their Tynemouth visit, the fishermen guessed. There was still a slight mist and visibility was poor, but soon they could be identified as battleships; and the Gamecock Fleet was right in their path. Growing a little anxious— it was not like the Royal Navy to ignore their easily recognizable identification lights—the smackmaster sent up a couple of green flares, and when this had no effect, ordered his fleet to steam to windward.

When the searchlights came on, sweeping their fingers in swift arcs over the sea, there was still only surprise among the trawler crews, and even the first shots that slammed into the water ahead of the battleship column were accepted for a moment as nothing worse than the prelude to night gunnery practice. It was rather to avoid a collision than because of the gunfire that the trawls were cut and full steam ahead was ordered on every boat.

Panic broke out among the fishermen only when the searchlights concentrated their blinding light on three of the trawlers 'like a ring of fire', and the sea around them was churned up by hundreds of exploding shells. The men still below poured onto deck, waving their arms and shouting at the tops of their voices. 'To show what we were, I held a big plaice up,' one fisherman told later. 'My mate, Jim Tozer, showed a haddock.'

It was going to take more than a fish or two to halt the Russian gunners now that they were getting the range, which from the *Suvoroff* was down to a hundred yards. There was certain to be a hit before long. 'Going on deck, I saw several ships which had covered us with searchlights and which were firing at us at once,' reported Albert Almond, a trimmer on the *Crane*. 'I ran below again, followed by the bo'sun—who had nearly reached the bottom of the ladder when he fell back. "I'm shot—my hands are off!" I turned to help him, but another shell burst, tearing away the flesh of my left arm.' The *Crane* was taking the brunt of the fire, shell after shell striking home. Joseph Alfred Smith, the skipper's son, was asleep when the guns started firing, and a shot came through the fo'c'sle, extinguishing the light above his head. When he rushed up on deck, he imagined it was daylight. The boat's engineer, John Nixon, was staring at Almond, who had been hit again, in the head this time. 'Who are you?' he was demanding helplessly.

Young Smith's father was already dead, lying across the deck headless, and the Third Hand had similarly been decapitated. Most of the rest of the crew had been wounded and there was blood all over the wet fo'c'sle of the *Crane*. The first mate was frantically waving a red lamp with one hand and trying to launch the boat with the other. But the winch had been riddled by shell fire and the trawler was already sinking.

The barrage died only when the Russian gunners recognized the more serious foe advancing on them, though the twelve- and six-pounder fire still remained heavy as the *Moulmein*, *Gull* and *Mino* steamed towards the stricken

Crane in an attempt to take off the wounded and the dead before she sank.

Comprehension of the blunder they were committing came slowly to the Russian squadron. The torpedo-boats which they imagined had mixed-in with the fishing boats had clearly been driven off, and only a scattering of badly battered trawlers was milling about like doomed moths in the glare of the searchlights. At the same time, on the bridge of the *Suvoroff* the signals from the confused and thoroughly frightened Enkvist, who should have been a full fifty miles to the south-west, and was returning the hail of fire with equal wild enthusiasm, were at last recognized as Tabulevitch, a system used only in the Russian Navy, and Rozhestvensky ordered the buglers to sound the cease-fire. 'Switch off searchlights!' he shouted at Captain Ignatzius. 'One beam up'—the squadron's code instruction to break off action.

The firing died slowly, shots ringing out intermittently for some minutes, and one or two searchlights from the *Alexander III* and *Borodino* still flitted about over the water. Only a few yards from the C.-in-C. an over-zealous gunlayer on the fore upper-bridge six-pounder could not be restrained. Rozhestvensky rushed at him, grabbing him by the shoulder and pointing at the battered, listing *Crane*. 'How dare you!' he screamed.

It was five minutes to one; the action had lasted just twenty minutes. With all lights extinguished and at full speed for fear of another attack, the battleship divisions steamed away south-west in ragged line-ahead three miles behind Enkvist's re-formed cruisers. Breathless and garrulous from their baptism of fire, the gun-crews squatted among the scattered shell cases beside their hot gun breeches, shouting their claims between cigarette puffs. Not one had seen less than a dozen enemy torpedo-boats darting in and out of the shell fire, caught and lost again in the white pin-points of the searchlight beams, and there were loud tales of torpedo trails skating past a hair's-breadth away. Slowly to their peasant minds came the realization that the enemy had attacked in force and had been beaten off. The Gamecock Fleet had raised the morale of the Second Pacific Squadron higher than it had been since the Tsar had wished them farewell at Reval.

In the wardrooms the excitement was equally intense as the action was discussed over glasses of vodka and tea. While everyone accepted that there had been a serious mistake over the identity of Enkvist's cruisers, few of the officers doubted that there had been Japanese vessels skulking among the trawlers, awaiting their arrival. All evidence supported this: the daily reports of assembling enemy boats from neutral ships, confirmed by official warnings from the Admiralty, those reconnaissance balloons, the attack on the *Kamchatka* a few hours before. That they had hit some of the covering trawlers (English no doubt—there was no limit to what the English would do for their allies) was generally accepted, but what could you expect in a night action? On the *Suvoroff* only the head surgeon was emphatic that there had not been a single torpedo-boat present. He had been an idle observer during the firing, for there had been no serious hits and no injuries on the flagship. His lone voice was soon suppressed.

Admiral Enkvist's medical staff had been busier. The *Oryol* alone had fired over five hundred shells, and there had been seven battleships in the line, at one time all firing on the *Aurora* and *Donskoy*. A hit or two had been inevitable at the close range and both cruisers had been struck in the upper works. On the *Aurora* a gunner had been injured, and Chaplain Afanasy mortally wounded 'by a 45 mm. shell which went through the priest's cabin and through the priest in it'. There was a moment's silence in the wardroom of the *Suvoroff* when this news was announced; then one of the gunnery lieutenants, a young man

noted for his dry humour, was heard to murmur as he
adjusted his pince-nez, 'That is not bad by way of a
beginning.'

There were no further alarms. As if exhausted after its
orgasm, the fleet did no more than carry away the trawls
of the next fishing fleet through which it carved its way at
four o'clock, and continued south-west across the North
Sea, a shade uneasy perhaps, but on the whole pleased
with its performance. It had been a hectic night.

There was a light fog at dawn on the 23rd, but it was
warmer and the sea was less choppy. Briefly to the east a
damp sun could be seen, and intermittently to the west the
cliffs of Dover, grey through a fine drizzle.

From vantage points all along the south coast of England as far west as Shoreham, small, curious crowds
gathered, watching the fleet steaming down Channel
beneath the dense black cloud of its own smoke, hugging
the three-mile limit as if seeking reassurance from
Britannia's might. Towards mid-day the second division
of battleships halted opposite Brighton's new Palace Pier
beside a pair of waiting colliers, and took on coal. For two
and a half hours the towering superstructures and heavy
gun turrets, the stocky dark silhouettes of the *Oslyabya*,
Sisoy Veliky and *Navarin* were clearly visible and drew
several thousands to the pier and the beach and the railings
of the Marine Parade.

In the afternoon the *Suvoroff*, followed by her three
sister ships, heaved to off Rottingdean, and the *Malay*,
which had been accompanying them, drew alongside and for
two hours transferred coal to the battleships' bunkers. Then
they too slipped off into the mist. Only the fishermen of the
Gamecock Fleet knew of the night attack in the North Sea.

Five hours after the last battleship disappeared over the
horizon down Channel, the *Moulmein* with her flag at half

mast led the damaged trawlers into Hull harbour. The
news of the disaster had preceded her, the wounded having
been landed from a hospital ship earlier in the afternoon,
and there were groups of anxious relatives and friends, and
a scattering of reporters, huddled on the quay when she
came alongside. Only a few of them were talking, pointing out to one another the shell-splintered deckhouses and
funnels of the leading boat, the *Magpie*, the *Gull*, the
Mandalay and the others which moored behind them. It
began to rain hard and the policemen were wearing their
capes when they carried ashore the coffins a few minutes
later. Like any fishing port, Hull was accustomed to sudden
death; but this was a new sort of disaster that for the
moment no one understood, and as the fishermen came
ashore, only murmured inquiries greeted them. The wave
of indignation gathered momentum slowly.

That night a deputation of Hull fishermen representing
the Gamecock Fleet was taken to London on the night mail
by the local M.P., Sir Henry Seymour King, and soon
after breakfast presented themselves at the Foreign Office.
The Foreign Secretary, Lord Lansdowne, was away, and
it was left to two of his officials to ask for evidence of the
attack that was already headlined in every morning newspaper in Europe. 'It's up at Hull,' one of the fishermen
told them. 'Two headless trunks.' But they were able to
produce some shell splinters from their pockets, and that
seemed to satisfy the Foreign Office.

For the British people the 'Dogger Bank Incident' as
Fleet Street at once named it, contained all the necessary
ingredients for a national feast of furious outrage. To a
country at the very peak of its power and wealth, with
ancient maritime traditions, dependent on the sea for its
trade, possessing the greatest merchant and naval fleets
the world had ever known, the attack was intolerable. To
the British, the fisherman 'battling in all weathers to bring
the catch home', facing unknown hazards to fill the nation's

larders, had always been the heroic symbol of a heritage; all the schoolbooks said so.

To the British, the symbol of Russia (of whom too much had recently been heard) was equally clear. It was, of course, a bear—a great, lumbering, stupid, cruel bear—grabbing whatever it could lay hands on without regard for manners or diplomacy; and his latest victim was the brave little Jap, who, by golly! was giving him a taste of his own medicine. There was little fear of Russia in Britain at the turn of the century; but like any noisy, marauding, predatory beast, the bear had to be kept in order. That it should dare to fire on and sink British trawlers on their lawful occasions, and kill innocent fisherfolk, was an affront to national pride.

Trafalgar Square was filled with protesting crowds that evening, the Russian Ambassador was booed as he left his Embassy, there were deputations to Members of Parliament, to Downing Street, and the Admiralty. The Navy must deal with this wretched Russian admiral fellow. . . . Now was the time to see some return for the millions spent on ironclads. . . . 'Jackie' Fisher would teach 'em, he'd stop that madman and have him shot as a murderer. 'Is this wretched Baltic Fleet to be permitted to continue its operation?' asked the *Standard*, 'with its inefficient commanders, its drafts of raw landsmen, its blundering navigators and incompetent engineers. . . .'

In the backwash of the wave of anger came sympathy for the bereaved and injured at Hull. Condolences were telegraphed to the Mayor from the King's private secretary, with a cheque for two hundred guineas, and a hundred pounds from the Queen, together with numerous private donations (and a tactful note of sympathy from the Mayor of Tokio) arrived the next day.

On the morning of the 25th of October, Britain became suddenly aware that the incident had developed into a serious crisis, and that in fact the country was on the brink of war with Russia. 'The mind of the Government, like the mind of the nation, is made up,' stated *The Times*. Justice was demanded—immediate justice, backed by all the power of the Empire.

Sir Charles Hardinge, the British Ambassador in St. Petersburg, handed in a strongly worded note of protest, demanding an explanation, an apology, and an assurance that the guilty officers would at once be severely dealt with. Later in the day Count Lamsdorf, the Russian Minister for Foreign Affairs, called on the British Embassy with a request to pass on to King Edward and the Government the Tsar's sincere regret. But this was a gesture only; the Russian Admiralty yielded no apology and demands to make public Rozhestvensky's itinerary were met with a firm refusal.

In the evening the war fever mounted with an Admiralty statement announcing that, 'After the receipt of the news of the tragedy in the North Sea, preliminary orders for mutual support and co-operation were, as a measure of precaution, issued by the Admiralty to the Mediterranean, Channel and Home Fleets'. This was received everywhere with satisfaction in the knowledge that the Royal Navy was ready, aye ready—great, grey men-of-war slipping silently to sea heading for their secret rendezvous in battle formation, decks cleared for action, live shells in the breeches, British tars alert for the enemy: this was the very stuff of jingoism, a late autumn harvest of heroics.

Nor was reality so very different from this romantic picture. From all sides the massive strength of the Royal Navy closed in on the bully scurrying down Channel. The Home Fleet under Vice-Admiral Sir A. K. Wilson with eight battleships and four cruisers left at once for Portland, and the eight battleships in reserve were brought to a state of readiness. Lord Charles Beresford, with his flag on the *Caesar*, had under his command the *Victorious*, *Hannibal*, *Illustrious*, *Jupiter*, *Magnificent*, *Majestic* and

Mars, as formidable as they sounded and each more than a match for a well-manned *Suvoroff*. Ammunition chambers, stores and bunkers were quickly replenished and the cruisers *Theseus*, *Endymion*, *Doris* and *Hermes* detached to shadow the Russian fleet. 'Situation critical,' was the Admiral's farewell message. 'Good luck.' Gibraltar was put on a war footing and the dozen battleships and forty-four supporting cruisers, destroyers and gunboats were recalled from their visits to Italian and Austrian ports.

By the evening of the 26th of October there were in all twenty-eight battleships with steam up or already at sea to intercept and destroy the Second Pacific Squadron at a word from Whitehall. Rozhestvensky was now 'the ham of a strategic sandwich' as a satisfied correspondent to *The Times* put it. But the Thunderer's opposite number in St. Petersburg considered that 'the lessons of the first days of the war have not been wasted, and the new and treacherous attack by the Japanese has been met by the vigilant and pitiless eye of our Admiral and the straight fire of our guns'.

CHAPTER FOUR

The Admiral is Unrepentant

CAPTAIN IGNATIZIUS, who commanded the *Suvoroff*,
also led the lighter element in the flagship's wardroom,
which even during the most crucial and monotonous periods
of the voyage never seemed to lose its gaiety. Ignatzius
was a happy fatalist, confident that the Japanese would, as
usual, concentrate their fire on the leading ship of the first
column and that the outcome of the battle had long been
decided by St. Nicholas and those other all-powerful
heavenly spirits. Whether he and his crew would die or
survive the ordeal had been settled before they sailed from
Libau—and there was nothing that he could do about it.

The future did not trouble Captain Ignatzius; for the
present this rotund, buoyant, jolly little man was concerned
first that everybody should be as happy as he was, which
was hardly possible, and secondly that his ship should be
run to a standard that would satisfy his Flag Admiral;
which, by a combination of tireless energy and enthusiasm,
he came nearer to achieving than any other of the squadron's commanders.

The favourite foil for Ignatzius's banter was Midshipman Werner von Kursel, a rough, tough, simple-minded
Courlandian who had led a precarious life all over Europe
and Asia, and at every opportunity, like a dog showing off
its tricks, would air his gifts as a linguist. Whenever the
captain put him to the test the results were ludicrous and
the outcome always the same. There would be a pause, and
then von Kursel would say slowly and seriously, 'I think

I'm better at German than any other language'; and the whole wardroom would join in the laughter.

Von Kursel was also something of a sentimentalist and was devoted to birds and animals of all kinds. Later, when they reached the tropics, the ship became like a menagerie and nearly all the crew had a pet monkey or parrot, or even a goat. In those early days in northern waters the only pets on the *Suvoroff* were the three ward-room dogs, Gipsy, a fox-terrier puppy, the dachshund Dinky, and the long white-coated mongrel half-dachshund Flagmansty, who spent most of their life tearing round and round in circles chasing champagne corks and scraps of paper tied to string. In the Bay of Biscay, in icy rain and with half a gale blowing, someone clipped Flagmansty, apparently in preparation for the hot weather ahead. It was von Kursel who led the outraged protest, claiming that the poor animal would die of cold. The chaplain was generally thought to have been responsible, but strongly denied the accusation.

The severe, strongly built artillery officer Sventor-zhetsky, the harassed engineer Politovsky, Clapier de Colongue, the Torpedo Flag-Lieutenant Leontieff, Semen-off, Colonel Filippovsky; all these and the other thirty ship's and staff officers got on well with one another, and there were rarely quarrels among them.

The only discordant note was struck by the staff officer Captain Nicholas Klado, a born conspirator and wily diplomat, a sort of Machiavellian Mahan, who had contrived to establish himself among the inner councils of the Admiralty as his country's leading naval strategist and theorist. His clever articles in *Novoe Vremya* were widely read and influential, and Birilioff, Wirenius and even Grand Admiral Alexis frequently sought his advice. Klado returned from his war service in the Far East, where he had been Alexieff's secretary and confidential adviser (and had not heard a shot fired), more pompous and self-opinionated

than ever. But he was the only staff officer with decided
views on the cause of past disaster and the future conduct
of the war, and he expressed them with such authority
that he had come to be regarded as the Russian Navy's
seer.

Klado returned to St. Petersburg at the height of the
preparations for the Second Pacific Squadron's departure,
when things were at their most chaotic and no one quite
knew which ships were going, how they were to be got
ready in time, how they were to be refuelled and provi-
sioned, or even whether they were to travel by the Cape
of Good Hope, the Suez Canal or Cape Horn. Klado produced the answers promptly and emphatically, and some of
them were acted upon. He was loud in his insistence that
every seaworthy vessel capable of making the journey
should be taken, claiming that the more the Japanese had
to fire at the less chance there was of their hitting the ships
that really mattered—the *Suvoroff* and her sister ships and
the new fast cruisers.

Captain Klado almost got his way. There were a dozen
or so armoured cruisers and coast defence vessels in the
Baltic which had been sent back from the Far East in the
1890s as being of no operational value and past repair. It
was only after long and violent argument that Rozhestvensky persuaded Birilioff that their ancient guns were
useless, that they would be millstones round his neck, holding the whole squadron to their speed in combat, and consuming priceless coal on the long journey. He partly won
his battle; the Admiralty compromised and made Rozhestvensky take only some of the less obsolescent among them,
and Klado retired defeated. For this he never forgave
Rozhestvensky, and after he had himself appointed to his
staff, a mutual dislike that soon turned to scarcely veiled
hatred inevitably developed between these two strong-
willed, short-tempered personalities—the crafty teacher's
pet who was not to be crossed, and the elderly Admiral

who had risen by virtue of merit and achievement. Rozhestvensky would have done anything to rid himself of his
nagging parasite.

The squadron's voyage down Channel in three widely-
spaced divisions had been without serious incident. Most
of the way it had rained, and when the rain ceased a thick
fog settled as they passed the Cotentin peninsula. Many
small land birds sought shelter on the decks and were fed
by the crews, and there were always little knots of sailors
to be seen by the rails tossing biscuit crumbs to the gulls
that swooped and hovered and dived about the warships'
sterns. It was rough and very cold in the Bay of Biscay
until the morning of the 26th of October when a warm sun
rose in a cloudless sky, as if the season had changed over-
night. Ahead of the squadron the sierras of northern Spain
shimmered in the heat haze, and beyond them they could
just make out the higher snow-capped peaks. This sudden
southern warmth, which few of the sailors had ever felt
before, was like a balm after the anxieties of the past
weeks, and the wide, smooth harbour of Vigo looked
peaceful and welcoming.

After the ships anchored, Rozhestvensky gave orders
that coaling from the five German colliers awaiting them
should begin at once. They had steamed eighteen hundred
miles, and the bunkers were low. He was still unaware of
the uproar he had created four days before in the North
Sea, and the sudden arrival of a cutter alongside the
Suvoroff bearing several port officials was accepted as a
normal routine visit.

But any displeasure caused to Britain was bound to have
wide repercussions, and Vigo provided only the first of
many cold welcomes for the Russians. The Spanish deeply
regretted that they must act within their rights. These
warships of a belligerent power, they insisted, were en-
titled to remain in neutral waters for only twenty-four
hours. Steps were being taken at once 'to prevent any

replenishment of stores by the ships'. Spanish policemen were in fact already boarding every ship in the squadron to prevent coaling and any other infringement of the regulations.

Rozhestvensky was furious. Didn't the Spanish authorities realize that his fleet had been in action? 'Some of our ships are damaged—that is why I have separated from the remainder of the squadron,' he told the officials. 'We have coal for only two more days' sailing. It is imperative that we stock up our bunkers.'

The Spaniards shrugged their shoulders, repeated their regrets and descended from the *Suvoroff's* bridge. Before they were back at the quayside, Rozhestvensky issued orders for the colliers to come alongside in order to be ready to coal at a moment's notice, and armed sentries were posted on the hawsers with orders to shoot anyone who attempted to interfere with them. If he was to be treated as a belligerent, Rozhestvensky had no compunction in behaving like one, and decks were cleared for action.

In the afternoon, after informing the Port Commandant that he intended to call on him, the C.-in-C. went ashore, and to his surprise and pleasure was received by a guard of honour and a military band. Having done their duty, it was the least the hospitable Spanish could do. In an easier atmosphere Rozhestvensky reassured the official that he had no intention of disobeying the order. We will arrange this peacefully and diplomatically, he told him, and the commandant agreed that that was the most sensible thing to do, in view of the fact that there happened to be a British cruiser squadron in the next bay. Soon after, as confirmation of this, one of Beresford's men-of-war steamed in and anchored uncomfortably close to the Russian battleships.

From the commandant's office, Rozhestvensky proceeded to the French Consulate, and the wires were soon busy with a stream of telegrams between Vigo and St.

Petersburg and St. Petersburg and Madrid. Meanwhile the bunkers of the *Suvoroff* and her sister ships remained empty.

It was not until the evening, when the Admiral returned and newspapers arrived on board and began to circulate, that the crews realized for the first time that they had set off an international crisis. War with Britain was imminent. Would France and Germany remain neutral? The Admirals and commanders of every ship involved were to be tried by court-martial. At the very least the ironclad divisions were to be sent back to Reval. . . . The Continental newspapers were nearly as outraged as the British. 'Monstrous and inexplicable', commented one German paper. The *Berliner Tageblatt* considered that the Russian commanders 'must be all the time in an abnormal state of mind', and Rozhestvensky was described as 'an exceedingly nervous gentleman, who gets into a state of boundless excitement over trifles'.

Rozhestvensky took it all cheerfully, confident that St. Petersburg would put an end to this nonsense, unalarmed at the size of the forces closing about him. Every naval correspondent had been busy with his latest copy of *Jane's Fighting Ships*, adding up the opposing ironclads. One of the articles Clapier de Colongue read to him in his cabin that evening told of the entire British Navy hovering outside Vigo, twenty-eight battleships poised to destroy him. This made the C.-in-C. laugh. 'A strange amusement, this,' he said, 'always counting up the ships. If we were to come to blows, then all we should be concerned with would be the first four ships. How many more there might be is all one to us.' Such nice logic was needed at this hour.

The situation appeared no less critical the following morning, and it was becoming obvious that the British government was determined that the Russian battleships should in effect be retained in custody in the port, with the Royal Navy on guard outside, until satisfaction was obtained from St. Petersburg. Conscious of his C.-in-C.'s predicament, but unaware of his *insouciant* reaction to it, the Tsar sent Rozhestvensky a message of cheer, which he read out to the *Suvoroff's* assembled crew on the quarter-deck.

'In my thoughts I am with you and my beloved squadron,' it ran. 'I feel confident that the misunderstanding will soon be settled. The whole of Russia looks upon you with confidence and in firm hope.' Rozhestvensky then read out his own answer: ' "The squadron is with your Imperial Majesty with all its heart." Is that not so, comrades?' he asked his sailors. 'What the Emperor orders we carry out. Hurrah!' And the cheers echoed across the harbour.

In the early afternoon news arrived from the Port Commandant that the Spanish government had relented to the extent of allowing the ironclads to take on four hundred tons of coal each, and no more, from the colliers. It seemed that England had agreed that they could be released on bail. Everyone, officers and men together, set to at once, with the promise that there would be two extra tots of vodka for the crew of every ship that refuelled quickly. Coaling went on all through the night, and by ten o'clock the next morning eight hundred tons were safely aboard each battleship. The crisis appeared to be over, and everyone thought they would now be sailing.

Only Rozhestvensky and Clapier de Colongue knew that this relaxation had been but a gesture of appeasement from Madrid and that the situation had not improved. At the request of St. Petersburg, Rozhestvensky sent two long telegrams giving the Russian version of the Dogger Bank Incident. 'The incident of the North Sea', he insisted, 'was provoked by two torpedo-boats which, without showing any lights, under cover of darkness advanced to attack the vessel steaming at the head of the detachment. When the detachment began to sweep the sea with its searchlights, and opened fire, the presence was also discovered of several small fishing vessels. The detachment endeavoured to spare these boats.' In the second telegram there was a conciliatory note. While suggesting that it was imprudent of 'foreign fishing vessels to involve themselves in this enterprise by enemy torpedo-boats', he begged, 'in the name of the whole fleet, to express our sincere regret for the unfortunate victims of circumstances in which no warship could, even in times of profound peace, have acted otherwise.'

These widely publicized messages—'indisputable facts which justify the action, not only in our eyes but in the eyes of every impartial observer', *Novoe Vremya* claimed—seemed momentarily to harden the Russian attitude. But the sudden passion in Britain was on the wane . . . two fishermen, one trawler! And, after all, the Russians had apologized, admitted their mistake. The way was open to peace, and after a meeting of the British cabinet on the 30th of October, Mr. Balfour, the Prime Minister, took the train to Southampton, where he was due to address the local National Union Conservative Association.

All was well. The Russian government, he said, had ordered the detention at Vigo of the units of the fleet concerned in the incident in order to discover which officers had been responsible. An international commission was to be set up to investigate; the Russian Emperor had shown great wisdom.

The nation was visibly relieved and the Continent no less thankful. The Rome *Tribuna's* 'Such a result is well worth a slight sacrifice of *amour propre*', was typical of the approving comment.

Understandably disregarding the provision that he should leave behind guilty officers, Rozhestvensky at once arranged for the appropriate witnesses to be released. Three were junior officers from the *Oryol*, *Borodino* and *Alexander III*, and from the *Suvoroff* he selected Captain Klado. It was a golden opportunity to rid himself of that persistent nagger, although later he was to regret deeply his choice. A lieutenant on the *Suvoroff* watching the banished captain descend to the pinnace murmured to an officer at his side, 'The rats are leaving before the ship sinks. . . .'

The battleships cleared Vigo harbour at seven on the morning of the 1st of November, escorted to the limit of territorial waters by a Spanish cruiser—which then handed over to foreign warships. The Royal Navy, whose watch-dogs were still there, had not yet finished with Rozhest-vensky, and for three days and two nights they remained faithfully with their charges. All the way to Tangier Beresford's cruisers made sport with the Russian battle-ships, darting ahead and crossing from port to starboard in beautifully executed movements, falling astern and then steaming past at full speed in perfect line-ahead barely half a mile away.

Sometimes there were only two or three English men-of-war in sight, at others half a dozen appeared over the horizon and joined in the play, as a hint of limitless reserves. At night their searchlights flickered on and off again, darting over the sea, pausing first on one another and then on the Russian battleships in turn, plodding along without lights at nine knots, as if to reassure them-selves that their prizes were still safe.

For a raw squadron that could scarcely maintain station in a flat calm on a steady course, it was hard to bear. 'It's disgusting to treat us like this,' a midshipman on the *Oryol* exclaimed angrily. 'Following us about like criminals!'; and that night Politovsky wrote bitterly in his diary: 'They are cunning and powerful at sea and insolent everywhere. How many impediments has this ruler of the seas put on our voyage?'

The ultimate humiliation came early on the morning of the 2nd of December when the *Oryol's* steering gear once again broke down and Rozhestvensky had to halt the division while the flag-engineer was sent over to her and repairs were carried out. As the British cruisers turned about and re-formed suspiciously to their rear in immaculate battle order, Semenoff, standing beside Rozhestvensky on the *Suvoroff*'s bridge while they watched this redeployment, was unfeeling enough to ask, 'Do you admire this?'

Rozhestvensky could bear it no longer; his carefully assumed indifference (until then he had done his best to ignore the provocative display) broke down, and half-sobbing he replied, 'Those are real seamen. Oh, if only we . . .' And he broke off, walked swiftly across the bridge and disappeared down the ladder.

The next day, the 3rd of November, was more cheerful. Beresford's cruisers at last drew away and left them in peace, and the special luncheon to commemorate the tenth anniversary of Tsar Nicholas's accession became a double celebration. Toasts were drunk to the Emperor and, less formally, to the destruction of the Royal Navy. In the seamen's quarters, vodka ran freely, and there were speeches and repeated cheers on deck. There was still plenty of spirit left in the Second Pacific Squadron; and there was a prospect of shore leave in Tangier that evening.

At three in the afternoon the four great *Suvoroffs* steamed slowly into Tangier roads and anchored alongside Felkerzam's ironclads and Enkvist's cruisers, from which they had become separated after the Dogger Bank Incident and its political repercussions. Packed with Russian warships, together again for the first time since Libau, and with their crews excitedly exchanging experiences with old friends, the roadstead was like school hall after a major misdemeanour. 'We had three hits,' 'I counted twenty Japs,' 'Didn't those British make a fuss?' 'Do you know what happened to —— ?' The shouted greetings and the messages flashed from ship to ship.

Even the *Kamchatka* turned up at the rendezvous, full of

her exploits, boasting of the three hundred shells she had managed to fire on that fatal evening; and hotly denying that her enemy had been the Swedish merchantman *Aldebaran*, the German trawler *Sonntag* and a French schooner.

But officers and crews were not given long to gossip. They were already far behind schedule and there were a dozen Hamburg-Amerika colliers waiting for them. There would be no shore leave that night—but there would be a prize of 1,500 roubles for the fastest ship. Everyone stripped to the waist and set to work to the encouragement of martial music.

The reunion was brief. Rozhestvensky had decided to split the fleet for the voyage round Africa, depriving Felkerzam of his flagship, *Oslyabya*, and sending him through the Mediterranean to Suez with the *Sisoy Veliky* and *Navarin*, three light cruisers and the destroyers. Nobody quite understood the reasoning behind this sudden change of plan, and there was much argument in the wardrooms. The official version, that the draft of the bigger battleships was too great for the canal, only added to the controversy, for everyone knew there would be six feet or more to spare. Perhaps he feared further torpedo-boat attacks in the narrow confines of the Red Sea; if so, someone pithily pointed out, it was curious that he was prepared to risk the two old battleships the Admiralty had insisted on his including against his wishes. A more charitable view was that he feared for the safety of the old ironclads on the longer and rougher Cape trip.

At nine in the evening the *Sisoy Veliky*, renowned for her prodigious coal consumption, led the detachment out into the Gibraltar Straits and headed east with her flock, belching a great cloud of black smoke.

The Sultan of Morocco had been delighted to welcome the Russians, and to prove his disregard for power politics and Western opinion, let the world know that they could stay as long as they liked. Rozhestvensky went ashore in the afternoon in full dress uniform to express his gratitude. At the head of the long wooden jetty he was met with a seventeen-gun salute from the shore batteries and received by a deputation of sheiks from the royal household and officials of the Russian consulate in morning coats and bowlers. Together the impressive party proceeded into the town for the exchange of courtesies.

Rozhestvensky wanted to get away the next day, but a gale during the night held up the coaling, and it was not until the early morning of the 5th that anchors were weighed. Although the crews had been deprived of their shore leave, the halt had not been without its diversions. In the pouring rain that followed the storm on the 4th of November, the local pedlars had taken advantage of the lull to swarm on to the warships with their wares. Business in postcards, white shoes and topees for the tropics, mats and nick-nacks and souvenirs of all kinds, had been brisk. It was a gala day for the local bazaar men.

Later in the afternoon, a thousand tons of frozen meat turned up in the *Esperance*, which meant postponement of the evil day when they would have to start on the salt beef barrels; and a contingent of nurses arrived in the *Oryol*, a twin-funnelled hospital ship of the same name as the battleship. She was to form a permanent part of the squadron, and the proximity of her clean white hull, contrasting with the muddy black of the warships', and her hundred white-clad nurses, even though they were so tantalisingly inaccessible, were to give comfort during the long months.

Rozhestvensky had started out on the voyage entirely lacking confidence in his commanders. Thirty-eight years' service had left him with few illusions about the quality of personnel in the Imperial Navy, and he knew that all the best senior officers had long since been drafted out to the fighting zone in the Far East. He had little more confidence in his staff, except the faithful, conscientious Clapier de Colongue, Semenoff and one or two others. The blunders of the first weeks had served only to confirm his low regard for his subordinates. From the beginning it had been his policy to keep his own counsel, limiting his communication with his captains and admirals to the briefest instructions, consulting no one but de Colongue. No one ever knew the squadron's sailing orders, which was to be their next port-of-call, nor where they were next to coal and provision. They were left only to hope that combat instructions would be provided before they met Togo.

This understandable reserve of the C.-in-C. had already resulted in some embarrassing moments, in ships being miles off course, calling for coal where there were no colliers, and adding to the squadron's general nervousness. When even the commanders could not confirm or deny them, all kinds of preposterous rumours ran rife.

So far the departure from every port had been markedly undistinguished, and it was additionally aggravating that there had always been a lot of people watching, with a scattering of newspaper correspondents among them. The departure from Tangier soon developed into a series of wild *faux pas*, a worse show than anything they had put on before. The ships of the new Cape squadron were given the briefest instructions to form up in the roads into a complicated cruising formation, which was to be maintained as standard throughout the voyage to the rendezvous with Felkerzam at Madagascar.

There were to be two columns, the *Suvoroff*, *Alexander III*, *Borodino*, *Oryol* and *Oslyabya* to starboard, and the *Kamchatka* (of all ships!) leading the *Anadyr* and the other transports to port. Enkvist was to bring up into a wedge at the rear the *Nakhimoff*, *Aurora* and *Donskoy*. Nothing so difficult had been attempted before; and no one had quite dared to ask for more elaborate details, like the speed they were to steam at, or the distance between vessels they were to hold.

The result was two and a half hours of pandemonium, with Rozhestvensky storming from one side of his bridge to the other while de Colongue desperately tried to sort out the mêlée according to his instructions. To complicate matters further, the *Anadyr* caught her anchor chain in a submarine cable. 'Cut it away!' her captain was ordered —and Tangier's communication with Europe was at once severed for four days.

When at last some sort of order was established, the *Suvoroff's* steering gear broke down, jamming hard to port, and the bewildered captain of the *Kamchatka* suddenly found the flagship steaming straight towards him. A collision was avoided by a few feet and the other transports scattered.

There followed days of comparative peace, with only an occasional breakdown to halt the fleet for a few hours, and the tiresome appearance on the horizon from time to time of their probation officers, the British cruisers. Speed was eight knots, the weather was clear and fine, the sea calm.

At Dakar ten colliers awaited them, carrying 30,000 tons of coal; beyond could be seen an inviting palm-fringed shore and cool white houses, but even before anchors were dropped, the coal ships were moving towards the ironclads. Work was to begin without delay, and the *Suvoroff*-class battleships, with their bunker capacity of 1,100 tons, were to take on no less than 2,200 tons. No one had been warned of this overloading, of course; no one but Rozhestvensky knew that the French had forbidden the fleet the use of Libreville, their next port-of-call, and that it was doubtful if they would be allowed into Great Fish Bay either.

Where was the coal to be stored? There might have been less dismay among his captains if Rozhestvensky had explained the necessity for this drastic intake. Captain Yung's second-in-command was distraught. 'What on earth are we to do?' he asked helplessly. 'I never heard of such a thing. How can I possibly keep the ships clean with a thousand tons of coal lying about in odd corners?'

Rozhestvensky was not at that time much concerned with cleanliness, only that the stuff should somehow be crammed into his ironclads. The 'Instructions for Storing Coal' that were issued from the flagship read like a glossary of an ironclad's anatomy: '. . . in any spare space on the upper deck, lower deck, gun deck, poop and in the cockpit, over closed watertight manhole covers, in the bathrooms, drying rooms, engineroom workshops, wing passages, fore and aft torpedo flats, twelve-inch gun turret passages, in bags between the 47 mm. guns, loose on the quarter deck, with some means to prevent it falling overboard. . . .' There were three pages of these instructions. Officers' cabins (up to the rank of commander) were not spared; any corner of the ship would do so long as the engines could work and the ship could be steered—and the crews did not actually asphyxiate. 'Compartments in which coal is stored should be from time to time ventilated by rigging windsails through the skylights', concluded a warning note in Rozhestvensky's orders. But because by the time the job was finished there would hardly be room for the men to squeeze below decks, asphyxiation seemed the least danger.

Dakar marked the beginning of this new ordeal by coal, a test of physical endurance and patience as gruelling as any the great pioneers and ancient sea explorers ever suffered. Heat and dust were the ingredients. The coal dust spread everywhere. Constantly stirred by the vibration of the ships' engines, it hung about in clouds in the still, damp air of these cramped, overloaded iron ships; in the gangways, mess decks, shafts and passages and cabins in which it was stacked, creating an atmosphere like that

of a mine shaft in a heat wave. For four months Rozhestvensky's crews worked and ate and slept with the bitter,
nauseating fumes of coal in their nostrils.

The coal dust stuck damply to the ships' iron and woodwork. The filthy irritant found its way into the food, into
clothes and everything the sailors possessed, into the
mouth and eyes, into the very pores of the skin to which
it clammily adhered. And when the furnaces had consumed
the fuel and the sailors seemed at last to be rid of the
stuff, there was once again the inevitable nightmare of
coaling—'black fever' or 'the feast of coal' as it was
called.

There was no escape from the coal; only a growing
hatred that soon affected everyone, from the commanders, who were unaccustomed to the extremes of
discomfort, to the rawest and most phlegmatic peasant-
sailors.

With the West African heat came the humidity, like a
warm, suffocating, invisible rain-cloud, as clingingly in-
escapable as the coal dust. The dampness deadened every
movement, made the simplest decision an effort and eating
a burden, saturated clothing and hammocks, rusted exposed
metal and warped the woodwork on the ships. All ports
and deadlights had to be closed; the fans rotated sluggishly,
barely stirring the steaming, dust-laden air.

Rozhestvensky's greatest achievements were to procure
against every obstacle this loathsome coal, and to sail his
raw, mixed fleet intact through that evil climate with no
more than a handful of casualties. Even the British believed
it impossible; only tremendous determination and bull-
headed obstinacy could have done it—and these were two
qualities that none of Rozhestvensky's critics could deny
him.

The French Port Admiral of Dakar came out in a launch
as the coaling began, and told Rozhestvensky that it must

cease at once. The Japanese and British governments were about to protest at the Russian fleet's entry into neutral waters.

Rozhestvensky was standing no nonsense. 'I intend to take on coal unless your shore batteries prevent me,' he said.

The two admirals eyed one another cagily. 'You surely must know that we have no shore batteries,' the Frenchman replied. The tension eased, there was some laughter, and a champagne toast to the success of the voyage was drunk.

With oakum or damp cotton waste stuffed into their mouths, the thermometer at 120 degrees and the humidity in the nineties, the crews set to work. Soon a black cloud rose and enveloped every warship and its attendant collier; and from the shore the harbour appeared to be filled with smouldering hulks. The sun looked like an orange ball from the decks of the men-of-war; while from the depths of the colliers' holds, where the men choked and coughed and sweated under their filthy black loads, it looked like a tiny, blood-red spot. When from time to time a man fainted, a bucket of water was thrown over him, and when he came round he picked up his fallen sack or basket and went on with his work. A few cases of heatstroke were treated more seriously, and on the *Oslyabya* the son of the Russian Ambassador in Paris, Lieutenant Nelidoff, fell down dead from the heat. The coaling continued without a pause, and it took over twenty-nine hours to empty the colliers' holds.

The blackened sailors were lying about exhausted on deck, resting with their tots of vodka before starting work on cleaning ship, when the Port Admiral set off for the *Suvoroff* again, more determined this time. He had received a cable from Paris, he informed Rozhestvensky; it confirmed his own original order. The French government expressly forbade the refuelling of the Russian warships in the neutral harbour of Dakar, and steps would be taken to prevent it if necessary.

No such steps would be necessary, Rozhestvensky re-assured the Admiral, thanking him with all the natural courtesy at his command; and gave orders to weigh anchor in three hours' time.

CHAPTER FIVE

'Withdraw Your Fleet at Once'

Now the *Suvoroff* and her sister ironclads were more unmanageable than ever, like sluggish, overloaded river barges. Their lower decks were almost awash and took on water in the slightest swell, and their armoured belts were submerged below their waterlines. When the ships had been at normal draft, and rolling only five degrees in a slightly choppy sea during the Dogger Bank Incident, the gunners in the lower ports had been half-swamped. Now the ships could not even be considered as seaworthy, let alone as fighting units, and they looked as if they might capsize in the slightest beam wind. With over two thousand miles to their next coaling base—which might have less sympathetic port officials—this was a risk Rozhestvensky had to take. Luckily the weather remained fair, and slowly the fleet staggered south, steaming at nine and a half knots when it could, but held up frequently by engineroom breakdowns on one or another of the ships.

A bearing on the *Borodino* constantly became overheated (she had been plagued with this trouble ever since she had sailed, and could never manage more than twelve knots); the *Donskoy* got sand in her Kingston valves after running on a bar; the old *Malay* held them up time and again, until recourse was made to a towing cable, and this broke so often that finally a chain had to be used instead.

And, of course, the *Kamchatka* made a contribution to their troubles. On the 22nd of November she was seen to be falling farther and farther astern. When called back to her station, she replied, 'Dangerously damaged—cannot proceed'. Finally the flag-engineer was detached to investigate the trouble, though the fleet's repair ship should really have been able at least to diagnose her own trouble. 'Trouble trifling,' the *Kamchatka* signalled shamelessly almost at once, and quickly resumed station.

It was on the *Kamchatka*, too, that the first signs of a restlessness occurred that on several ships later flamed into mutiny. The civilian stokers engaged for the voyage were under orders from naval engineers, and, as always, it was the stokers who suffered most from the intense heat and suffocating atmosphere—'pale and haggard so that one wondered if they could hold out'. Strikes threatened, groups of the men refused further duty, and the troubles spread to the other auxiliaries.

Rozhestvensky took firm action at once and threatened to put the lot of them off in open boats.

There were incidents on the warships, too, cases of mild insubordination which the politically unreliable sailors tried to fan into mutiny. Their seriousness usually depended on the action of the junior officer present; some tried severity, others realized that the exceptional conditions called for leniency.

On Captain Lebedeff's *Dmitri Donskoy* discipline was unusually lax. At two o'clock one morning the *Suvoroff's* searchlights sweeping the sea in a surprise mock alarm, picked out one of the *Donskoy's* boats making its way to the hospital ship. 'Three dissolute officers', as the C.-in-C. described them in the next order of the day, had been escorting a Sister of Mercy back to her quarters: 'an example of extreme depravity; tomorrow we may reap the consequences.' The consequences for Lieutenant Vaselago and Midshipmen Varzar and Selitrenikoff were immediate arrest and return to Russia for court martial, the captain being severely reprimanded and his ship placed under Enkvist's supervision, with orders to 'cure her of her innate corruption without delay'. All the nurses were well-connected ladies, mostly daughters of noblemen; and two were nieces of Rozhestvensky. There is no record of what happened to this particular one.

To offset the tedium of their slow progress towards the equator, Rozhestvensky began filling in the periods between breakdowns with practice attacks by the cruisers on the ironclads, simple manœuvres and formation changes, and simulated night torpedo attacks. 'The confusion which is bound to take place during the first exercises,' the C.-in-C. benignly concluded his order, 'must not be minded, but the task completed and repeated.'

Tall and taut, his head thrust forward, his hands gripping the rail on the *Suvoroff's* bridge, Rozhestvensky watched the overloaded ships struggling to carry out his orders in the heavy South Atlantic swell. At the start of every exercise it was clear that he was determined to be tolerant; then as mistake after mistake was made his staff could see his patience rapidly becoming exhausted, like a well-intentioned, irritable schoolmaster with a classroom of backward children. For a time there would be a tense silence, his head would go farther forward and he would turn pale with anger.

Suddenly he would swing round to Clapier de Colongue and shout, 'Signal to the captain of the *Borodino* "You don't know how to command your ship".' Then he would pace rapidly from side to side of the bridge, pausing momentarily to raise his glasses to one or other of the guilty ships, cursing them in turn and demanding to know what sins he had committed to be burdened with such a horde of incompetents. 'I have signalled you four times,' he told the *Nakhimoff*, 'all without response. Four days' arrest for the officer-of-the-watch.' And the vessel would be ordered to break line and take station to starboard of the *Suvoroff*, the position of ultimate disgrace.

As one day of exercises followed another, Clapier de Colongue learned to anticipate every stage of his chief's

exasperation until it became almost a ritual. But, however
hard they tried, there was little improvement in the standard of seamanship: months of careful, patient instruction
were needed to transform these untrained recruits and
rusty reservist officers into a working unit, and months
more of gunnery practice were required to make the
Second Pacific Squadron into a fighting fleet. But the guns
had been fired once only, on that wild night in the North
Sea a month before, and these makeshift manœuvres *en
route* served only to drive home to even the simplest-
minded Ukrainian peasant their hopeless incompetence.
Time was needed; if only there were six more months to
spare. But every hour lost reduced their chances of turning the tide in the Far East.

The little French colony at the mouth of the Gaboon
estuary was without a telegraph, and the Lieutenant-
Governor had had no warning of the approaching Russian
fleet. On the morning of the 26th of November he was surprised to see three large auxiliaries approaching and
anchoring off shore. Next a pair of cruisers hove into sight,
and then a column of battleships. Gigs were lowered from
the ironclads, each with two leadsmen and two flag buoys,
which were towed by pinnaces steaming in line abreast
ahead of the fleet to mark out the anchorages.

Gaboon had never seen anything like this before. The
Governor had heard of the war in the Far East, but nothing
of this fleet and its misdeeds. Thankful that they appeared
to be just outside territorial waters, he took a launch
loaded with flowers and tropical fruit and a crate of champagne to the flagship, to present his compliments and
invite the officers ashore.

The atmosphere in Rozhestvensky's cabin was cordial
and the exchange of courtesies bordered on the extravagant. 'There will be some German colliers here the day
after tomorrow,' the Admiral told the Governor as he was

leaving, 'and if the weather permits, we shall coal outside French territory.'

That night the chaplain on every ship sent prayers to Nikolai Ugodnik—Nicholas the Just, the sailor's patron saint—for a calm sea until the colliers arrived. Doubtless there were prayers ashore, too; the Governor was without instructions, or a precedent, for such a situation.

The next day there was shore leave for officers and crew members who were not on watch; for the first time for six weeks they could escape from the heat and the damp and the filth of their overcrowded ships, from the clinging smell of rusting ironwork, paint and pervading coal dust. The sailors came ashore in the ships' boats by the hundred, looking in wonder at the strange tropical trees, the luxuriant undergrowth and the great, exotic flowers. There were birds of a size and vivid colour they had never dreamed of, monkeys swinging high in the branches, moths a foot long, turtles basking on the sands—strange sights, strange scents, strange sounds. These Russian sailors who, a few months before, had known of nothing outside their drab, laborious lives, nothing but a colourless world of soil and distant horizons, were given a brief glimpse of paradise: for a few hours the Odyssey touched its Land of the Lotus Eaters; and in the evening the sailors returned to the familiar drudgery of their ironclads, numbed and bewildered. It was all beyond their comprehension.

The officers strode ashore self-confidently, intent on exploration and a good time. They found eighteen-feet-long boa-constrictors, watched the natives preparing monkeys for consumption by soaking them in the bogs for tenderness, helped search for the cannibals who had recently eaten two white men, traded trinkets for parrots and baby monkeys; and called on the king.

They found he was 'just a wild nigger', asleep in a grubby hut with one of his wives. The next day the reception was more impressive, and he met them in ancient

naval cocked hat, frock coat, loose necktie, starched cuffs
and ceremonial sword, lacking only shirt and trousers.
Surrounding him were his court ladies and wives, all stark
naked, and by his side was the ancient Queen Dowager,
who let down the tone by begging for money and demanding to be photographed arm-in-arm with her seventy-two
years'-old son. The officers also unwittingly transgressed
court etiquette by sitting on an innocent-looking wooden
box in a corner of the hut which, it was revealed, contained the body of the late monarch who had died only
two days before.

At Gaboon, too, the crew of the *Alexander III* lost their
shipmate 'Andrew Andrewitch', a native who had been
stranded on the battleship at Dakar. At first he had been
furious, storming and weeping in turn as he fled about the
decks, and complaining that his wife would be stolen. But
later he came to enjoy his role of ship's mascot and ate and
slept, worked and played with the bluejackets, and even
learnt some Russian. He was quite reluctant to leave in
the end, and had to be comforted with a bonus of sixty
roubles before he could be packed home on a coaster.

The squadron had already crossed the equator when the
Suvoroff's navigator by mistake made landfall thirty miles
south of Gaboon. But the official ceremony took place
three days after they left the estuary, after a brief call at
Libreville, on December 2nd. It was celebrated on every
ship in the traditional manner from nine in the morning.
On the *Suvoroff* a procession formed up at the stern and
moved slowly forward to the music of the ship's band.
There were devils and barbers with giant razors, half-
naked painted savages, peasants in native costume, and
preceding the gun carriage carrying Neptune and Venus, a
peasant carrying in a shawl one of the wardroom dogs,
whose tail was constantly twisted to simulate the howls of
a baby.

The procession halted at the fore twelve-inch gun

turret, on which had been erected a great canvas bath, and the dipping, lathering and shaving proceeded to the accompaniment of shouts and screams of laughter from a packed audience in the bows, while others of the initiated cheered from the masts and yards and cross-trees.

On the bridge above, Rozhestvensky looked on tolerantly with his Staff, while skulking seamen and officers, and even Captain Ignatzius himself, were sought out and ducked. The war seemed far away on that warm December morning.

The Commandant of the Portuguese colony at Great Fish Bay had been carefully instructed in what action he was to take if the Russian fleet tried to use his sheltered waters for coaling; 'Britain's oldest ally' was to brook no compromise. Sure enough, three colliers arrived on December the 5th. The Commandant telegraphed for naval support, and when Rozhestvensky's ironclads steamed in and dropped anchor by the sandy spit which gave protection from the swell, a tiny Portuguese gunboat, the *Limpopo*, bustled out officiously and came alongside the *Suvoroff*.

Rozhestvensky tried humouring the captain when he came aboard, offered him champagne and asked for news of the war, but was met with a cold response.

'I have instructions from my government to order your departure at once,' he was told.

'But we are outside territorial waters,' Rozhestvensky answered reasonably enough. 'We can do what we like here.'

The captain was definitely not to be trifled with. 'You are anchored in the bay. That is the point. Kindly withdraw your fleet at once, or I shall be forced to take drastic action.''

Coaling was already in full swing when the gunboat steamed off, demonstrating her prowess by darting in and out of the anchored ironclads, while the Russian commanders awaited with interest the first broadside from her single three-pounder gun. Instead the *Limpopo* indicated that she was leaving for Benguela to protest and obtain support from British naval units.

'Good-bye, little one,' Rozhestvensky signalled the gunboat as she dipped her stem into the heavy rollers offshore. 'Pleasant passage. By the time you have crawled to the Royal Navy for help, not one of us will be here.'

Mercifully the weather had cooled and the south-west trades brought low scudding clouds at dawn and clear skies by mid-day for the journey south from Great Fish Bay. The only port on the entire 18,000-miles voyage where they could be sure of a welcome was Angra Pequena in German South-West Africa. This was Rozhestvensky's last port-of-call before Diego Suarez in Madagascar, which by agreement with France was to be their base for their reunion with Felkerzam's squadron and for a general refit before the long haul across the Indian Ocean. Somehow or other more than 2,300 tons of coal were to be taken on at Angra Pequena by the big battleships for the weary, dangerous trip of 3,000 miles round the Cape.

On the 11th of December they steamed cautiously into the narrow bay, a boat from each ship taking soundings ahead, and anchored close against the narrow rocky peninsula that divided the harbour in two.

The British had ceded Angra Pequena to Germany, retaining only two small islands off-shore. Powerless to prevent the Russian invasion, they were reduced to sending a protest. The story of the British reception soon spread from ship to ship, giving delighted satisfaction, and the German Governor, known simply as 'the Major', became a legendary figure among the officers and crews.

'What squadron? Where is it lying?' he was reputed to have demanded of the British delegation as he strode on to his veranda and looked across the empty water. The Russian ships were packed so tightly that the auxiliaries and cruisers were forced to anchor at sea, but the peninsula just hid them all from view.

The Major became outraged when it was suggested that he should take a boat and see for himself. 'I'm a military man,' he protested. 'I'm not going cruising around in a native canoe looking for mythical Russian battleships.'

This, and other incidents—the arrival of a battalion of German soldiers to put down a rising of the Hereroes, and the dining and wining of their officers on the *Suvoroff*— compensated a little for the worst coaling battle of the entire voyage. The harbour was not so sheltered as it appeared, and the wind, which had been blowing in squally gusts when they arrived, increased to a full gale. For two days Rozhestvensky waited impatiently for it to blow itself out, then in desperation ordered up the colliers.

Rolling and pitching in the heavy sea, the coal ships struggled to come alongside, and time and again crunched against the hulls of the ironclads. The *Suvoroff's* twelve-pounders pierced her own collier like the prongs of a fork, damaging gun barrels and torpedo booms, and after an hour the operation had to be called off. Lacking lighters, they tried transporting the coal in the ships' launches. This proved a slow, laborious and equally dangerous procedure; after battling all day and by the glare of searchlights through the night, only a few hundred tons had been taken into the battleships' bunkers.

The delay was maddening and Rozhestvensky, who always responded to this sort of frustration by fits of uncontrollable rage, made life unbearable for Clapier de Colongue and the rest of the Staff. In that tight little storm-swept bay, all the commanders became infected by the tension and irritability on the flagship, and there were sharp outbreaks of indiscipline among the seamen that flared and died again. A sailor on the *Korea* lost his reason, and a sub-lieutenant on the *Oryol* went berserk, racing round the deck sobbing, 'The Japs are waiting for us. We shall all be sunk! We shall all be sunk!' until he was locked in his cabin under guard. They had already been at sea for more than two months, without mail or news from home, out of touch with the world, travelling, it seemed, without purpose or destination, suffering endless discomfort, boredom and hardship.

The launches struggled unceasingly from the colliers to the warships and back again with their filthy sackloads, the ironclads heaved at their moorings, and the wind blew day after day, whistling through the shrouds, scuffling up grey clouds of coal dust, and beating at the trees on the gaunt shoreline.

At last on the night of the 15th of December the storm died, and in the morning the sea had fallen to a fog-shrouded gentle swell. With coaling going on in earnest, the Major came out to luncheon on the flagship at mid-day. He brought bad news with him. 203-Metre Hill, overlooking Port Arthur, had been captured at last by the Japanese after a bloody struggle.

'And what is 203-Metre Hill?' Rozhestvensky asked.

'It overlooks the entire harbour and roadstead of Port Arthur,' he was told. 'It may mean the end of the fortress.'

Rozhestvensky shrugged his shoulders. He did not understand military matters. He was much more interested in the warning which the Major brought from one of his own agents that sailing schooners at Durban were being fitted out with torpedo-tubes. With full British co-operation, it was said, the Japanese Rear-Admiral Sionogu was preparing to intercept the Russian fleet with these camouflaged vessels.

Rozhestvensky might have expected it. After their attack (as he still believed it to have been) in the North Sea, after failing to deprive him by diplomacy of coaling bases over the first 8,000 miles, the crafty Japs were going to make a last attempt to destroy his fleet before he could reach the war zone.

Simultaneously a signal arrived from the Russian Admiralty quoting a note just received from London which said bluntly that 'a repetition of the Hull incident would be most undesirable' if the Russian fleet should pass within the vicinity of the well-established fishing grounds off the coast near Durban Those wretched British again! And what an extraordinary coincidence!

Rozhestvensky instantly dispatched a cable to St. Petersburg in clear instead of in code, so that the whole world should understand, threatening that he would 'ruthlessly destroy all Durbanese fishing craft who attempt to break through my squadron or come within torpedo range . . .'. The Admiral was not going to be caught unprepared a second time.

The Second Pacific Squadron left African shores for the last time on the 17th of December, steaming out awkwardly, loaded more heavily than ever before, past the British islands and into the South Atlantic swell. Good wishes of farewell followed them from the Major, 'Happy voyage and all success in your venture. . . .' It was comforting to know they had one friend in the world.

Two days later they were celebrating the Feast of St. Nicholas, the Tsar's name-day, with banquet luncheons in the wardroom and a special meal, with the vodka flowing freely, on the mess-decks. Cape Town and Table Mountain had already slipped by seven miles away when the last toasts were being drunk below; from the shore the fleet could be seen through the slight haze as a score of distant straggling dark shapes, moving eastward very slowly beneath its perpetual great black cloud. The barometer was falling and the wind was rising. There was heavy sea ahead of them.

The irregular, restless swell broke into a full storm during the night. In any other circumstances Rozhestvensky would have sought shelter for his heterogeneous squadron of overladen vessels. But time was pressing, and in any case there was no harbour within a thousand miles that would receive them. Instead everything was battened down, wedges were jammed under shores and struts, the loose sacks of coal about the decks secured as far as possible with cables, and they prepared to ride it out.

For two days and nights the ships pitched and tossed helplessly, all but the mastheads disappearing from sight as they dipped deep into the troughs of the great waves, propellers racing wildly, and then struggled up on to the crests again, exposing their ram bows. The water swept over the decks even of the biggest ironclads, crashing against the turrets, reaching up to the conning-towers and bridges and swirling down into the stokeholds and engine rooms in a black, coal-strewn flood. No corner of the ships could escape; and the ironclads would have capsized very soon if they had not been running before the gale.

The tug *Roland* disappeared entirely and was presumed to be lost. The old *Malay*, which should never have attempted the voyage at all, had an engine breakdown when the storm was at its height. As the other ships passed, wave after wave was pounding over her and when one struck her amidships she exposed her red belly and keel like a dying whale. It seemed impossible that she could remain afloat. But when last seen far astern her crew were still struggling to hoist makeshift sails to keep her head into the seas while repairs were completed.

The *Kamchatka* had her troubles, too, and it was in character that her signal to the *Suvoroff* when things were at their most critical should carry a hint of the bizarre. 'My coal is very poor. Request permission to throw 150 tons overboard,' she begged.

In streaming oilskins on the *Suvoroff*'s bridge, Rozhestvensky read the message incredulously. Then he turned to the signalman and bawled into his ear, 'Tell the *Kamchatka* that we're all using the same coal and that my orders are that only the culprits are to be thrown overboard.'

Shortly afterwards, the squadron's incorrigible repair ship flashed, 'Do you see torpedo-boats?' In spite of the impossible conditions, which would have swamped one of those 300-ton cockleshells, and certainly made it impossible for even a battleship to fire a shot, the general alarm was sounded before the *Kamchatka* could apologize and explain that the signalman had been confused into using the incorrect code. 'I meant we are all right now.'

On the night of the 23rd of December the storm at last abated, and on the following day the squadron was able to halt to take stock of their condition and clean up and dry out. The *Borodino* had her old bearing trouble again, the steering gears of both the *Oryol* and the *Suvoroff* required attention, and few of the ships were without some sort of damage after their pounding.

Within twenty-four hours the rocky southern extremity of Madagascar was sighted, and the fleet at once turned and proceeded up the eastern coast. Now that the worst seemed to be over, more than half their journey completed, the storm overcome, Admiral Sionogu frustrated, and with a safe anchorage ahead, everyone felt a great sense of achievement and satisfaction. The *Malay*, and even the little *Roland*, they heard, had survived and were on their way.

Now they had only to link up with Felkerzam's squadron, refit and set sail for Port Arthur. Never before had the fleet enjoyed such a sense of buoyant self-confidence.

CHAPTER SIX

The Fleet Stagnates

SAINTE MARIE was perhaps the least salubrious port-of-call of the entire journey, a steaming, unproductive little island off Madagascar's eastern seaboard, which the French had been reduced to using as an overflow penal settlement for Devil's Island. Nor were the natives particularly agreeable; they had, in fact, recently murdered two white officials, and when one great man-of-war after another steamed in and anchored offshore, they were convinced that retribution—on a formidable scale—had arrived at last, and fled to the hinterland.

Rozhestvensky, too, was glad enough to leave when a rising wind from the south-west made coaling impossible, and the French administrator canoed out to the *Suvoroff* to suggest that the estuary of the Tang-Tang river a few miles further north would be more suitable.

Rozhestvensky was impatient for news of Admiral Felkerzam, who should by now have arrived at Diego Suarez with his Suez detachment and have dispatched a cruiser to meet the main fleet. He was worried, too, about the unprotected colliers which had already been waiting for some time to coal the combined fleets, and were obvious targets for any Japanese armed merchantmen, many of which were known to be loose in the Indian Ocean.

'Bungling commanders, inefficiency! They cannot carry out even the simplest arrangements,' he exclaimed, and ordered the tug *Rousse* to Tamatave to try to find out what had happened to Felkerzam, and then Enkvist to take the *Nakhimoff*, *Aurora* and *Donskoy* as protection for the vital coal ships and with instructions for Felkerzam to rejoin the flag immediately.

Shortly after they left, a single collier turned up with a message from Felkerzam saying that, in accordance with orders received direct from the Admiralty, he was 'overhauling his tired machinery' at Nossi-Bé, an island-studded bay five hundred miles away on the other side of the island, and that he regretted that he would be unable to proceed to sea for at least two weeks.

Rozhestvensky burst into one of his dreadful rages. How dared those interfering idiots at St. Petersburg alter the fleet's plans without reference to the C.-in-C. and send orders direct to his subordinates! He was equally furious with Felkerzam who had had the temerity to incapacitate his ships and then belatedly inform his Commander-in-Chief by means of a collier. And why Nossi-Bé? Diego Suarez, as he knew perfectly well, was to be their rendezvous. 'If they are so old that they can't steam,' he stormed at Clapier de Colongue, 'then they may go to the devil. We have no use for rubbish here. . . . But I'll go there myself,' he added with relish, 'I'll dig them out fast enough.'

Rozhestvensky's impatience was understandable. Although he affected little knowledge of military matters, he had no illusions about the Far East war situation and he knew that in the Second Pacific Squadron lay Russia's only hope (and a forlorn one) of regaining command of the sea and turning back the Japanese advance. His plan was to coal, carry out minimum repairs and set sail with his combined fleet to unite with the First Pacific Squadron as soon as possible. There had been enough maddening delays already: speed was vital.

It was the little tug *Rousse*, steaming back perkily from her reconnaissance mission to Tamatave, that brought the disastrous news which at once altered the prepared functions and intentions, the entire *raison d'être* of the fleet, added immeasurably to Rozhestvensky's already vast load of problems of logistics and organization, and incidentally explained why Felkerzam's detachment had anchored at Nossi-Bé instead of Diego Suarez.

Reduced to their simplest terms, the consequences of the *Rousse's* commander's news that Port Arthur was about to fall and that the fleet in the harbour had already been entirely destroyed, were that they were no longer a reinforcing squadron, and that they had lost their only adequate base in the Pacific. The Major had been right: a few hundred shells from 203-Metre Hill, overlooking Port Arthur harbour, had wiped out the powerful force of modern battleships and cruisers which, allied to Rozhestvensky's squadron, would have given them at least a numerical superiority over the Japanese. Now the Second Pacific Squadron, untrained, untested, lacking modern equipment and with their engines in need of overhaul, would have to face Togo alone.

But it was the ice-cold comfort at the end of the message, intended to instil him with new hope, that finally broke Rozhestvensky's spirit and sent him, bent and despairing, to his cabin, with Clapier de Colongue at his heels. Another supporting fleet, he was informed, with the ludicrous title 'Third Pacific Squadron', was being hurriedly assembled at Libau, and would join him as soon as possible.

So Nicholas Klado had won after all. To Rozhestvensky, his victory over the Board of Admiralty was as serious as the Japanese success at Port Arthur. It was the victory of pure arithmetic over pure logic. After testifying at the International Commission[1] investigating the Dogger Bank Incident in Paris, Klado had returned to St. Petersburg

---

[1] The Commission in its report published in February 1905, condemned Rozhestvensky for opening fire and leaving the scene of the incident without giving aid, and awarded damages to the British of £65,000, which included the value of the fish in the nets. A majority of the Commission considered that no torpedo craft had been present.

ILLUSTRATIONS

VICE-ADMIRAL ZINOVY PETROVITCH ROZHESTVENSKY

THE RUSSIAN BATTLESHIP ORYOL, SISTER SHIP TO THE BORODINO, ALEXANDER III AND THE FLAGSHIP, SUVOROFF

BANK INCIDENT. FISHERMEN FROM THE *GULL* RESCUING SURVIVORS FROM
THE *CRANE* UNDER RUSSIAN SHELL-FIRE

CAPTAIN NICHOLAS KLADO

REAR-ADMIRAL FELKERZAM

BATTLESHIPS OF THE *SUVOROFF* CLASS COALING AND REFITTING AT NOSSI-BÉ, MADAGASCAR

THE FLEET PASSES SINGAPORE

REAR-ADMIRAL NEBOGATOFF, AND ONE OF THE COAST-DEFENCE SHIPS OF THE THIRD PACIFIC
REINFORCING SQUADRON WHICH SAILED UNDER HIS COMMAND

'MOB IS THE ONLY WORD LITERALLY TO EXPRESS OUR FORMATION AT THIS TIME.' AN ARTIST'S SOMEWHAT IMAGINATIVE IMPRESSION OF THE RUSSIAN FLEET RECEIVING THE FIRST JAPANESE SALVOES AS IT EMERGES FROM THE STRAITS OF TSU-SHIMA

JAPANESE TORPEDO-BOATS PRESS HOME THEIR ATTACKS ON THE *ORYOL* DURING THE
NIGHT ACTION

'YOU PERFORMED YOUR GREAT TASK
HEROICALLY . . . I PAY YOU MY HIGHEST
RESPECT.' ADMIRALS TOGO AND ROZHEST-
VENSKY AFTER THE BATTLE

ADMIRAL HEIHACHIRO TOGO
(1847–1934)

and persuaded the 'dry land admirals' of the Higher Naval
Board that, with the imminent destruction of the Port
Arthur Squadron, it was more than ever essential to
strengthen Rozhestvensky with everything they had in
reserve. 'All these old ships,' Klado claimed again, 'could
be used to attract the enemy's fire and consequently
diminish the number of projectiles which might otherwise
strike the modern ships.'

Klado's arguments now seemed incontrovertible. Already
the ancient, rusting coast defence vessels were being fitted
out for the voyage east. And Rozhestvensky's instructions
were that he must await their arrival—in perhaps eight or
ten weeks' time!

There was only one thing left for him to do. 'Telegraph
to St. Petersburg,' he instructed de Colongue, 'that I wish
to be relieved of my command.' Then, feeling suddenly
exhausted and ill, he retired to his bunk.

The last news the squadron had received from home was
at Angra Pequena where the Major had managed to procure
some St. Petersburg newspapers for them. But these had
been dated October 16th, the day they had sailed from
Libau, and requests made at West African ports for permission to telegraph *Novoe Vremya's* office for information
about the war had been refused. Anxiety among the crews
had slowly given way to a feeling of isolation and detachment. Forgotten by the authorities, they became reconciled to steaming for ever about the oceans of a hostile
world.

The news of Port Arthur's fall quickly spread among the
Suvoroff's officers, and within hours had circulated down to
the crew rooms of every ship in the squadron, wrenching
them back to harsh reality. Details of the disaster were
passed by word of mouth in wardrooms and crews' quarters
and spread like an icy flood, causing depression and a sense
of outrage. Their mission, which before had appeared to

be hopeless enough, was suddenly seen as suicidal. Nothing could save them now.

Among the seamen, the news of the formation of a supporting squadron of old Baltic reserves made little impression for the present, serving only to confirm that their country was determined to persevere with the war and that they would not be returning home. 'Food for the fishes —that's all we're good for now, comrade. . . .' Still without letters from their wives and families (the Admiralty was as ignorant of the importance of mail in sustaining morale as of everything else), even their earthy, phlegmatic humour momentarily dried up.

In the wardrooms, although there was a closer analysis of their position, the depression was as acute. A number of the officers backed Klado and pointed to the additional firepower the old ships would provide, forgetting that their obsolete guns had an absurdly short range and that their antiquated engines would reduce the speed of the fleet even further. But they all agreed that it was the fall of Port Arthur that had caused the French to yield to Japanese and British pressure and deny them the use of Diego Suarez; that the war was to all intentions already lost; and that nothing but defeat awaited them. A fatalism they were never to throw off had gripped even the most loyal of them.

'To declare ourselves to be incompetent, to turn back and run the risk of being branded as cowards', wrote Flag-Officer Semenoff, one of Rozhestvensky's staunchest supporters, '—these ideas never entered my head. If, however (and I mean to be ruthlessly candid about this) at that time St. Petersburg had grasped how utterly hopeless—not to say criminal—our adventure was, and if they had sent us categorical orders to come back, I should have said, "The Lord be praised".'

Already the alarming suspicion had begun to grow that the units of the Second Pacific Squadron were being regarded in St. Petersburg as political rather than strategical pawns, with Rozhestvensky as the reserve scapegoat, and the lives of the ten thousand sailors as expendable.

Christmas morning (by the Russian calendar) arrived *en route* to Nossi-Bé in a flat calm, with a faint haze covering the sea and half obscuring the sun. The temperature was rising into the nineties in a damp, clammy atmosphere when the decorated ships heaved-to on the ocean for the celebrations, beginning with Mass at 8.30. At ten o'clock the unexpected order was given for the crew of the *Suvoroff* to assemble on the quarterdeck for the C.-in-C. to address them, and the nine hundred men gathered together quietly.

The shock and the anger caused by the recent news had given way to a depression that was as heavy as the humidity, and for the present lacked even the stimulus for indiscipline. As simple in their responses and emotions, and as inarticulate, as young schoolchildren, they were aware only that their families were a long way away and that they were unlikely ever to see them again. They awaited their Admiral's arrival in sullen silence. It was a melancholy Christmas morning.

Rozhestvensky, looking bent, drawn and twenty years older, left his cabin and made his way aft with Clapier de Colongue, the only man on the ship who knew what he had endured and that he had asked to be relieved of his command. No one had seen the Admiral for two days, and there was a ripple of faintly hostile curiosity as he climbed on to the aft twelve-inch turret and stepped forward to give his address, the glass of champagne in his hand contrasting oddly with his air of defeatism.

He began quietly, so that few could hear what he said, and there was 'an uncertain ring in his voice'. Then, as if forcing himself out of a coma, he raised his drooping body, his head came up, and drawing on his reserves of nervous energy, he began suddenly to shout with the vigour and enthusiasm of an orator.

'God grant that, after serving your country well and faithfully,' he called across the heads of the ship's company, 'you may be vouchsafed a safe return and a happy meeting with the families you have left behind.' When he warned them of the hard work and dangers that lay ahead, he suddenly became more and more excited, as if gripped by some deep emotion, perhaps of compassion for these hundreds of men whom he already believed to be doomed. 'This can't be helped,' he went on, 'it is war. It is not for me to thank you for your services. You as well as I serve our country side by side. But it is my right and my duty to report to the Emperor how you are doing your duty, what fine fellows you are, and he himself will thank you in the name of Russia.'

Now he raised his hat above his head in his left hand, his voice fell again, and the words of his toast were broken by his audible sobs. . . . 'May God help us to serve her honourably, to justify her confidence, not to deceive her hopes. To you, whom I trust! To Russia!'

Rozhestvensky drained the glass and then held it high above his bared head, while the cheers rang out across the water and caps were thrown in the air. 'Lead us!' 'We won't give in!' 'We'll do it!' Rozhestvensky heard them cry. Their arms were raised and he could see that many of them were in tears. Then the crash of the guns firing the salute drowned all other sound.

At sunset that evening four unidentified cruisers were reported approaching from the south-east, and the gun crews were at action stations until dawn. In spite of all her handicaps and inadequacies, the *Suvoroff* would have made a formidable foe that night.

The fleet could not have had a more suitable or more magnificent base in Madagascar than Nossi-Bé. The main island which gave the port its name was surrounded by a number of smaller islands. The peninsula of Angaboka to the south-east, a barrier of reefs to the west and the dominating conical peak of Nossi-Comba to the east, all gave shelter from any gales. High, thickly wooded hills fell down to Hellville, named after the French Admiral Hell who had taken possession of the bay in the name of France sixty years before.

From the bridge of the *Suvoroff* Hellville looked a pretty little town of white houses and red clay native huts, and the whole prospect was so enchanting and the anchorage so perfect for the fleet's requirements, that Rozhestvensky could not understand why the French had allowed him the use of it when political pressure had deprived him of Diego Suarez. What was more, anchoring berths had been laid out for all his ships, and as the *Suvoroff* led the squadron cautiously in through the maze of uncharted islets, a torpedo-boat carrying the tricolor darted out and cut its way through the still waters of the bay towards them, flashing 'Welcome' from its bridge. The Messageries Maritimes workshops, Rozhestvensky learnt later, had been warned of the likely demand for skilled labour and machinery, and a contingent of dockyard workers had been sent to the town from Diego Suarez. Great quantities of provisions, including a thousand bullocks, had been made available, and obviously everything possible was going to be done to make the stay pleasant for the Russians and profitable for the hosts.

The French had already displayed an extraordinarily inconsistent attitude towards the Second Pacific Squadron, the authorities (sometimes with full approval from Paris) again and again acting against their loudly declared intentions by permitting coaling. Rozhestvensky had been puzzled by this, and it was not until he had been in Madagascar for some time that he began to understand that, as usual, France was trying to please Japan and Britain without causing too great displeasure in Berlin and St. Petersburg. Of course France would cancel her contract permitting the Russian fleet the use of Diego Suarez, the French Ambassador had assured the Foreign Minister in Tokio; but on the same day Russia had been told that there was nothing to prevent their using Nossi-Bé, which was, in any case, quite as suitable. For France, the Second Pacific Squadron's voyage was a seven-months-long juggling sequence, with the act becoming progressively more complicated as the Russian fleet approached the war zone.

In that splendid harbour on the 10th of January, 1905, the crews managed to forget for a few hours the hardships of the voyage and their anxieties for the future in the excitement of the reunion. Felkerzam's ships, as comforting as the appearance of old familiar friends in a crisis, were anchored at the far end of the bay, their crews in topees lining the rails and waving. Under a scorching sun, the ironclads' bands struck up on the quarterdecks, signals flashed from ship to ship, the guns cracked out, and as soon as the anchors were dropped, boats were lowered and visits exchanged. Discipline was relaxed for the afternoon, at every party the vodka ran freely, and later hundreds of the bluejackets went ashore, shouting and singing and roaring through the streets of the little town with their arms linked. There had never been such a night of celebration in Hellville.

Felkerzam, it appeared, had had an easier journey than the main fleet, though it had not been without its difficult moments. On shore leave at Canea in Crete, for example, the crews had got out of hand, and in drunken brawls with the natives a Russian bluejacket had been killed and a dozen more stripped in the town square. The passage through the Suez Canal had been an anxious time, too, with some provoking displays of hostility and obstructionism by a couple of British cruisers. There had been reports of Japanese torpedo craft in the Great Bitter Lakes and along the shores of the Red Sea. Rozhestvensky's second-in-command was able to give him all this latest news and details of his communications with St. Petersburg over luncheon on the flagship on that day of reunion. The heavily bearded Enkvist was there as well, and this was one of the few occasions during the voyage when the two divisional admirals conferred directly with their C.-in-C. Of the future, Rozhestvensky told them nothing, and this time his reticence could be justified, for he knew as little as they. He referred briefly to the report that 'the broken old Baltic hulks' might yet join them, and hastened his guests away as soon as he decently could. He had never felt at ease with his admirals, and found their company more than ever trying at this critical time.

For the first few days at Nossi-Bé the officers and crews were given no opportunity to worry about their future. Rozhestvensky's orders were that the ships were to be overhauled, revictualled and coaled at top speed as originally planned, and in the steaming heat of the sheltered bay the work went on in two shifts without a break. Conditions were as bad here as at Dakar, Gaboon and the other tropical coaling points, with the stripped, filthy and exhausted sailors falling asleep amongst the scattered coal on the decks the moment their watch was completed. Cardiff coal dust lying heavily in the damp, fetid air made any thought of rest below decks impossible, the humidity deprived the men of all appetite, and even the water which they drank in prodigious quantities was warm and unattractive distilled sea-water. By the end of the fourth day when the coaling was at last completed, they all looked like the survivors of a mining disaster, grey-faced and staring-eyed, with torn, blackened trousers. Sunstroke had killed one man and laid out dozens more, dysentery was already breaking out on many ships, two sailors on the *Borodino* had been suffocated by the heat and dust in a wing passage, and on the *Ural* an officer had been killed and another injured by a Temperley crane slinging coal from a collier.

Revictualling followed—fifty thousand cases of potatoes from Cape Town, flour and meat and vegetables, chocolate, biscuits and preserves from the stocks judiciously laid in by the French, and now sold at a handsome profit. Knowing Russian officers' tastes, they had also prepared supplies of fancy foodstuffs and drink for the wardrooms, and lighter-loads of crates were slung aboard the big *Suvoroff*-class battleships. 'Never before has any fleet laid in such stores of champagne and liqueurs', reported *The Times'* correspondent.

Several of the keenest young officers were already preparing plans for hunting in the mountains and jungles of the hinterland, and inquiries were being made at a number of houses about short-term letting. If they were to be granted a few unexpected weeks of remission, then they were determined to enjoy themselves.

Their Admiral, on the other hand, still nursed hopes of getting them away the moment his ships were fit for sea. With the refusal of his resignation, St. Petersburg had cabled confirmation that a Third Pacific Squadron was being prepared to support him, and that with this combined force, in spite of the loss of the Port Arthur squadron, Rozhestvensky was to reclaim command of the sea and cut off the Japanese communications. The Admiralty, the message concluded, would appreciate Rozhestvensky's assessment of the new situation.

The C.-in-C. replied promptly. He had known from the moment he received the news of the destruction of the battleships and cruisers in Port Arthur that he could never hope to carry out his original commission, that the most he could now hope to achieve was the relief of pressure on the Russian armies by harrying the Japanese supply ships. But now, more than ever, success depended on speed; every day that passed was a gift to Togo, another day for him to refit his own tired vessels that had been at sea on patrol continuously for twelve months. Their gun barrels were smooth, their machinery in desperate need of an overhaul. The fall of Port Arthur had given the Japanese their first respite since the opening of hostilities.

Rozhestvensky concluded his message with a brief, pointed summary of the situation. 'I have not the slightest prospect of recovering command of the sea with the force under my orders,' he cabled. 'The dispatch of reinforcements composed of untested and in some cases badly built vessels would only render the fleet more vulnerable. In my view the only possible course is to use all force to break through to Vladivostock and from this base to threaten the enemy's communications.'

It was the only policy that gave them an even chance of survival and an opportunity to damage the enemy, but Rozhestvensky had about as much chance of being allowed to carry it out as he had of defeating the Japanese in open battle. The influence of Klado's strange strategical principles was as strong as ever in St. Petersburg and the Admiralty's mind was made up: the Japanese could still be beaten at sea, but only by simultaneously pitting the entire strength of the navy against Togo. They had read Klado's highly praised articles in *Novoe Vremya* which exposed as the cause of the Russian Navy's defeats to date their policy of meeting the enemy piecemeal. Time and again, Klado pointed out, the Japanese had picked off isolated small units when the combined Far East fleet at the beginning of the war (disregarding the Baltic and Black Sea fleets) could have overwhelmed Togo by concentrating its strength and going out to meet the enemy. They were determined not to allow this to happen in the final trial of strength. The C.-in-C. must await reinforcements.

While officers and crews struggled with coal and stores for an imminent departure, Rozhestvensky, fretful, harassed and frustrated, fought on in his cabin for their survival,

dispatching cable after cable to Russia begging to be
allowed to proceed. 'No one really knows what the Admiral
has to go through,' Clapier de Colongue confided to one of
the *Suvoroff's* officers. 'Sometimes I bring him a deciphered
cable. He reads it. He crumples up the paper in his hand.
He masters himself. He begins to dictate the reply. Often
he changes the form, makes improvements, gets furious
with me. I hold my tongue. I know that his anger is not
directed at me. . . . Or he suddenly says, apparently quite
calmly: "Leave me alone, by and by I will—I will write it
myself", and on going out I hear him breaking the pencil
he has in his hand, trembling with suppressed rage, calling
"Traitor!" '

To add further to his troubles, Rozhestvensky was suddenly faced by another crippling handicap. As far as Madagascar the German coaling organization had been beyond
criticism, and the Hamburg-Amerika line, spurred on by
the huge profits in their contract, had adapted themselves
to the vagaries of French policy with efficiency. But now
Russian disasters in the East were making themselves felt
politically. Within a few days of their arrival in Nossi-Bé,
Japan had protested strongly at this infringement of
neutrality, and a naval spokesman in Tokio had threatened
that 'any colliers discovered in the vicinity of the Russian
squadron would instantly be fired on and destroyed'.

The collier crews soon made clear that they had signed
on to supply coal, not to engage in naval battles, and the
Germans regretfully informed Rozhestvensky that in the
circumstances they would not be prepared to extend their
contract to cover the fleet's voyage across the Indian
Ocean.

This was too much for Rozhestvensky. Betrayed by his
Admiralty, deprived of fuel and sabotaged by his allies,
how could he ever hope to reach Vladivostock? With fine,
experienced crews and commanders, with modern well-
tried ships and support and encouragement from home, his

task would have been fearful enough. Clapier de Colongue became reconciled to the final disintegration of his C.-in-C.'s will when, for the second time, Rozhestvensky retired ill to his bunk. He was suffering, de Colongue informed the Staff, from acute neuralgia, was in great pain, and was demanding ice. But he was to be deprived even of this comfort: in spite of an intensive search, with picket boats threading their way from ship to ship, no ice could be found for the Admiral.

'Day followed day like the links of a chain', the great ironclads, the armoured and light cruisers, the bulky, high-sided auxiliaries and transports, the diminutive tugs and destroyers, 'the three score and ten ships at anchor, in the calm sea, their hulls set steadily in the oily-looking waters, and the whole atmosphere oppressively still and damply hot'. In that steaming tropical bay during those long January and February weeks, the fleet began to assume the appearance of a weird naval review, without end or purpose, forgotten by the world.

At first, while Rozhestvensky was fighting to bring some sense of reality to their situation, and the ordeal of the coaling was over, the men were possessed by a sort of wild fatalism. Speculation about their future soon became tedious; whatever was to happen to them, it would be for the worst, and few among them believed they would ever see their homes again. Next week, next month, next year, they would inevitably meet Togo's battleships and be blown to pieces.

Meanwhile there was fun to be had in Hellville, which ceased to be a small, thriving and well-administered colonial town, inhabited by a few French traders, Malays, Jews, Indians and natives, and began to live up to its name. Felkerzam's crews had already succeeded in bringing the tone of the place down before the main fleet arrived, and when daily shore leave was granted the men found brothels, bars and gambling saloons set up for them in requisitioned native huts and corrugated iron shacks. Women had flocked to Hellville from all over the island, and vast supplies of liquor of all kinds were imported to meet the boom. Everything went soaring up in price, but money meant nothing, either as winnings or losses, at the gambling tables, for no one was allowed to send his pay home, and hundreds of useless trinkets and souvenirs were thrown overboard as soon as the men arrived back on their ships.

Demand for everything exceeded supply and inflation ran riot. The canny proprietor of the town's largest bar, a nameless broken-down hut, enlarged his premises and put up a garish sign, 'The Parisian Café'. 'I'm retiring to Paris after you all leave,' was the half-caste's explanation to his patrons; while above the hastily-erected stalls of his neighbours, roughly painted signs proclaimed, 'Purveyors to the Russian Fleet' and 'Russian Buyers Especially Welcome'.

'Our men despaired of escaping from the war with their lives,' wrote Novikoff-Priboy of the *Oryol*, 'so they drowned thought in drink, dicing and drabbing. The officers, who usually went ashore in mufti, turned a blind eye to their inferiors' misconduct, being afraid that a reprimand would provoke insolent replies. The bluejackets openly disregarded the voice of authority. They reeled through the streets, or lay dead drunk where they fell. Others crawled about on all-fours.'

Bottles of liquor, cheap bangles and beads, head scarves and native sandals were not the only things the sailors brought back to their ships on the leave boats. Keeping pets soon became a craze, and parrots and porcupines, chameleons, frogs and dogs, hares and monkeys and pigs, all bought at high prices, were hoisted aboard every evening to join the oxen, cows and sheep which were kept in pens as reserve fresh meat for the voyage ahead. There they ran wild, excreting on the stacked piles of coal, over the decks and between decks, in the crews' quarters, the torpedo flats and gun turrets and in every gangway, turning the ships into open zoos. A crocodile was somehow smuggled into one of the battleships; on another a snake bit an engineer and his leg swelled until the surgeon despaired of his life, though he finally succeeded in saving it. A cow slung on to the *Suvoroff* with its calf went berserk, charging about the deck and scattering the bluejackets. For days after the cow was at last secured, the burning issue aboard the flagship was whether it would ever again yield for its calf, who was not thriving on tins of condensed milk. On another battleship, the favourite sport was getting monkeys and dogs drunk on champagne and inciting them to fight one another. The smallest issue became a diversion; anything was good enough to pass away the time until the next wardroom party, the next beat-up ashore.

Because of the low quality of Rozhestvensky's commanders, indiscipline and demoralization were complete after two weeks at Nossi-Bé. While the Second Pacific Squadron's C.-in-C. lay sick in his cabin, nursing his breakdown, there was nobody to care, nothing to prevent the fleet from declining into a state of anarchy.

Complaints from the local French administrator, M. Titeau, at last aroused Rozhestvensky from his sick bed and brought him, withered and pale but roaring like a lion, from his den. It was in the interests of a boom town to tolerate a certain amount of rioting and debauchery when every drop of liquor was paid for in good Russian gold, but a gang of bluejackets from the *Groznyi* had started tearing down native huts, and if that practice was taken to its logical conclusion Hellville as a leave centre would soon cease to exist.

Only an impulse like this could have regenerated the dynamo, and these sailors from the *Groznyi* provided it. Horrified and outraged at what had been going on during his confinement, Rozhestvensky hastened into action with all his old vigour, reprimanding officers and commanders ('Your men and your ship are a disgrace to the fleet'), and within a few days transforming the lives and standard of conduct of his 10,000 men. Shore leave for officers and men, except on High and Feast days and Sundays to selected and approved personnel, was banned forthwith, all pet animals were to be thrown overboard or put ashore. . . . The flow of daily orders, which had dried up for nearly two weeks, poured forth in a torrent, and a rigorous new routine of ship-cleaning, brass-polishing, physical training and small-arms drill instituted.

'We work now until we drop', wrote home one officer, and *The Times'* St. Petersburg correspondent quoted another officer: 'Rozhestvensky is thoroughly hated on account of his arbitrary orders, and we have lost all faith in his strategical competence. Among other brutal orders is one that anthems and chants for the dead should be performed day after day on board the hospital ship, a measure which exercises a terribly depressing effect upon the invalids.'

But the spirit of the fleet at Madagascar ebbed and flowed, as restless as the tides in Nossi-Bé, as unpredictable as the temper of the Admiral. It was the political news from home that broke the mood of sullen hostility caused by the harsh regime, and fanned up the first dangerous flames of mutiny. On February 13th, a small reinforcing detachment of cruisers, auxiliaries and destroyers, which had been delayed by mechanical faults or non-completion, arrived at Nossi-Bé with the most recent St. Petersburg newspapers the fleet had seen since Felkerzam had joined them.

These newspapers were intended only for the wardroom, but no censorship could have prevented their filtering through to the lower decks, where they were excitedly seized upon and read from cover to cover. The earlier issues of *Novoe Vremya* contained a series of articles by Klado, the opening rounds in his campaign against Rozhestvensky which he had already won, full of the jargon which sounded so authoritative, condemning the folly of sending out the Baltic Fleet piecemeal 'to certain defeat', and provided fascinating if hardly reassuring reading to a squadron about to go into battle.

But the later foreign newspapers were even more sensational, carrying the full stories of the great riots and upheavals against the Tsarist regime, the overtures to Russia's bloodiest year of unrest and violence and revolution: student riots, strikes and demonstrations at Baku, St. Petersburg and Moscow, martial law in many big cities and, most terrible of all, details of the Winter Palace massacre of demonstrators.

This news of revolt against a decaying and corrupt regime could not have found a more fertile breeding ground than Nossi-Bé, with its ten thousand angry and disillusioned sailors, and of course it provided triumphant justification for the subverts scattered throughout the fleet, who 'decided to prepare for future events by forming an organization which should keep the most advanced elements of the squadron in close touch with one another'. If two thousand had died under the Cossack cavalry charge before the Winter Palace, they had died for a cause in which they believed, not purposelessly at the hands of an unknown enemy in a distant sea.

With the wet season now set in and the rain pouring down from the low scudding black clouds day after day, sweeping across the bay and washing clean the steel decks, the revolts and strikes at home were the sole topics of conversation among the bluejackets. In groups as they worked, as they ate on the mess decks, quietly in their hammocks at night, they talked of nothing but the ferment that was stirring in their country and the desperate restlessness in their own hearts.

If the news had arrived while Rozhestvensky was ill it would have sent a spontaneous and probably uncontrollable wave of revolt through the fleet; every unit would have become a battleship *Potemkin*, with no Imperial troops to wreak revenge. Instead, by a combination of alertness and ruthlessness, the C.-in-C. just succeeded in retaining control.

Mutiny broke out first on the *Nakhimoff*, whose officers were particularly weak and self-indulgent, without a thought for their men. The crew of the *Nakhimoff* had not tasted bread since they had left Libau, although all the other big ships had their own bakeries, and now even the dry biscuits were going mouldy. At supper one evening the entire crew of four hundred refused to eat any more, throwing their food overboard, and later, as dusk was falling after prayers, disobeying the order to dismiss given by the officer-of-the-watch. 'Give us fresh bread!' they called, and began milling about the deck, shouting at the tops of their voices and grabbing weapons.

The mutineers were preparing to rush the bridge and the officers' quarters when the captain appeared, and by drawing their attention to the big guns of the *Suvoroff*, which had swung round and were pointing straight at them, succeeded in silencing them. Fourteen of the arbitrarily selected ringleaders were shot, and a number more were sentenced to long terms of detention.

Rozhestvensky's iron rod ruthlessly beat out the fires of revolt flickering up all over the fleet. Suddenly courts martial became almost daily events. On the *Ural* an officer was sentenced to dismissal and deprivation of rank for beating his captain insensible; on the *Suvoroff* four sailors who had stolen crates of champagne from the wardroom and hidden them among the idle boilers were ordered to a detention battalion for three years; the *Kamchatka*, *Borodino*, *Alexander III* and many other ships all had their courts martial; and at last, in an effort to clear the fleet of its worst elements (and also to avoid pressure on the over-crowded lockups), Rozhestvensky decided to get rid of the old *Malay* and send her home with the worst offenders, together with a few of the most seriously ill.

But before the prison ship could be got away, a full-scale mutiny broke out on board, and this time the desperate men succeeded in gaining control, locking up the officers and crew in their own filthy cells in the bowels of the ship. Unluckily for them, the uproar was heard across the harbour. Once again the *Suvoroff*'s guns were trained on a unit of her own fleet, and a strong boarding party was sent to put down the revolt. After a short, sharp struggle, during which a number of shots were fired and several men wounded, the *Suvoroff*'s sailors succeeded in regaining control and cornering the mutineers.

Rozhestvensky's strongest ally during this crucial period was the climate. Apathy and listlessness dampened the men's spirit more successfully than the examples of shooting parties and courts martial. It was easier to charge the barricades in St. Petersburg's winter snow with a thousand others at your side than to organize a mutiny with the humidity at 98 per cent. It was energy rather than courage that Rozhestvensky's men lacked. 'More and more frequently there falls on me complete oblivion to my surroundings', Engineer Politovsky of the *Suvoroff* wrote home to his wife. 'I have such attacks of endless despair, such fancies, such horrible thoughts, that, by God, I do not know what to do, where to hide, or how to forget myself.'

The depressive effect of the Madagascan climate was beginning to get a grip on everyone by the third month, and the unsuitable food—the endless vegetable soup, made now from local manioka instead of fresh cabbage—encouraged stomach ailments and provided little protection against disease. According to the settlers, the European expectation of life was not much more than three years,

and 'malaria, dysentery, tuberculosis, boils, mental de-
rangement, prickly heat and fungoid infections of the ear
wrought havoc among us'.

By early March the death rate was running at an alarming level, and there were funeral services every day.[1] The
hospital ship was packed, the Sisters of Mercy run off their
feet, and the sick bays on every ship overcrowded. Some
of the worse cases of lunacy were sent home with the
mutineers on the *Malay*, but there was nothing to be done
with the milder melancholics who 'roamed the ships in filthy
uniforms, muttering to themselves "Do you fear death?"'

It was not death that the bluejackets of Rozhestvensky's
fleet feared; the fear of death had been worn away by the
months of hardship and mistreatment, boredom and home-
sickness. Death had become the ultimate anti-climax. With
the snuffing out of the last flames of insurrection, their only
fear was that they had all been condemned to the living
hell of Nossi-Bé for eternity.

Only Admiral Rozhestvensky's health appeared to remain unaffected by the Madagascan climate. Since his recovery from his breakdown, his remarkable vigour and
fund of nervous energy had driven him on relentlessly, and
he had been working eighteen hours a day on the vast
problems his fleet faced, as well as on minor administrative
routine which should have been the responsibility of his
Staff. As far as St. Petersburg was concerned, he was to
remain at anchor until the reinforcing squadron joined him
at some unspecified date. Perhaps because the breakdown
in the coaling arrangements ensured this delay, it appeared
to Rozhestvensky that the Admiralty was remarkably un-
concerned about the Hamburg-Amerika Company's breach
of contract.

[1] The *Kamchatka* almost succeeded in adding to these when a
saluting shell honouring one of her dead turned out to be live, and rico-
chetted off her neighbour, the cruiser *Aurora*.

The C.-in-C. decided, therefore, to reopen negotiations himself. He began by pointing out to the company that failure to meet their commitments would involve them in a lawsuit involving hundreds of thousands of pounds, and a great deal of goodwill. When this failed to have any effect, he offered, according to *The Times* of March 25th, to buy ten of the colliers outright on behalf of the Russian government, intending to sail them with scratch crews across the Indian Ocean with his fleet.

Tact and diplomacy were not among Rozhestvensky's gifts. But by a sustained campaign of bullying and by employing all manner of threats, he slowly wore down the supercargo representing the Hamburg-Amerika line and persuaded him to accept the offer.

The Admiralty knew nothing of these negotiations, nor did they discover until it was too late that Rozhestvensky had capped his victory by persuading the German authorities to allow four more colliers, carrying a further 30,000 tons, to follow him across the Indian Ocean at a discreet distance and meet him at Saigon.

While the final rounds in the most important coaling battle of the voyage were taking place, Rozhestvensky decided that, with boilers now cleaned and repairs to machinery completed, the fleet should begin their first serious training programme. The guns had not been fired since the night of the Dogger Bank Incident and manœuvres had been limited to the simplest changes of formation. Although all his ships had been commissioned since the previous autumn, the Second Pacific Squadron was no more of a fighting force now than it had been when it left Libau.

'We must work hard, not sit still with our hands in our laps,' Rozhestvensky told his captains and crews. 'We cannot afford much ammunition for target practice, but everyone must become familiar with the telescopic sights. . .' The new Barr-Stroud rangefinders, fitted since the outbreak of the war, were almost as mysterious instruments as these new-fangled telescopic sights, and were treated, even by the regular gunnery officers, with some suspicion.

The shortage of spare ammunition was equally serious. Supplies had been awaited anxiously since they had first anchored in Nossi-Bé, and at last on March the 11th, the supply ship *Irtysh*, reputedly carrying large stocks of twelve- and six-inch shells, had arrived from Reval. But all she had on board were 12,000 pairs of boots and vast quantities of fur-lined winter coats to combat the cold. On the three occasions when the fleet put to sea for gunnery practice and manœuvres, only a few large-calibre shells could be fired, and the gunners had to make do with aiming rifles, their triggers connected to the firing mechanism, secured above the guns. This, the Flag Gunnery Captain explained, provided the gun crews with all the necessary drill and routine, and the effect lacked only the noise and recoil—and the evidencè of the fall of shot.

The result of the first of these sorties is shown in Rozhestvensky's order of the day issued the following morning. The fleet had steamed out of Nossi-Bé, and after taking up station, the ships were ordered to turn together eight points and stop engines in line abreast while the targets were set. The flagship did not set the best example to the rest of the squadron:

'Nearly an hour elapsed before the *Suvoroff* could up-anchor,' ran the C.-in-C.'s order, 'the reason for this preposterous delay being that the windlass, clogged with rust and mud, would not work. In an hour, ten ships did not succeed in forming line, although the leading vessel went dead slow. Everybody had been informed that towards noon, the signal would be given to turn together and stop engines in line abreast, but the captains lost their heads, and instead of forming a single line abreast, the ships became a mere jumble in which they were steaming about in every direction. One feels really ashamed to speak of the firing,' went on Rozhestvensky. 'In practice destroyer attacks, the small calibre guns did not succeed in scoring a single hit, although the target differed from the Japanese torpedo-boats to our advantage inasmuch as they were stationary.' And of the battleships' main armament: 'The costly projectiles of twelve-inch guns were used for trial shots, when small calibre weapons would have given the requisite information. Sometimes, after several minutes of absolute silence, the fire of twelve-inch guns would be resumed, without any rectification of aim, although in the interim there had been marked changes in the wind, the direction and the range. . . .'

In the subsequent manœuvres the *Suvoroff* did succeed in making one hit, on the bridge of the *Donskoy*, which was towing the target, and at the end of that day Rozhestvensky appears to have run out of adjectives, for 'Unpardonably bad!', 'Wretched performance!' occur again and again, with every justification. Some of the weaknesses revealed would have produced startling results in action. When the flag signalled a formation of destroyers to form line abreast, the boats scattered in every direction, and only a careful post-mortem proved that most of the squadron had not yet been issued with the new signalling code books adopted by the Imperial Navy six months before.

Nor were the torpedoes any less erratic than the shells. They were too precious to waste, but on one occasion Rozhestvensky ordered a salvo to be fired. Of the seven that left their tubes, one jammed, two swung ninety degrees to port, one ninety degrees to starboard, two kept a steady course but went wide of the mark, and the last went round and round in circles 'popping up and down like a porpoise' and causing panic throughout the fleet.

That was the last time they went to sea on exercises.

By the first week in March the word was racing through the squadron that their departure was at last imminent.

The rumour travelled, as all news travelled in the Second Pacific Squadron, with remarkable speed, and was without apparent origin, although as usual it proved to be true. The fleet's divers were working night and day in an attempt to remove some of the weed and barnacles that had grown on the hulls during their long tropical anchorage, reducing the top speed of the battleships by at least two knots and increasing their coal consumption at cruising speed from 100 to 130 tons daily. Somehow the word had spread that their C.-in-C. had persuaded or (more likely) bullied the Germans into supplying them with coal to their destination, and it was observed that the wardrooms were taking on considerable supplies of perishable foodstuffs.

The Russian Admiralty had heard no news from Rozhestvensky for some time. 'We know nothing of his whereabouts or his intentions,' the St. Petersburg correspondent of the *Petit Parisien* was told rather huffily by a spokesman. They had issued their orders, and that was that. But knowing their Admiral's stubborn nature, and remembering the long argument they had had with him, they must have feared he might take independent action, and as a precautionary move they gave him no information on the progress of the supporting squadron, controlling its movements directly from St. Petersburg.

Their fears were justified. Rozhestvensky had made up his mind several weeks before that his fleet's only chance of survival was to leave Nossi-Bé as soon as possible, to do battle with Togo if this could not be avoided, but above all to attempt to reach Vladivostock while there was still time, and before the ancient old wrecks from the Baltic reserves arrived to encumber him.

By the 10th of March even the Japanese appeared to have realized that the Russian departure could not be long delayed. Coasters and passing merchantmen brought reports of a squadron of Japanese cruisers less than a hundred miles away, and several times a Russian destroyer was sent out of the bay to investigate suspected roaming auxiliary cruisers.

The symptoms of tension among the Russian crews were reflected by an increase in the rate of suicides, which now became almost commonplace, and the reports of hypothetical 'reconnaissance balloons' high up in the hazy blue sky. Everybody was on edge, tempers flared easily, and there were several cases of sailors leaping overboard at night in an attempt to swim ashore.

It was an unofficial report from the friendly local French naval commander that decided Rozhestvensky to leave without further delay. The Third Pacific Squadron, he was informed, was coaling at Crete on its way through the Mediterranean and had been ordered by St. Petersburg to proceed with all speed to link up with the main force. The 'self-sinkers' were much nearer than he had imagined, and if he was going to disregard the authority of the Admiralty, he must hasten to lose his fleet in the vastness of the Indian Ocean.

Clapier de Colongue knew that his C.-in-C. was committing an act of insubordination compared to which the *Nakhimoff's* mutiny was a minor misdemeanour. But he made no comment when Rozhestvensky told him, on the evening of the 15th of March, that a general signal must be made to prepare for departure the following morning. It was inconceivable for de Colongue to comment on his C-in-C.'s instructions. 'Yes, sir,' he said, and withdrew.

There was little sleep for anyone that night. For the first time for many weeks, the quiet of the tropical night in Nossi-Bé was broken by the sounds of shouted commands, the hollow clang of hurrying footsteps on steel decks, and, deep below, of powerful machinery throbbing into life. By dawn the smoke from a hundred funnels was drifting and spiralling upwards to form an immense black cloud that blew slowly over the coast and dispersed far away over the mountains.

Anchors were weighed soon after one o'clock, and one by one the forty-five ships formed up into awkward line-ahead and steamed out of the bay under the fierce mid-day sun. Escorting the flagship on either side was a pair of trim white-painted French torpedo-boats, seeing their guests to the open sea with the 'Bon Voyage' signal flying at their yards; while at the stern of the *Suvoroff* the ship's band played the Marseillaise. Only the *Kamchatka*, after signalling that she was sinking, remained stalled at her anchorage, her crew desperately trying to pump out waist-high water in her engine room. But soon the trouble was traced to a cracked pipe, and by three o'clock she was scurrying off in pursuit of the squadron.

Sitting in the armchair which had been specially provided for him on the flagship's bridge, Rozhestvensky read the latest reports of the Russian army's fight for Mukden, the key centre in the battle for Manchuria. Already the Russian casualties ran into tens of thousands, General Kuropatkin was retreating in disorder; and soon the truth that he had known for weeks must become clear to the whole world: that Russia's last hope of averting defeat lay in the fleet under his command.

An hour later he was interrupted by a signal from the *Oryol*, which had broken formation and was slowing. 'Port engine failure', he read.

'Reduce the squadron's speed to five knots,' he instructed, adding irritably: 'And order the *Oryol* to hasten with her repairs.' He was becoming obsessed by the thought of those 'self-sinkers' seeking him out and dragging him back by the coat-tails.

CHAPTER SEVEN

Reinforcements from Home

THE Admiralty had chosen Rear-Admiral Nebogatoff to
command the squadron intended to reinforce Rozhestvensky and to compensate him for the loss of the Port
Arthur force. By Russian naval standards, Nebogatoff was
a mild-mannered officer, approachable and friendly, with a
natural sympathy for the men under his command, and
immensely patient and tolerant. No more strongly contrasting admiral to Rozhestvensky could ever have served
in the Imperial Navy. He was fat and small, with none of
Rozhestvensky's impressive presence, his chubby face
decorated with a short beard and 'disfigured by chronic
eczema'. His eyes were small and protruding. In short, he
was an unprepossessing figure. He talked quietly, rarely
raising his voice, and moved about his flagship with little,
awkward steps. He was invariably referred to as 'Grand-
dad', although he was only in his mid-fifties.

While Rear-Admiral Nebogatoff's task was nothing like
so formidable as Rozhestvensky's, to sail his old ships
with their accompanying auxiliaries and colliers to the Far
East and place himself under the unwelcoming command
of an Admiral he neither liked nor respected was a chal-
lenging enough mission. He flew his flag from the old
9,000-ton battleship *Tsar Nicholas I*, armed with a pair of
twelve-inch and four nine-inch guns, all old weapons with
a slow rate of fire and a short range, and to support him
he had the cruiser *Vladimir Monomakh*, an older sister ship
to Rozhestvensky's *Dmitri Donskoy*, and three 4,000-ton
armoured coast defence ships, the *Ushakoff*, *Apraksin* and

Senyavin, all with a low freeboard and shallow draft for shore bombardment, nicknamed by the fleet 'the goloshes' or 'flat irons'. They were armed with ten-inch guns, and at the time of their construction they were never intended for ocean travelling, let alone for steaming in the line.

Considering what he had to contend with, Nebogatoff succeeded in preparing his old vessels for sea and gathering his crews together with remarkable speed. There was no question of overhauling the ships; there was time only for a dab of paint here, a touch of grease there—and with the dockers of Libau seething with unrest and strikes at the height of the winter revolution, that was difficult enough. As for his crews, like the ships Rozhestvensky had rejected, he had to be content with the left-overs, the scabby scrapings off the streets, pardoned convicts, and old reservists who had served under sail and had no use for steam power.

The night before they left, the *Senyavin's* officer-of-the-watch was stabbed to death, and a bo'sun wounded. 'You're only being sent to make a demonstration. You'll soon be home again,' the Port Admiral reassured one of Nebogatoff's anxious captains. 'You don't really think you're going to fight?'

Nebogatoff's firm but mild authority and the winter sea voyage down Channel, across the Bay of Biscay and through the Mediterranean, seemed to have a mellowing effect on the Third Pacific Squadron's wilder elements. There were few outbreaks of insubordination. The crews were kept alert and disciplined by continual gunnery practice, and, at night, by simulated torpedo attacks with all lights extinguished, for Nebogatoff did not believe in searchlights. As for coaling, he was blessed by good weather and good personal relations in the neutral harbours at which he stopped. It was difficult to create a fracas over this gentle gentleman with his quaint little collection of vessels.

Nebogatoff had been given explicit instructions not to communicate with his future C.-in-C. At Suez he cabled St. Petersburg for instructions on where to rendezvous with the main force and learned that Rozhestvensky had already left Madagascar after signalling simply 'I am on my way east'.

'Continue to Jibuti and await further instructions,' St. Petersburg ordered; and at Jibuti the Admiralty were even less explicit. 'You are to join up with Rozhestvensky, whose route is unknown to us . . .' ran the message.

Nebogatoff did not need to be told that Rozhestvensky was being outrageously insubordinate and that he regarded the Third Pacific Squadron's ships as unwanted guests, but luckily Nebogatoff had not started off with any illusions about the sort of welcome he was likely to receive.

At last, after coaling at Mir Bat Bay on the Arabian coast and safely crossing the Indian Ocean, he heard at Singapore that St. Petersburg had received news of Rozhestvensky. He was given the name of the port where, if he did not linger (and Rozhestvensky kept the appointment) he might yet be able to add his force to the Second Pacific Squadron.

For more than three weeks Rozhestvensky's armada was lost not only to the Admiralty authorities but to the world. From March 16th until the evening of April 8th it steamed some 3,500 miles without seeing another ship, for only the last few days within sight of land, and for much of the time more than two thousand miles from the nearest shore. Several bluejackets had leapt overboard during the first few days, victims of the fleet's growing anxiety neurosis; the rest were carried slowly, never at more than eight knots, across the vast expanse of the Indian Ocean, halting every four or five days for the inevitable back-breaking coaling and the more frequent breakdowns.

As one clear tropical day followed another, the men's curiosity and anxiety about their future were slowly exhausted, and in their detached, uncertain half-world encompassed by the deck rails of their ships and the endless unbroken horizon, they passed the time talking about their families and home lives, exchanging stories, playing cards and deck games, in the evening singing songs to the balalaika or the concertina, and grumbling at the shortage of matches and cigarettes and the poor quality salt beef when the last of the cattle had been slaughtered and eaten. The journey might have lasted another three months and the conversation, the stories, the sad songs and the occasional laughter would surely have sounded the same.

Even on the flagship, where Rozhestvensky fretted and cursed at every delay, sent scathing signals to the transports towing the destroyers every time a cable snapped in the swell, only poor de Colongue, whose life was made a misery, was much affected by the violence of his C.-in-C. The rest of the ship's personnel simply became sunk in their daily routine.

When land at last appeared on the morning of April 5th, and they swung round in a long straggling line along the coast of Sumatra, it was the scent, after the weeks of clean salt air, rather than the sight of it that was at once apparent: the familiar, heavy, rich odour of tropical vegetation that stretched out to them like an enveloping cloud.

As if reflecting the sense of urgency that the sight and scent of land brought with it, the signal came from the flagship for the two fastest cruisers to steam ahead as lookouts, while the fleet reformed protectively with the two battleship divisions on either side of the colliers, auxiliaries and transports. The destroyers were released after their long tow and darted off on reconnaissance. 'Keep a sharp look-out for suspicious vessels,' Rozhestvensky ordered. 'The enemy will be informed of our approach.'

Soon the reports from alert look-outs in makeshift

crows-nests began to come in, at first hourly and then more frequently as they entered the main shipping routes from Singapore. The *Oleg* had a penchant for submarines, her fellow cruisers discerned concealed guns on every passing merchantman, and from the bridge of the *Oslyabya* Admiral Felkerzam signalled that he and his officers had positively identified not less than twelve torpedo-boats steaming behind a British East Indiaman. Once again, as orders were issued for guns to be manned day and night, tension mounted through the fleet.

At two o'clock on the afternoon of April 8th, the news suddenly spread through the streets of Singapore that a great naval armada had been sighted steaming towards the town, and thousands flocked to the waterfront and crowded the windows of buildings with a view over the sea. At first there was some uneasiness. Where had these great battleships and cruisers come from? What was the object of this demonstration of naval might? Certainly no Royal Navy vessels were expected, and they were not Japanese. 'Russian,' the word went round at last. 'The Russian Baltic Fleet—off to fight Togo.' And the onlookers remembered the Dogger Bank Incident and how the vaunted armada had faded from the news weeks before.

'It was a splendid spectacle,' cabled *The Times*' correspondent, and the forty-two ships were certainly as impressive a sight as the British Navy had ever provided for the naval base. 'All the ships were burning soft coal, and the smoke they made was visible for miles,' reported Reuter. 'The ships, magnificent but foul, were proceeding at about eight knots, and it took them fifty-five minutes to pass a given point. All the vessels showed signs of their long voyage in tropical seas, about a foot of seaweed being visible along the waterline, and the decks were laden with coal. . . .'

But this sudden reappearance of the lost fleet, whose

progress as far as Madagascar had been closely followed and reported daily in every newspaper, was much more than a stirring spectacle. It proved that Russia not only possessed great naval strength, but that she intended to commit it to battle against the Japanese who, with the fall of Mukden, had seemed to have gained their objectives and all but won the Far East war. In every country there was praise for the Admiral who had made such a ludicrous start to his long cruise six months before, had somehow contrived to bring his squadron half across the world, and was now ostentatiously seeking out the enemy. Rozhestvensky was suddenly the game fighter who does not know when to give in. 'We have suffered many things at the hands of the Russian navy during this war', wrote one London leader writer. 'Nevertheless, the news that Admiral Rozhestvensky and the Baltic Fleet, scorning evasion and concealment, have stood on down the Straits of Malacca, have passed Singapore, and have sailed proudly into the China Seas, will send a thrill of admiration through all Englishmen who read it.'

Without the authority or knowledge of the Russian Admiralty ('We have absolutely no news of the squadron,' a spokesman had told a St. Petersburg correspondent the day before), Rozhestvensky had won Russia's first great moral victory of the war, and the Japanese government was now faced by the threat of a powerful fleet in being on its doorstep.

On the *Suvoroff* at the head of the straggling column, the crew was lined along the port rails staring at the town. There, a few tantalizing miles away, were the facilities they needed so badly—a wide sheltered bay, dockyard installations, the stores from which to replenish their ships, the equipment to clean and overhaul them, the quiet security of an anchorage before they sailed to meet the enemy. But the nearest Russian harbour was Vladivostock, still three thousand miles away, beyond the Japanese fortified bases and Togo's patrol lines. Through their glasses the officers could identify two English cruisers in the harbour and could see a number of merchantmen at anchor or along the quaysides. On the bridge, Rozhestvensky stood for several minutes in silence, staring at the town through his powerful binoculars, then passed them to Clapier de Colongue. 'In a few minutes,' he told his Chief of Staff with satisfaction, 'the telegraph will report this to the whole world.'

As Raffles Island fell behind them a small steam launch was sighted sailing parallel to the fleet and clearly trying to catch up and make contact with the flagship. For a moment there was some alarm at her appearance, and the destroyer *Bedovyi* was sent to intercept her. Then it was seen that she was flying Russian colours and was signalling that the local consul had important dispatches and would like to come on board for an interview with the Admiral.

'Tell him we can't stop—it's far too dangerous,' Rozhestvensky told de Colongue. 'The *Bedovyi* can pick up any papers.'

Undeterred by this cold reception, the consul did as he was told, and then steamed close up the line of first division battleships, calling out through a megaphone the latest news from home and from the war front. 'Mukden has fallen,' he shouted out. 'General Kuropatkin has been dismissed and replaced by General Linevich. . . . I have got together all the newspapers I could lay my hands on, but you didn't give me much time.' Then news of more immediate moment to the fleet: 'Admiral Kamimura's cruiser squadron called at Singapore three days ago, and is now believed to be on its way to North Borneo, and twenty-two more warships under Togo's flag which came in sight of the town are now at Labuan. . . . Admiral Nebogatoff with the Third Pacific Squadron has sailed from Jibuti to join forces with you. . . .'

It was a broken, barely audible message, and many of

the words were carried away on the wind, but the news was confirmed in the dispatches and papers that the *Bedovyi* delivered to the flagship, which Rozhestvensky read through in his cabin that night. The Russian armies were fleeing north before the Japanese in Manchuria; already they had lost 30,000 killed, 40,000 prisoners and vast quantities of stores. On land there seemed to be no hope of retrieving the situation, and nothing short of a great naval victory could save his country now.

And victory would have to come swiftly. For what were the orders that the Admiralty had at last succeeded in getting to him? The crucial military situation did not appear to have altered in the slightest degree the overall strategical plan. Rozhestvensky was to sail with the Second Pacific Squadron for Kamranh Bay on the Cochin China coast, there to await Admiral Nebogatoff's Third Squadron. There was also a hint in the newspapers, though it was not yet confirmed in his orders, that Nicholas Klado had persuaded the Admiralty that yet another squadron should be prepared from the surviving remnants of the Baltic Fleet—the vessels that even Nebogatoff had refused because of their age and unseaworthiness—and dispatched to ensure overwhelming victory.

As a final insult, Rozhestvensky read in amazement that after destroying the enemy in battle and on his arrival at Vladivostock, he was to hand over command to Admiral Birilioff, who was already *en route* to the Far East by the Trans-Siberian railway. Rozhestvensky was outraged. This time the corrupt and incompetent clique in St. Petersburg, by suggesting that he should wait more weeks and even months, while the Russian armies bled to death and Togo completed refitting and preparing his navy for battle, had really overreached themselves. And after defeating Togo, who had already destroyed piecemeal a fleet much stronger than his own, and regained command of the sea, he was to hand over to Birilioff, the man who liked to be called 'the fighting Admiral' though he had never been in action! It was clear that the crucial moment had arrived when he must either act independently, disregarding the outrageous commands from St. Petersburg, or prepare to sacrifice his fleet uselessly.

Shortly after the fleet had sailed past Pedro Branco Island into the South China Sea, Rozhestvensky called a conference of Clapier de Colongue, Semenoff and his Flag-Lieutenant, in his cabin for two o'clock on April 10th— the first occasion on which his most trusted intimates had gathered formally together.

Semenoff has left a vivid picture of the Admiral in a state of acute nervous tension at that conference. It was clear that his highly developed sense of discipline was being hard-pressed and his loyalty strained beyond endurance. Sometimes he sat deep in his chair, drawing abstractedly on a piece of paper, and then he would leap up to pace to and fro across the cabin floor behind the chairs of his Staff, muttering to himself and occasionally asking them their opinion of the situation.

It was not easy for them to answer because he had to'd them nothing, of his orders from St. Petersburg, of the progress of Nebogatoff's squadron, of the rendezvous at Kamranh Bay; or even whether he intended eventually to attempt to slip past Togo or deliberately face him in battle. Slowly, by careful questioning, they managed to learn something of the dilemma their C.-in-C. faced, and for the first time it was revealed, if only by suggestion, what they had long suspected, that the reason for their hasty departure from Madagascar lay in Rozhestvensky's fear that they might be saddled with Nebogatoff's 'self-sinkers', and his hope that he might better be able to persuade the Admiralty of their folly from the war zone than from the security of Nossi-Bé.

'So they've sent Nebogatoff on all the same!' Semenoff exclaimed. 'Without giving him a rendezvous? Just simply at haphazard!' It was preposterous, unbelievable! They were being chased half around the world by this 'archaeological collection of naval architecture'. The Admiralty had taken leave of its senses!

But it was true. 'It's all over,' the Flag-Lieutenant whispered to Semenoff in one of Rozhestvensky's moments of abstraction. 'We've not managed to escape.'

The opinions of the three officers were unanimous. It would clearly be suicide, the Flag-Lieutenant suggested, to await the arrival of the Third Pacific Squadron. Their only chance was to act immediately and in defiance of instructions in an effort to force a passage to Vladivostock. If they succeeded in evading Togo, so much the better; if they met him, then they must put their trust in God and pray for victory.

'Forward, and let come what may!' Semenoff confirmed more dramatically. But his effort to instil some fire into the meeting fell flat. Their C.-in-C. nodded a brief acknowledgement, and without raising his eyes dismissed them.

The atmosphere as they filed silently from the cabin was grave and defeatist, with Rozhestvensky slumped deep in his chair, his chin on his chest, staring down at the floor.

It is doubtful if Rozhestvensky slept at all that night, and all through the following day it was obvious to everyone who came into contact with him that he was still in a state of agonizing indecision. It may have been the appearance of the British armoured cruiser *Cressy*, passing close by on an opposite course early in the morning, that decided the issue. After saluting the Admiral's flag with thirteen guns, it disappeared astern, but shortly afterwards another British cruiser appeared, and this left Rozhestvensky in no doubt that he was being shadowed, and that already details of his course and position were being radioed to the Japanese fleet.

Again and again that day ships appeared on the horizon

and vanished from sight, just as Lord Beresford's Channel Fleet had toyed with him off the coasts of Spain and Portugal. One British merchantman, steaming closer to the fleet than the others, signalled, 'Have seen Japanese torpedoboats. Beware—and look out for attacks by night', it advised. It was as if the whole world was sniggering while it played a giant game of bluff with this fleet of ten thousand men voyaging towards their fate.

Things were no better the following morning; Rozhestvensky's loyalties were clearly still in violent conflict. 'The Admiral is so odd today,' Semenoff recorded, 'so restless, so taciturn and irritable . . . running about nervously, appearing first on one bridge, then on the other, then disappearing for a short time in his cabin; after that he moves about again on deck, looks through his notebook, notes something down in it . . . and finally he starts talking to himself.'

But later in the morning, Clapier de Colongue and the rest of the Staff were left in no doubt that he had at last made up his mind and had decided to act independently when the order was given to heave-to and take on coal from the accompanying colliers, only sixty miles from the shelter of Kamranh Bay. After issuing this order Rozhestvensky spoke to no one, pacing up and down the *Suvoroff's* bridge with his head thrust angrily forward, occasionally glancing at one or another of the ironclads to see how the coaling operations were proceeding.

Just before luncheon Rozhestvensky ordered the Flag Navigating Officer, Colonel Filippovsky, to come to him, and they were seen to be in deep conversation for some minutes before an officer went off and returned with a rolled sheet under his arm. Word from the charthouse soon revealed that the chart covered the route from Hong-Kong to Vladivostock. After a few minutes Rozhestvensky abruptly turned away and ordered an immediate report on the condition of the engines of all the ships to ensure that they were fit for a further long ocean voyage, and then went down to luncheon, at which he spoke to no one.

At one o'clock Rozhestvensky reappeared on the bridge and briskly ordered Clapier de Colongue to make a general signal to all ships to report their coal situation. One after the other the replies came in: the *Oryol* 2,000 tons, the *Borodino* 2,100 tons, the *Oslyabya* 1,800 tons. Only the *Alexander III* hesitated. 'Repeat the signal by semaphore,' Rozhestvensky ordered, and a few minutes later the answer came back. The reason for the ironclad's hesitancy could be understood, for the figure was 400 tons less, in spite of the five hours' coaling, than the figure she had reported at the regular daily morning report. 'There must be a mistake,' Rozhestvensky commented. 'Tell the *Alexander* to repeat the figure.'

'Have you made a mistake?' the *Suvoroff* signalled, and this time the answer came back promptly, 'No'.

What appeared to the rest of the fleet as a minor miscalculation, and perhaps a rather ironic one by the ship that was officered by 'the élite of the Russian nobility', that throughout the voyage had won every fastest-coaling prize and had proudly carried the efficiency pennant all the way from the Baltic, was to Rozhestvensky a calamity. By his somewhat haphazard method of basing his reports of estimated consumption of coal against estimated intake from the colliers, instead of on actual measurement of the stock, Captain Bukhvostoff of the *Alexander III* had frustrated his C.-in-C.'s plan to sail at once for Vladivostock.

The *Alexander III*, one of the squadron's four modern battleships, was to all intents and purposes now an ineffective unit. By an ironic twist of mathematics, the coal she carried was just insufficient to take her directly to Vladivostock, the holds of the colliers accompanying the fleet were now empty, and fresh supplies of coal would not arrive at Kamranh Bay for many days. Rozhestvensky could not possibly afford to leave the *Alexander III* behind; no Commander-in-Chief could sail into battle with his first line of attack reduced by a quarter. It appeared, therefore, that his old enemy, coal, had defeated him after all.

'There will be no victory . . . but we will know how to die,' Captain Bukhvostoff had responded to the toasts to the fleet's success at Libau six months before. Now this same captain, by his careless miscalculation of a few hundred tons of coal, had succeeded in fatally obstructing their advance, where the Japanese, the British and Portuguese, the Hamburg-Amerika Company, and even Captain Klado, had failed.

For some minutes Rozhestvensky stared silently at the piece of paper in his hand. Then he waved his arm in a gesture of hopelessness in the direction of the *Alexander III* and descended from the bridge, murmuring in a tone of resignation to Clapier de Colongue as he passed, 'Issue orders for the fleet to proceed to the coast as arranged.'

The sudden impulse of rebellion had been killed by that signal still flying from the *Alexander III's* yard-arm. In his cabin, Rozhestvensky collapsed into a state of melancholia which endured until Togo's battle squadrons were sighted in the Straits of Tsu-Shima.

By dusk that evening the hills of the Cochin China coast loomed over the horizon in undulating silhouette, and the squadron heaved-to in a gentle swell close to the Pandarin Light at the entrance to Kamranh Bay. The next morning elaborate precautions for the entry were taken: picket boats were lowered from the ironclads to lay down anchoring buoys in the basin, the destroyers spent the day zigzagging slowly and carefully across the wide expanse of water searching for mines, while the squadron's cruisers were given orders to patrol up and down the coast in search of any Japanese warships, or any indications that they had recently been in the area.

One more night was spent at sea, and then at half-past eleven on the morning of the 14th of April, the dirty, begrimed, weary ships cruised slowly in past Tague Island, through the narrow entrance into Kamranh Basin, a wide, calm stretch of water, a safe and perfect natural harbour.

In bringing his forty vessels over 4,500 miles from Madagascar without once anchoring, without any of the normal facilities for coaling or revictualling, without assistance of any kind, Rozhestvensky had completed one of the most remarkable voyages in maritime history. He had halted his fleet five times for coaling in mid-ocean, each time in a swell that made the operation difficult and immensely tedious, thirty-nine times for the repair of the tow-ropes hauling the destroyers, and more than seventy times for mechanical failures of one kind or another. Yet he had succeeded in crossing the Indian Ocean unseen, in navigating his squadron successfully through the island-studded Malacca Straits and deep into the South China Sea, all without a single casualty.

This should have been a moment of triumph for the C.-in-C., his officers and crew. Instead, Rozhestvensky hovered on the brink of a nervous breakdown, and his men sank into a state of weary disillusionment. Two days before, it had been common knowledge throughout the fleet that at last they were to sail towards Togo; and after the months of false alarms, delays and disappointments, the prospect of having to face Japanese shell-fire had seemed almost welcome in preference to the continued anxieties of this endless voyage.

But the feeling of anti-climax was only one reason for their depression. It was hot and steamy in that sheltered bay, little less uncomfortable than the atmosphere at Nossi-Bé, with only an occasional draught of cool air blowing down from the hills. Shore leave was not granted, and because a provision ship had not yet arrived, there was no relief from the dispiriting diet of sour salt beef and hard tack the crews had been consuming for weeks. And, once again, there was no mail from home, no newspapers, no news of how things were in Russia, no word of how the war was going.

As a final, ironical blow the *Gortchakoff*, one of the fleet's transports which was believed to be bringing letters from home, arrived the following day, still carrying on board the sailors' mail which they had posted at Nossi-Bé a month before. Even during the worst periods at Madagascar, the fleet's morale never sank so low. 'I can only wring my hands', Politovsky wrote home to his wife, 'and feel assured that no one can escape his fate'; while another of the *Suvoroff's* officers in a letter published in *Russ* long after Tsu-Shima, wrote, 'What hope is there for us now? We are fated to die; there is no turning back.'

Kamranh had once been a thriving French fortress town, but that had been many years before. Now it was distinguished only by the air of sombre decay of a settlement that has long since died. Across the narrow valley of the Petite Pass leading down to the sea there were the crumbling remains of an old stockade formed from caissons joined by rusting chains; scattered about the hinterland were rotting barrack buildings; the hills above the marshes surrounding the basin, with their patches of rough foliage over grey stone and sand, resembled moulting, scabby animals; and where the town had once been, only five or six of the houses were inhabited. No more appropriate place to match the depression and sense of fatalism of the Second Pacific Squadron could have been found.

Now resigned to obedience, Rozhestvensky cabled the Admiralty from the small signal station manned by an idle Annamite official: 'Have arrived Kamranh Bay. Await orders.'

'Remain until the arrival of the Third Pacific Squadron,'

answered St. Petersburg once again, adding plaintively
this time, 'And please keep informed of movements.'

'British cruisers are constantly shadowing me and radioing reports of my movements to Tokio,' Rozhestvensky
complained. 'I will not telegraph again before the battle.
If I am beaten, Togo will tell you. If I beat him, I will let
you know.' In this last message there seemed to be a
defiant hint that he still intended to sail forth independently
to meet the enemy, but in fact, so far as he was now
capable of logical thought and planning, Rozhestvensky
was resigned to his fate, for until fresh supplies of coal
arrived, there was no escape from this unsavoury shore.

For the next few days the fleet lay at anchor in Kamranh
Basin without action of any kind, as if prostrated with
fatigue after its long journey. The only sign of movement
came from the destroyers which constantly patrolled up
and down the coast keeping a lookout for Japanese scouts,
and at night formed their searchlights in a bar across the
entrance to the bay. No efforts were made to clean the foul
bottoms of the ships, there were no signals from the flagship ordering gunnery practice or exercises, no orders, no
abuse even; only a torpid silence suggesting that the
Admiral had gone into a coma.

At last, on the 15th of April, the four Hamburg-Amerika
colliers with 30,000 tons of coal steamed in, looking almost
as grimy and forlorn as the men-of-war, and the squadron
was forced out of its state of numbed exhaustion, stimulated by some mail at last, and by the first fresh cabbage
soup they had had for weeks, made from vegetables
brought from Saigon.

One of the colliers had also brought back a deserter from
the *Nakhimoff* who had thrown himself overboard at night
under the impression that the lights of Malacca were con-
siderably nearer than six miles away. By a miraculous
piece of luck (or perhaps misfortune, for later he was
ordered to be shot), the bluejacket survived eleven hours

in the water and was picked up by a Messageries Maritimes steamer and taken to Saigon, thence to Singapore, where he was put in the charge of the consul. 'It was rather an ordeal being taken on board the steamer,' the sailor recalled. 'They all looked at me as I had nothing on.'

With all the ships fully loaded again, and washed-down after the coaling, a new sense of activity stirred through the fleet. Limited leave was granted, and some of the sailors swarmed ashore to sample the arid delights of the decayed town and foothills. Among them went the *Bezuprechnyi's* mascot, a young goat the crew had brought from Nossi-Bé, nursing it with tender concern on the tiny destroyer through all the dangers of the voyage, and feeding it conscientiously on an unvarying diet of paper. Even the wardroom visiting cards had been consumed by the time they anchored, but when after a run ashore, the goat was provided with a feed of hay, he would have none of it. Only the local French newspaper would do.

Admiral Rozhestvensky was still ignorant of the political repercussions of his sudden appearance in the Malacca Straits, as well as of the world's excited admiration at his feat. But the Japanese government was not taking lightly the threat of his advancing armada, and, as one naval correspondent put it, 'Tokio appears to be as much under the spell of pure arithmetic as St. Petersburg.'

In fact the threat was more serious and more subtle than this, for overshadowing the direct menace of the battle squadron to Japanese naval power, was the very real danger of Rozhestvensky's creeping through the Japanese defensive barrier into Russia's last surviving Pacific port, from which he could provide pressure and a strong bargaining point in any peace negotiations. For Japan, peace would have to come soon. If she had the goodwill of almost the entire world on her side, sixteen months of war had exhausted her slender resources and bled her white, and not even Great Britain or the United States would further extend her credit. Within a desperately short time the 'banzai' cry of her troops would be silenced—by their government's inability to buy them the weapons and ammunition. So it was as urgently important for Togo to intercept and destroy the Second Pacific Squadron as it was for Rozhestvensky to reach Vladivostock.

Ironically, and for directly opposite reasons, Togo was just as anxious as Rozhestvensky to seek battle before Admiral Nebogatoff's reinforcements could arrive, for while Rozhestvensky dreaded the approach of the Baltic Fleet's cast-offs, Togo viewed their twelve-inch and ten-inch guns as a grave threat.

Time and again the Japanese foreign office had complained to France about her indulgent attitude towards the Russian fleet. These protests were repeated forcefully the moment Tokio heard of Rozhestvensky's arrival off the Cochin China coast, in a tone that could not be ignored, particularly in view of her recent sweeping successes in Manchuria. Japan made it amply clear to every government, friendly or otherwise, that she was determined to stand by her rights.

For the first time, with the fleet's approach close to the Philippine Islands, the question of American neutrality arose, though United States opinion appeared to be firm. 'But for the connivance of the colonial administration, and the contributory negligence, or worse, of the French government,' wrote the New York *Evening Sun*, 'Rozhestvensky would not be able to offer battle to the Japanese fleet. Indeed it is now seen that his voyage would have been a hopelessly mad enterprise without an understanding with the French.' *The Times'* naval correspondent, commenting on the surprise of American sources at the sudden reappearance of Rozhestvensky off Singapore, considered that American naval officers 'are inclined to think, however, that Admiral Togo will relieve American authorities of all responsibility'. As a precautionary measure, however, Rear-Admiral Train of the U.S.N. ordered the cruiser *Raleigh* and two destroyers, with a dispatch boat, to patrol round Sulu archipelago and Parawan to prevent the approach into territorial waters of any Russian warships.

Now that it was known that Rozhestvensky was coaled and ready for sea, the excitement throughout Japan and in every country in Europe mounted. Again and again the vital statistics were presented to newspaper readers by naval experts, figures which on paper demonstrated the near equality of the Japanese and Russians and provided endless scope for argument. In every country except Japan, where a curious respect for Russian naval power still existed, the low morale, inferior seaworthiness and gunnery of the Russians was accepted, but no one could deny Rozhestvensky his tremendous achievement in bringing his vessels to the very gateway of Japan, and his 50 per cent[1] superiority in twelve-inch guns, even before the arrival of Admiral Nebogatoff, could not be ignored by the theorists. According to accepted naval theory the heavy naval gun was all-powerful and was certain to be decisive in any fleet action, and Rozhestvensky's shooting would have to be very poor to compensate for this disparity.

'A decision is hourly expected', announced *The Times* on the 15th of April, and a few days later twenty Japanese men-of-war were reported off Saigon steering east. From Singapore, from Manila, Malacca, Saigon and Hong Kong and the large Chinese coastal towns, the rumours of battle began to pour in. 'Togo's fleet intercepted and utterly destroyed by Rozhestvensky', 'Many warships sunk in great naval battle in South China Sea', 'Togo destroys

---

[1] The sinking of only one first-class Japanese battleship had been announced by Tokio; that of another, by mine, had been kept a closely-guarded secret.

Russian Baltic Fleet'. Honours were equally shared between the two opponents, but always the battle was stupendous and always the result decisive and overwhelming. After a week or so of this, newspaper editors decided that their readers had had enough, and once again Far East naval activity was reduced to a few lines at the bottom of an inside page. 'The first flush of surprise and delight over the discovery that Rozhestvensky really possesses an effective squadron is wearing off,' said *The Times* on the 29th of April, 'and people are reverting to a condition bordering on indifference.'

It was only in Japan that tension continued to mount as Nebogatoff's reinforcements daily drew nearer and Rozhestvensky continued to flaunt the neutrality laws under the protection of French hospitality, awaiting his arrival. His prolonged stay was causing extreme indignation in Japan, and uneasiness elsewhere, especially in the United States and Britain, as Japanese protests to Paris became more outspoken and now contained barely veiled threats. The British Foreign Office tried to impress on France the seriousness of the situation, and on a visit to the French capital King Edward spoke warningly to Delcassé, the French Foreign Minister.

It was not, of course, simply dogged devotion to the Russian cause that prompted France's indulgent attitude towards the fleet; no one, except possibly the Germans with their coaling contract, was finding the six months' voyage so profitable. Over almost the entire distance it was the French who provided the necessary provisions— the fresh fruit and vegetables, livestock and dead meat, flour and preserves, all sold at outrageously inflated prices, and the even more profitable luxury foodstuffs and wines and spirits for the warships' wardrooms. The French colonial governments' reluctance to speed the parting guests could be understood.

Two days after their arrival in Kamranh, Rear-Admiral

de Jonquières, the second-in-command of the French squadron in Chinese waters, arrived on the cruiser *Déscartes*. Rozhestvensky at once expected trouble, but charming de Jonquières, a tall, grey-haired aristocrat of the old school, was most sympathetic on this visit, and appeared more in the role of a *maître d'hôtel* concerned for the welfare of his guests than of an unwelcoming frontier official, and when he left there was a message of good wishes flying from his yard-arm.

But on the 22nd of April, his cruiser slipped into the basin again, and this time it was clear that he had received new instructions from the local administrator. Still in the most gentlemanly manner, de Jonquières pointed out that according to international law it was illegal for the fleet to be in the bay for longer than twenty-four hours, and that, with the utmost regret, he would be obliged to ask them to leave the next day.

Promptly at one o'clock the next afternoon, anchors were weighed and one by one the ships steamed out through the narrow entrance in accordance with the order. 'Assembling outside Kamranh Bay,' as *The Times* described them, 'the ships formed an immense arc extending from Cape Varela to the head of the Kamranh Peninsula.'

Rozhestvensky had, however, made one condition to his immediate compliance, which permitted the Russians to leave behind their auxiliaries and transports in order to save precious coal, on the understanding that the fleet would not conduct any reconnaissance or interfere in any way with neutral shipping even if it was bound for enemy ports.

De Jonquières accompanied the flagship to the limit of territorial waters, and then tactfully signalled his headquarters, 'The Russian squadron has left the coast of Annam in an easterly direction. Its destination is not known.'

That evening Rozhestvensky called a second conference

on board the *Suvoroff*, this time of his entire Staff and all ships' commanders. It was not an inspiring meeting for any of them. Forced to leave his hiding place, forbidden to advance on the enemy without the reinforcements that were still many hundreds of miles away, and so desperately short of coal that he dared not even take his ships on exercises, it was clear that their C.-in-C.'s dilemma was more crucial than ever. The expression of hopelessness on Rozhestvensky's face as the officers filed into the cabin could be forgiven.

This time Rozhestvensky was not seeking anyone's advice, nor, it seemed, was he intent on inspiring confidence in the future. He began by explaining to them the predicament and the causes that had led up to it, and then announced his policy for the future. 'I shall keep at sea,' he told them, 'outside territorial waters in the neighbourhood of Kamranh Bay, where I am leaving behind some supply ships and non-fighting vessels. My orders are to wait for Nebogatoff. I shall wait. I shall wait until we have just coal enough left to take us to Vladivostock. If Nebogatoff does not arrive by then, there is no help for it—we go on without him. Forward! Always forward'—the histrionics now muted—'Pray keep this always before you.'

Within a few days the reason for the assembly of his senior officers became even more obscure. Rozhestvensky appeared to have solved his dilemma in the simplest possible manner, and 'always forward' had been interpreted as the next bay farther north. This was the wide, sheltered inlet of Van-Phong, suitably quiet and uninhabited except for a few native fishermen, a delightful out-of-the-way spot without any sort of communication with the outside world. Here, surely, was the perfect place for his fleet to await in safety the arrival of Nebogatoff in about two weeks' time.

The operation went off smoothly, and within a couple of hours the squadron was anchored in five parallel lines, with the big ironclads closest to the mouth of the bay, all set for a long stay. But by a stroke of the worst possible luck they were not to be undisturbed, for no sooner had the last ship stopped engines, than a little coaster, which once a month called to collect the local fishermen's catch, entered the bay and left again almost at once. It was hardly likely that the presence of some forty men-of-war in this unlikely place, where a funnel on the horizon created a stir, would pass without comment, and Rozhestvensky knew that it was only a matter of time before he was ejected like an insolvent hotel guest.

Meanwhile there was Easter to be celebrated, an important event in the Russian calendar, with religious ceremonies and feasts and Mass in great makeshift tarpaulin chapels decorated with potted tropical plants. But Easter this year was to be marked on the *Oryol* by an outbreak of indiscipline that led to one of the squadron's most serious mutinies.

The crew of the *Oryol* had always been a restless lot, and her officers some of the most self-indulgent and least effective in the fleet. This time the trouble arose over a diseased cow which had been brought aboard, along with other head of cattle, from Kamranh and kept in a pen on the upper deck of the ironclad. On hearing a report of the cow's condition from the ship's butcher, Commander Sidoroff ordered, 'Slaughter her at once; she'll do for the men's dinner tomorrow'—not the most diplomatic way of handling the position when it was known that for their Easter Day feast 'the head cook was preparing roast fowls, cakes and other dainties for the wardroom'.

That Saturday night there was heavy drinking of locally brewed hooch in the crew's quarters, broken by outbursts of angry shouting which grew so loud that the officer-of-the-watch appeared and, after a scuffle, arrested one of the noisiest bluejackets. At the assembly of the ship's company after Mass, Captain Yung was received in hostile silence instead of with the traditional cheers. When he had withdrawn, the men became more riotous than ever, and there was talk of raiding the officers' wine store. The crisis was reached when the men refused to eat their ceremonial dinner (of diseased cow) and threw their bowls overboard, shouting for Sidoroff and demanding that their comrade should be released and fresh food supplied.

As a full-scale riot threatened, the officers dining and celebrating in the deck-cabin at last became aware that something serious was afoot, armed themselves with revolvers and barricaded themselves into their cabins. Meanwhile, Sidoroff, in full dress uniform, bravely made his way to the upper deck, appeared above the men and demanded silence.

'Feed us on carrion, would you?' the sailors shouted. 'Set the prisoner free!'

'I can't liberate anyone on my own authority,' Sidoroff shouted back. 'That is a matter for the captain. I will instantly communicate your demand to him.'

This set the pattern for the complete capitulation that followed. After Sidoroff and Yung had discussed the situation in the comparative security of the conning-tower, Sidoroff reappeared to meet the catcalls, this time with the prisoner at his side.

'Here he is, my lads,' he told the men. 'Now then, no more trouble. I am going to order you a new dinner. Appoint a few delegates to choose two of the best bullocks, which will immediately be slaughtered.'

Peace came to the ship. The men sobered down, while the cooks set about preparing the feast for the crew of nine hundred. But it was not the end of the affair. The next day Rozhestvensky arrived in a steam pinnace, mounted the starboard ladder (from the head of which coal had frantically to be cleared), and made his way to the upper deck, where he could look down on the entire ship's complement assembled below.

'He did not salute us as was customary,' one of the seamen described him later, 'but remained standing, plunged in thought, towering by a head above the members of his Staff. His great stature, his rank of Vice-Admiral, his title of chief aide-de-camp to the Tsar, and his position as commander of the squadron, seemed to set him apart from the common herd, almost as if he were a god. His face was as dour as the sea in a storm.'

After a long and dramatic silence, Rozhestvensky suddenly shouted out, 'Traitors! Rascals! Mutiny would you?' and proceeded to hurl imprecations and abuse at them, quite beside himself with fury. 'I will not tolerate treason. This scandalous ship will be bombarded and sunk by the rest of the squadron. . . . Hand over the ringleaders. Where are they?'

When officers had picked out haphazardly eight men and brought them up alongside Rozhestvensky on the upper deck, he thundered at them: 'Look at them, these enemies of Russia. They are more like beasts than men. . . . What price did you get for selling your country? . . . Their pockets bulge with Japanese gold. Look, all of you, at their pockets, bulging with gold!'

The officers were then given a scarcely less severe dressing-down in front of the men: 'As for you, only in the sea fight, and in your own blood, can you wash out your sins . . .' he told them. Rozhestvensky paused in a final effort to control his violent emotions and, as if overcome by the pathos of his fleet's situation, left them with the parting words, heard by only a few: 'We are all stuck in the same hell. Who ever does not do his duty is a rogue. I am doing mine.'

Later that day signals from on shore indicated that they were once again *persona non grata*. The little coaster had left word of their arrival with the French administrator at Nhatrang, twenty miles to the south, who had immediately set off on the long and thoroughly uncomfortable cross-country trip to demand their departure by signal from the shore. But it was going to take more than one French official to stir Rozhestvensky now, and it was not until de Jonquières' arrival again, as courteous as ever but very firm, that he reluctantly agreed to leave the shelter of Van-Phong.

'I shall remain in the vicinity for twenty-four hours to ensure the execution of my instructions,' de Jonquières signalled warningly to Rozhestvensky; and again to his headquarters: 'The Russian squadron sailed in an easterly direction. Destination unknown.'

The fleet did not sail far to the east, however. Rozhestvensky had by now given up all pretence of dignity, and after the French cruiser had disappeared over the horizon, he slipped shamelessly back into the shelter of the bay. The stakes in this game of cat-and-mouse were too high for him to worry about the rules.

Nebogatoff was drawing near. Every day rumours of his progress flashed through the fleet, and betting on the date of their meeting with him became an important activity on every ship, many of the ironclads running totalisators. The odds narrowed when news arrived on the 8th of May that Nebogatoff had passed Singapore at four in the morning three days before, and Rozhestvensky at once detached four of his light cruisers to meet the reinforcements and direct them towards Van-Phong.

The cruisers had no sooner left than de Jonquières reappeared again, this time in a noticeably larger cruiser, anchored alongside the flagship and came aboard. His tall, erect figure was seen mounting the companion ladder, at the head of which Rozhestvensky, looking gaunt and terribly worn, awaited him. After exchanging courtesies, the two Admirals talked together amicably for several minutes, on the French side with much shrugging of shoulders and many gestures of regret—with the result that the forty ships were at sea again that night, cruising at three knots off the coast, showing no lights and keeping station only with difficulty.

At eleven on the morning of May 9th, the four cruisers returned and rejoined the fleet, without having sighted the Third Pacific Squadron. But that the reinforcements were near was suggested by the interception by one of the cruisers of radio messages in Russian between two ships with unfamiliar code names. Rozhestvensky at once issued orders for the entire fleet to sweep south with lookouts at the mastheads. Four hours later, seven miles off the coast of Van-Phong, in clear, sunny weather, with the sea running in only the gentlest of swells, a distant grey patch of smoke appeared on the horizon, and the mastheads, superstructures and tall funnels of Nebogatoff's fighting ships appeared.

One by one the warships were recognized by the crews packed on the upper decks, and greetings were roared out as they passed the fleet in line-ahead formation. At the head of the column was the old *Nicholas I*, Nebogatoff's flag flying at her masthead and looking ludicrously unfashionable; then the three coast-defence ships—the 'flat irons' or 'goloshes'—armed with ten-inch weapons, which had miraculously survived the storms of the Atlantic, the Mediterranean and the Indian Ocean; and, leading the four transports, the hospital and repair ships, the cruiser *Monomakh*, a tall-hulled survivor from the days of sail.

But nothing could deprive this moment of its solemnity and drama as the two squadrons slowly approached and sailed past one another on opposite courses, the signal guns crashing out the salutes and the sailors waving their caps and shouting across the water. From the *Suvoroff's* yard-arm flew the signal: 'Welcome, congratulations on the success of your voyage. Congratulations also to the squadron upon this reinforcement'; while the *Nicholas I* hoisted an acknowledgement and good wishes to her comrades.

Nebogatoff swung his squadron around in a wide semi-circle at full speed, funnels belching smoke like black water from a dozen taps, and drew them up in perfect line on Rozhestvensky's starboard beam.

The last of Russia's naval power was united in a majestic armada of more than fifty vessels, on a calm, foreign ocean sixteen thousand miles from its base. 'I consider that we ought to entertain feelings of great respect for the fleet which has come out to join us,' ran the C.-in-C.'s order number 229. 'Our strength is on a par with that of the Japanese, and in point of numbers we are stronger. . . .' All that remained to be done was to seek out the enemy and destroy him.

Later in the afternoon Rozhestvensky sent a signal to Nebogatoff requesting his presence aboard the flagship, and soon the two Admirals—the one short and lacking in dignity, the other tall, gaunt and stooping—were embracing one another at the head of the *Suvoroff's* gang-ladder before they disappeared with de Colongue and the Staff into the C.-in-C.'s cabin.

As Nebogatoff had expected, his reception was coldly formal, in spite of the welcoming signals and the little demonstration before the cheering bluejackets on deck. 'After half an hour of general conversation, he intimated that I should return to my own flagship,' Nebogatoff wrote later. 'My first idea was that the Admiral had no mind to disclose his plans in the presence of his Staff, and that soon he would give me a private interview. We never discussed a plan of campaign. He gave me neither instructions nor advice.' Nebogatoff had planned to make his way to Vladivostock by way of La Perouse Strait if Rozhestvensky had succeeded in eluding him, but he was given no opportunity at that meeting to express his opinion that it would be suicide to try to force a passage through the Straits of Tsu-Shima. 'I only once saw Rozhestvensky in the whole course of the cruise. . . . He did not again invite a visit, nor did he come on board the *Nicholas I*.'

After suffering a stroke, Admiral Felkerzam had been dangerously ill for some days, but Rozhestvensky did not feel it was necessary to pass on this news, nor to point out that in the event of his death, Nebogatoff as the next senior Admiral would automatically assume the position of second-in-command of the combined fleets.

In Kua-Bé, close to Van-Phong, the ships of the Third Pacific Squadron spent the next three days coaling and carrying out some of the more urgent repairs to their machinery, while Rozhestvensky hovered impatiently off the coast, nipping quickly into Van-Phong at dusk one night when de Jonquières was out of sight and returning to sea at daybreak.

On the 14th of May the two squadrons rejoined and took up cruising stations for the last lap of their voyage, with de Jonquières darting about the re-forming fleet like a nervous nursemaid suddenly relieved of her recalcitrant charges. 'Happy voyage and good fortune,' he signalled in parting, and Rozhestvensky answered with grateful thanks for the French courtesy and hospitality.

It was May Day by the Russian calendar, a double cause for celebration. On the *Suvoroff* the officers cracked a crate of Mumm's Extra Dry and toasted the Tsar and Tsarina, their fatherland, their Commander-in-Chief—and victory.

CHAPTER EIGHT

'Battle Flags are to be Sent Up'

'WE will be under the orders of Admiral Togo,' wrote home a Japanese officer a few days before the Battle of Tsu-Shima, 'a fact in which we all ought to rejoice. Notwithstanding that, I am very glad to have command of a destroyer and to be at a certain distance from him. He is an unpleasant neighbour for his inferiors.'

Admiral Heihachiro Togo had all the fierce characteristics of the man of iron will who drives himself to the top by zeal, unwavering self-confidence and burning patriotism. Although his country possessed one of the most powerful fleets in the world before he became its Commander-in-Chief, Togo was popularly known as 'the father of the Japanese Navy'. Contemporary British opinion liked to regard him as a benevolent genius, beloved of his men and idolized by the people, a sort of twentieth-century Lord Nelson; and he was even awarded the honour of a companionship to the Order of Merit.

The British view of the Russo-Japanese struggle as the gallant little Jap beating off the clumsy mauling attacks of the giant Russian bear can now be seen in its true perspective as just one more round in the endless struggle for power in that unhappy corner of the Far East; and Count Togo, O.M., who died at the venerable age of eighty-six in 1934, as one of the most effective exponents of early Japanese expansionism.

Admiral Togo commanded little love in his men, but unlimited respect as an administrator and tactician; to them he was the master whom they revered second only to the Mikado himself; and for the Japanese, who demanded none of the appealing eccentricities of a Patton or a Montgomery, that was enough. He was immensely courageous, a rigid disciplinarian with a passion for efficiency, and in a nation entirely devoid of naval tradition, his appreciation of the principles of naval warfare, his clear thinking and decisiveness were remarkable. He is unquestionably one of the half-dozen great naval commanders of the past century.

Togo's life spanned three of the great eras of naval development. When he was born sail still predominated and men-of-war were unarmoured and little different from those which had fought at Copenhagen and Trafalgar, and when he died the aeroplane had already made obsolete the battleship and its heavy guns. Togo fought his battles when the armoured fighting vessel was supreme and before the submarine's torpedo and the aerial bomb seriously threatened. He and Rozhestvensky were the only Admirals ever to lead their fleets into a full-scale and decisive gunnery battle. Tsu-Shima was the ironclad's finest hour, the one occasion in its brief history when it fulfilled its functions without interference.

Togo fought his first battle armed with two swords and a matchlock, and the enemy was a force of seven warships of the Royal Navy which had come to exact revenge for the murder of two British subjects and for local interference with British shipping. He was just sixteen, one of the hundreds of local boys who rushed to defend Kagoshima Bay against the threatened invasion, 'wearing a tight-sleeved haori, a short hakama and a round hat adorned with the family crest'.

During the brief engagement, in which the Royal Navy set fire to two fishing boats and retired at leisure without damage, Togo was seen to be less excited than his fellows and appears to have remained impassive under the shell fire.

Forty years later this half-savage youth was in command of more than a hundred fearfully complicated men-of-war, directing them in patrol and shore bombardment, manœuvring them in the elaborate motions of a fleet action against the enemy. His career epitomises the extraordinarily rapid development of his country to Western standards of technology and sophistication.

The episode at Kagoshima Bay was followed by the intensive development of the Japanese Navy, and Togo and two of his brothers were among the first to join up, fighting in a number of rebellions up and down the country. Like most navies of the nineteenth century, the Japanese based their organization on British practice and most of their ships were built in British yards to British designs. In 1871 Togo was selected for training in England, served two years on the *Worcester*, did a course in gunnery on the *Victory* (the Trafalgar Day celebration on the old flagship was one of the few occasions when he seems to have been visibly moved) and a course in mathematics at Cambridge. While one of Japan's earliest battleships was being built at Greenwich, Togo filled in his time with a course in naval engineering, and when the *Hiei* was completed, he sailed on her back to his homeland, arriving in 1878. In England he had studied conscientiously, applying himself with the peculiar zeal of his race, and within a few years of his return, he was given his first command.

As captain of the *Naniwa* he opened hostilities in the Sino-Japanese war by sinking the Chinese troopship *Kowshing en route* to Korea in 1894, just as his torpedo boats fired the first rounds against the Russian fleet at Port Arthur ten years later. His reputation was made in the Chinese war and confirmed early in the Russo-Japanese conflict, when, now as Commander-in-Chief, he followed up the first crippling blow with his unremitting blockade of Port Arthur and the naval action of the Battle of the Yellow Sea. Of course he was lucky, lucky to have killed

Makaroff, the one potentially great Russian naval commander, and even more fortunate in killing Witthoft with the opening shot at the Battle of the Yellow Sea, and above all fortunate in his foe, who ventured forth piecemeal, tentatively and only rarely to meet him.

On November 14th, 1904, the Mikado presided over a long secret conference of the naval and military general staffs at the royal palace in Tokio to prepare plans for the interception and destruction of the Second Pacific Squadron, which had sailed a month previously. For the Japanese, who never underestimated their enemy, the problem was formidable, for by then their effective battleship force had been reduced to four vessels, all of which had been on almost constant patrol since the beginning of the war.

The most important result of this conference was the formation of a Special Service Squadron of armed merchantmen to patrol the approaches to the war zone; and the decision to put in hand immediately a programme to refit the guns and worn machinery of the fleet, and a comprehensive training programme to keep up the high standard of efficiency of the crews during the period of waiting. For all this Togo was ultimately responsible, and, with no foreknowledge of the Russian fleet's long sojourn in Madagascar and its further delay awaiting coal and reinforcements, nor of the Port Arthur fleet's imminent destruction, it seemed impossible to complete the immense task in time.

In fact Togo had completed the refitting of almost his entire fleet by late February 1905. He had worked out his plans to the last detail and had chosen as his base the wide, sheltered waters of Chin-Hei Bay on the south-eastern coast of Korea long before Rozhestvensky left Madagascar. The whole of the Sea of Japan north to Vladivostock, the Korea Straits as far south as the island of Quelpart, were divided into numbered squares which were kept under constant patrol by the fast ships of his Special Service Squadron and formations of light cruisers, while the main force—the first and second squadrons, the battleships and the numerous powerful eight-inch gun cruisers under the command of Admiral Kamimura—lay in wait in the security of Chin-Hei Bay,[1] occasionally proceeding to sea on exercises and for gunnery practice.

'Togo is now in the picture of health. He said that now that the fleet had been refitted, the ships were as good as new'; and, 'Nothing could be better than the temper of the personnel of the Japanese Navy or the condition of their ships', ran the last reports from the two Royal Navy officers attached to the fleet as it lay in wait behind the elaborate net spread around the approaches to the only Russian base. For Rozhestvensky to escape from that net and to avoid a full-scale fleet action appeared impossible— and the tensely expectant enemy he would meet was supremely confident in its ability to inflict a crushing defeat.

'I think we have reached the culminating point in our adventures. Tomorrow the decision must be made.' On the *Suvoroff* Lieutenant Zotoff, the wardroom bore, had been pontificating for far too long. By the evening of May the 26th the *Suvoroff's* restless officers did not need to be told that the supreme crisis was near at hand. For the past few days as they had steamed north-east from Formosa in driving rain, low mist and chilling winds, the tension had been building up so that the nerves of even the gay and gregarious flagship's officers were near to breaking point. Lieutenant Zotoff could consider himself fortunate not to be silenced by a vodka bottle as he droned on: 'Presumably Togo is no greater fool than us and knows that the only course for us is the east side of the Gulf of Korea. I assume that he also knows how to use a pair of compasses and is acquainted with the four rules of arithmetic. . . .'

[1] The Singapore Russian consul's report was erroneous: no Japanese men-of-war had recently been in the vicinity.

Within twelve hours they would be entering the Korea Strait, the narrow channel between the island of Tsu-Shima and the Japanese mainland. There was no doubt now that this would be their route, although some of the officers had been surprised that they were not attempting the passage around Japan's eastern seaboard and through the Straits of La Perouse. But, as Togo had calculated, Rozhestvensky had judged this to be too dangerous in view of the difficulty of coaling in the rough Pacific waters without the aid of a single sheltering bay, and with the constant danger of torpedo-boat attack over a distance of some 1,500 miles. In any case there was no chance of circumnavigating the enemy's homeland unobserved, and Togo would have ample time to steam north to intercept them on their four-hundred-mile passage across the Sea of Japan. As usual it was no use denying the truth of Zotoff's clichés; they had already passed the point of no return.

The remarkable thing was that the Russian fleet had approached so close to Togo's bases without apparently having been observed. Until that morning, it is true, the weather had favoured them, and there had even been suggestions that in the poor visibility they might yet slip through unnoticed. But the morning of the 26th dawned bright and clear with a strong sun reflecting off the calm sea ahead of them. And still there was no smudge of smoke from Togo's scouts on the horizon. The intercepted radio messages from the powerful enemy observing station on the Goto Islands confirmed that Rozhestvensky's armada had somehow got to within a hundred and fifty miles of the Japanese islands without being seen. 'Last night . . . nothing . . . eleven lights . . . but not in line . . .' the Russian telegraphists had picked up from a jumble of code.

In the evening the fleet closed up as if in self-protection, and a welcome mist wrapped itself about the vessels, making station-keeping without lights more difficult but adding a further reassuring sense of security. The fleet was steaming in two columns, to starboard the seven battleships and the *Nakhimoff* of the original Second Pacific Squadron in line ahead, to port Nebogatoff's *Nicholas I* leading his coast-defence ships and four of the cruisers, while between them steamed the seven destroyers, the *Kamchatka*, the three transports, the *Rousse* and the *Svir*, and the two hospital ships. Fanned out about the fleet as scouts were the five other cruisers.

Day and night since they had entered the danger zone the gun crews had been at action stations, and full preparations for the battle had been taken. The fleet's superfluous colliers and transports had been shed some days before, and several of the armed merchantmen dispatched into the Yellow Sea and towards Japan's eastern seaboard in an attempt to create a diversion. Last exercises were carried out only that morning, the one occasion on which the fleet attempted manœuvres as a single unit. 'Prepare for action,' Rozhestvensky signalled as his ships slowly, awkwardly assumed battle formation. 'Tomorrow at the hoisting of colours, battle flags are to be sent up.'

On all the ships the tables and chairs, the wooden fittings and anything combustible that was not vital to their fighting efficiency from the mess decks, cabins and wardrooms had been hurled overboard, the decks hosed down (and sprinkled, like the guns, with holy water), the boats filled with water. Makeshift shields of sodden tarpaulin, hammocks, sailcloth and ropes as shell-splinter protection had been erected at vulnerable points, and heaped piles of coal sacks had been placed around the unprotected quick-firing-gun positions.

On the ironclads, the surgeons had been preparing for the casualties. 'Fifteen hundred first-aid packets had been put together for individual use', on the *Oryol*, 'each containing sterilized gauze, a piece of oilsilk, and a bandage; the whole wrapped in oil paper and enclosed in a cardboard box. These boxes, sealed and stamped with the Red Cross, were kept in store on each of the bridges, in the conning tower, in the turrets, in the casemates. . . .' Bamboo stretchers, operating tables with the sterilized instruments laid out alongside . . . 'all was ready for the morrow's harvest of death'.

Early in the day the sailors had gone through their sea-bags, sorting out their letters, keepsakes and small valuables for consignment into the ships' treasure chests; and although there was no chance of posting any mail before the battle, most of the sailors—many of them slowly and painstakingly—had written letters home. Everyone turned in early that night, and even among those on watch there was little talk.

Later that night Semenoff made a tour of the flagship and noticed the strained silence that hung heavily over the decks, where the men slept uneasily, stretched out beside their guns. The mist had thickened and the only sounds were the creaking of the plates as the ship rose and fell in the gentle swell, and the regular beat from a nearby destroyer invisible on the port beam. It was a relief to be able to climb down the iron ladders deep into the engine room with its bustle and life, where the air carried the purposeful scent of hot oil and quivered with the pulsating throb of the powerful great engines and the sound of hissing steam from the pipes and the clatter of moving machinery. The lights gleamed brightly on the connecting rods and the furnaces sent a warm glow across the damp steel floors. Here, far from the forbidding paralysis above, was a safe, detached world where the men still moved and acted normally and shouted at one another.

In the wardroom at three o'clock a few officers still lounged about, some asleep, some sipping tea, all preoccupied with their thoughts or too tired to care.

Back on deck, Semenoff saw that the moon had risen in its last quarter; 'against the mist, dimly whitened by its silver rays, the ship's funnels, masts and rigging were sharply outlined. . . . Again on all sides this dreadful, painful silence'. On the forebridge it was almost a surprise to discover that the ship was, after all, under human control, and that the men were alive and watching.

'What are you doing wandering about?' Captain Ignatzius asked.

'Just having a look round.' Semenoff nodded towards the still form of Rozhestvensky in his armchair. 'Gone to sleep?'

'Just persuaded him to. And why shouldn't he? Daybreak in a couple of hours.' Ignatzius was not in the least depressed nor apparently even affected by the atmosphere of foreboding. They were nearly safe, he thought. 'It's 200,000 to 1 against anyone running into us accidentally. But I don't like this breeze,' he confessed. 'It's freshening —hope it doesn't break up the mist. If it does, tomorrow will mean the end of the *Suvoroff*. We'll give them the slip yet if only the mist stays.'

And how were the Japs feeling, Ignatzius wondered, who still did not know where their enemy was, or when the action would be fought? This thought appeared to amuse the irrepressible captain. 'What a stew they must be in!' he exclaimed. 'What fun!' And he began to laugh so loudly that he had to stuff his handkerchief into his mouth to avoid waking up Rozhestvensky.

The mist was still there at dawn, but the wind had increased from the south-west, turning it to damp, swirling, half-opaque clouds that almost obscured the deep-red sun rising ahead of them, and the horizon had dissolved into the uniform blue-grey of sea and sky.

The fleet's second division was still there, holding station well on the port beam, while behind them sailed the cruisers, 'kicking and plunging in the lumpy seas', a correspondent to *Blackwoods* described them, 'as if protesting at the little flutter of bunting from the *Suvoroff* which kept them churning their propellers behind the obsolete iron coffins when they should have been patrolling the passage now looming up in front of them'.

The visibility varied from moment to moment; sometimes it was as much as ten miles, and the distant dark smudge of Tsu-Shima could just be made out between the whipped-up spray; then it would fall to less than a mile, bringing a brief, false feeling of security to the officers on the *Suvoroff's* bridge.

The mist was at its thickest, joined now by flurries of fine rain, when the flagship's look-out called down to the bridge that there was a strange vessel approaching them rapidly from the starboard. A dozen pairs of binoculars at once began to sweep across the murky water, but for a full minute nothing could be seen. Then the mist drew back like a stage curtain, revealing in sudden nakedness a two-funnelled ship cutting through the water less than a mile away, its two six-inch guns clearly visible.

It was the Japanese auxiliary cruiser *Sinano Maru*, travelling at a great speed and heeling hard over as she shied away from the fleet. But before a gun could be brought to bear on her, the mist closed in again and she had gone. Captain Ignatzius's 200,000 to 1 chance had come up.

CHAPTER NINE

The Meeting at Donkey's Ears

'I have sworn to God to accomplish my task. He has already strengthened my nerve, and has in His infinite mercy protected us in the stress of the operations we have already accomplished. I pray that God may strengthen my right hand, and that if I fail to fulfil the oath I have sworn, He may purge my country from shame with my blood.'

Vice-Admiral Zinovi Petrovitch Rozhestvensky
(Fleet Order No. 294).

THE Russian fleet sailed on through the rising seas at a speed of nine knots. It was hard going for the little destroyers, which heaved and bucked about like twigs in a mill-race, disappearing from sight every few seconds. Even on the ironclads the rollers were sometimes lifting up over the bows and sweeping across the foredecks and pouring in through the lower gun ports.

For a time the shore line on the port beam was no more than an indistinct, tumbling blur. But the mist thinned a little as the morning advanced, revealing the precipitous cliffs of Tsu-Shima, the forests beyond—and, reaching high into the heavens above them, the cleft mountain peak of The Donkey's Ears, pert and mocking, a travesty of a landfall. They had come eighteen thousand miles to be greeted by an ass.

For more than an hour they were left in peace. No one appeared to be interfering with their progress. In forty-eight hours they would surely be steaming into Vladivostock. . . . That scouting cruiser must have been a ghost ship, their brief glimpse of it through the swirling mist an hallucination.

Just after six o'clock the *Ural* came up from astern at full speed, signalling by semaphore that there were four Japanese light cruisers shadowing them from astern. The radio operators were beginning to intercept messages in Japanese code, too, in an ever-increasing stream. The air was humming with orders and reports, all incomprehensible but by their very bearing and volume suggesting sudden enemy activity all around them. Still nothing could be seen from the flagship, only glimpses of Iki-Shima to the south and to the north-west the Donkey's Ears of Tsu-Shima.

The fast armoured cruiser *Idzumo* was the first Japanese warship deliberately to expose herself to the fleet, appearing out of the haze to the north-east, with black smoke streaming from her funnels, and swinging round to sail parallel with the advancing columns. She made no hostile move, and might almost have been an envoy sent by the Mikado to welcome and escort them in.

Rozhestvensky at first made no attempt to interrupt her peaceful spotting, as if deluding himself that she did not exist. It was not until eight o'clock, when she was less than six miles away on a closing course, that Ignatzius sent an order to the aft twelve-inch turret of the *Suvoroff*. But even as the great guns swung round and slowly raised high their barrels, the *Idzumo* turned sharply to starboard and steered away at full speed. She was beyond range before fire could be opened.

The *Idzumo* was replaced on the port beam of the fleet by three more armoured cruisers and the battleship *Chin-Yen*, headed by a light cruiser. For an hour these ships examined the Russian fleet at leisure, just beyond effective range, until they, too, slipped away, and were relieved by four light cruisers. It was clear that Togo intended to strike out in his own time and was prepared to wait and hold back his battleships until Rozhestvensky had cleared the Straits of Tsu-Shima, which restricted manœuvring.

Behind them The Donkey's Ears faded from the sight of the Russian fleet.

'The ship's company was unusually cheerful and talkative,' wrote Novikoff-Priboy of that morning of waiting, and a spirit of lighthearted gaiety affected all the crews now that the climax of tension had passed. At last, after all these months of anxious cruising, they were to fulfil their function, and the outcome of the battle that lay ahead seemed suddenly of trivial importance. Before sundown they would know the answer, and that was all that mattered.

By a happy chance, today was the anniversary of the Tsar and Tsarina's coronation and there could be no more appropriate moment for the celebration functions to take place than this, with His Majesty's battle squadrons sailing towards the enemy, decks cleared for action. The ceremony of raising the St. Andrew's flag at the stern and at the mastheads and the Thanksgiving Service, with the chaplain in full canonicals, that followed on the decks of the battleships, perfectly matched the mood of the men. Even the most incorrigible subverts added their voices to the patriotic hymn, *Long Live the Tsar*.

There was a tot of vodka for every man after the service, and at twelve o'clock as the column swung round on to a north-easterly course for Vladivostock, the officers of the *Suvoroff* hurried down to the wardroom, where the stewards had prepared rows of brimming champagne glasses for the loyal toast. The laughter and the excited chatter were silenced by the senior officer present, the Admiral, the captain and most of the Staff still being up on the bridge, and for the last time in that wardroom, which had heard so many toasts since the previous September, glasses were raised. 'On this, the great anniversary of the sacred coronation of their Majesties, may God help us to serve with him our beloved country. To the health of the Emperor! The Empress! To Russia!'

Before the cheers died away, before the glasses could be drained, the call to action stations sounded through the ship, and the officers hurried back to their posts. The four light cruisers, which had slowly been converging on the fleet, had been joined by a group of destroyers, which, it was feared, might dart ahead at any moment and attempt to lay mines across their bows. Ever since the conclusion of the thanksgiving service this detachment had been comfortably within range of the battleships' main and secondary armament, and the commanders of all the ironclads had been impatiently awaiting the signal from the flagship to open fire. A few well-placed salvos would blow these impudent Japanese scouts out of the water, but the C.-in-C. appeared as if paralysed, standing motionless on the bridge of the *Suvoroff* with only an occasional uninterested glance at the shadowing cruisers.

Captain Yung of the *Oryol* could endure the waiting no longer. It was madness, besides being bad for the men's spirit, to allow those little ships to hover about them like this; monstrous that a detachment had not been dispatched to deal with that first auxiliary cruiser, the *Idzumo*, and the others. Yung had less confidence in Rozhestvensky than any of the other commanders, though no one feared the Admiral more than he did, and it may have been that he ordered his six-inch guns to open fire on his own authority in the confident knowledge that he would never have to answer for his insubordination.

The sudden sound of that first salvo shot through the fleet like a spasm. The *Oryol* had used smokeless powder, and the keyed-up gunners, who had had their sights trained on the cruisers for some time, took it as a signal from the

Suvoroff that the action was to open. Broadside after broadside crashed out before the hastily raised signal from the flagship to cease fire, 'ammunition not to be wasted', had any effect.

'Ships' companies to have dinner at once.' The crews tumbled down the ladders to the mess-decks like gangs of triumphant schoolboys, shouting and laughing, braced and excited by their baptism. They had fired on the enemy, and he had turned away and fled, lobbing back as he ran a few stray shells which had missed. This wasn't going to be so bad after all.

For the past few hours the first, second and third divisions of ironclads had been in single line-ahead battle formation, Nebogatoff's coast-defence vessels at the rear being followed by the transports, hospital ships and destroyers, protected by Enkvist's light cruisers. But at this point, Rozhestvensky suddenly gave the order for the first and second divisions to turn eight points (or ninety degrees) to starboard in succession and at the same time to increase their speed to their maximum of eleven knots. No one will ever know what strange reasoning prompted the Admiral to carry out the manœuvre, the first positive step he had taken beyond the order to take up battle stations. Perhaps he had formed the notion—and it could have been no more than a guess—that the Japanese would approach him from the east, and that the most powerful units of his fleet must therefore be placed to act as the spearhead of their attack. Rozhestvensky issued only two fleet orders at Tsu-Shima, both of them before the fleets engaged, the first causing mystification and dismay, the second a state of chaos that gave the enemy an advantage of initiative that he never lost. If no Commander-in-Chief has ever suffered such a long and exhausting prelude to an engagement, none can have led his forces into battle with such calm irresolution.

Before the second division, led by the *Oslyabya*, could

complete the movement, cruisers reappeared from the north-west again, and Rozhestvensky, as if uncertain whether these now formed the van of Togo's main squadrons or were merely reassuring themselves of his course and disposition, changed his mind and cancelled the order in time to prevent the second division from following him, and with the *Alexander III*, *Borodino* and *Oryol* trailing behind him, turned again through ninety degrees so that his first division lay on a course parallel with and slightly ahead of the rest of the line.

It was at this crucial and dangerous moment, with the Russian forces divided and confused, that Togo's main battle fleet, headed by the flagship *Mikasa*, appeared on the horizon as a long, steady line of grey hulls and towering superstructures beneath a streaming cloud of black smoke. From the fore bridge of the *Suvoroff* Rozhestvensky watched them through his binoculars for a few moments in silent satisfaction. His trap could hardly have worked better; Togo could not have selected a bearing more favourable to the Russians on which to make his approach.

The cautious Semenoff, standing beside his Admiral, was less confident. He had been at the Battle of the Yellow Sea, at which Togo had cleverly divided his forces, and was anxious in case Kamimura's armoured cruisers might now close in from the other side, forcing them to divide their fire.

'No, they are all there,' Rozhestvensky replied confidently, and was proved right a few minutes later as the eight-inch gun ships, each more formidable than the most powerful Russian armoured cruiser, hove into sight behind Togo's first squadron of ironclads. At a range of ten miles the whole strength of the Japanese Navy exposed itself, marking at last the conclusion of all the bluffs and alarms and deceptions of the past seven months. This was the ultimate, decisive moment, on which hung the lives of twenty-five thousand men confined to their cages of steel, the climax of the bitter struggle for power into which their countries had thrown them.

It was Togo who acted first, carrying out two successive movements of breathtaking rashness, which could have

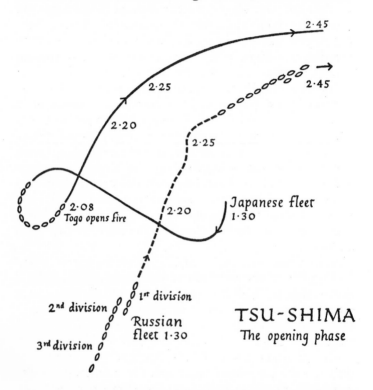

2·45

2·45

2·25

2·20

2·25

2·08
Togo opens fire

2·20

Japanese fleet
1·30

1ˢᵗ division

2ⁿᵈ division

Russian
fleet 1·30

3ʳᵈ division

TSU-SHIMA
The opening phase

been contemplated only by a Commander-in-Chief with complete confidence in the skill of his subordinates and the meanest regard for the skill of his enemy. He turned his single battle line first to starboard in a south-westerly direction, crossing, while still out of range, from starboard to port of the two enemy columns, and then, as he proceeded at full speed on an opposite parallel course, suddenly reversed the direction of his two squadrons in succession, ship by ship in turn, through 180 degrees, on to the Russians' weaker flank.

Rozhestvensky countered by issuing his second and final order, signalling his four detached battleships to return and re-form in a single line ahead of the rest of the fleet, but failing to slow the one column or increase the speed of the other, so that the ships of the first division had to squeeze back into their old position at the van as well as they could, forcing the second and third divisions to reduce speed, and even to stop engines. 'One vessel had to turn to starboard and another to port,' Nebogatoff later described this moment, 'so that there was absolute confusion. . . . Mob is the only word literally to express our formation at this time.'

Rozhestvensky, who either preferred to ignore or was unaware of the pandemonium astern of the flagship, watched Togo's beautifully executed double movement and reversal in silent admiration before making off, still without a word, for the head of the ladder that led to the conning-tower below. Clapier de Colongue, following hard on his heels, turned before disappearing. 'To your stations, gentlemen,' he told the little knot of officers who were following their departure anxiously.

Admiral Togo's cabin was plainly decorated, in marked contrast to the ostentation of Rozhestvensky's. It was furnished with a roll-top desk under the porthole, a chart rack beside it, a round table and a smaller table beside the sofa on which lay a folded rug and blue pillow. On the mantelpiece was a bunch of artificial flowers made from feathers, a present from the people of the city of Kobe; placed on china dishes on each side of the imitation fireplace was a pair of dwarf trees, a five-hundred-year-old cedar, and a fir, both gifts from his old friend, Count

Okura. Two paintings hung from the walls, one the work
of his steward, of which Togo was especially proud, showing the fleet bombarding Port Arthur, the other of a
training squadron which the Admiral had commanded
before the war, depicted in a typhoon on a voyage to Aus-
tralia. The only other decorations were a Russian shell
which, had it exploded when it struck the ship's bridge,
would have blown him to pieces; the other the whisker of
a torpedo which had lodged itself in the *Mikasa's* net one
night. This cabin had been Togo's living quarters for
almost a year and a half, and it was here that he received
news at 5.15 a.m. that the Russian fleet had been sighted
by Captain Narikava of the *Sinano Maru.*

Togo read the message which he had been anxiously
awaiting for the past two days and nights, laughing, it is
said, for the first time since the war began. 'The enemy is
in square 203, and is evidently making for the eastern
channel.' Perhaps it was just a coincidence that the name
of the height which Japanese soldiers had captured at such
terrible cost, the key to Port Arthur from which the last
ships of the Russian Far East fleet had been destroyed by
artillery fire, had been 203-Metre Hill. But Togo considered it a good omen, important enough for the news
to be circulated to every crew member of every ship of the
fleet.

'Having received warning that the enemy fleet is in
sight,' Togo telegraphed to Imperial Headquarters, 'the
combined squadrons will go out to meet and defeat it. We
have fine weather, although the sea is rough.' At Chin-
Hei Bay, almost a hundred miles north of Rozhestvensky's
position at dawn, there was only the faintest trace of the
mist that had permitted the *Sinano Maru* to approach so
close to the Russian fleet, and visibility was 12,000 yards.
The rough seas, high enough for Togo's five torpedo-boat
divisions to have to seek temporary shelter, 'caused in-
convenience', ran an official report, 'from the water dash-

ing through the turret and casemate ports, and from the spray that constantly wetted the object glasses of the sighting telescopes'. But the whole fleet was clear of Douglas Inlet and steaming west towards the Sea of Japan before seven o'clock.

All through that long morning the wireless reports poured into the flagship from the *Idzumo*, the battleship *Chin-Yen* and later from Admiral Dewa's light cruisers, giving exact details of the ships in Rozhestvensky's fleet, their disposition and their every move. No Admiral could have been better served by his intelligence, and only the visibility could affect the moment at which they would sight the enemy.

When contact was at last made just before half-past one, Togo's Staff tried to persuade him to move down to the conning-tower. But the Admiral would have none of it. He had fought all his actions from his bridge, exposed to every passing shell splinter, and he was not prepared to leave it now. It was a good example to the men, he considered, and besides, you could see better out in the open. 'I am getting on for sixty,' he told his Chief of Staff, 'and this old body of mine is no longer worth caring for. But you are all young men with futures before you, so take care of yourselves and continue living in order to serve your country.'

And there he remained, this tough little grizzled man with the brilliant black eyes, determined, protruding under lip and tightly pursed-up mouth. Above him on the foremast streamed the signal: 'The fate of the Empire depends upon today's event. Let every man do his utmost.' The Nelson touch was not inappropriate: he was leading his ships into combat with all the incautious brilliance of the victor of Trafalgar.

There is a story that when, after the Battle of Tsu-Shima, the Mikado asked Togo to bring before him the most gallant sailor from the Japanese fleet, he summoned

Captain W. C. Pakenham, R.N., to the Royal Palace. Pakenham, the Royal Navy's observer, attached to the battleship *Asahi*, was certainly a striking figure, and even the most fervid, banzai-screaming Japanese bluejacket could not have acted more fearlessly during the action. In the course of his fourteen continuous months with the fleet, when he had been in every action and had not once stepped ashore, he established an intimate relationship with the C.-in-C., who often consulted him on decisions of policy and strategy. It is doubtful if Togo ever admired anybody, but he certainly had the highest respect for the austere, dignified British officer, who always dressed so immaculately, with a freshly starched high collar, even under the most difficult conditions. He was also tall and he wore a monocle, which alone distinguished him on any Japanese warship; in fact Pakenham became a legend long before he suffered the storm and fury of Tsu-Shima from a deck chair, placed in the most exposed position on the quarter-deck of the *Asahi*, taking notes of the battle's progress with appalling *sang-froid*.

In his dispatches Captain Pakenham recorded vivid glimpses of the battle from the moment when Togo first turned to cross the Russian's 'T', when 'it was possible to see down the length of the Russian lines. In the right column the four biggest battleships loomed enormous, dwarfing all others into insignificance. It was not easy', he went on, 'to realize that the battleships of Japan were probably producing at least equal effect on the minds of the Russians.'

Rozhestvensky's first ranging shots were fired before Togo swung round so dramatically and to such effect through 180 degrees, the first shell falling only twenty-two yards astern of the *Mikasa*, 'and being rapidly succeeded by others that fell almost as close'.

These opening Russian salvos were unpleasantly disillusioning for the Japanese. There was none of the wildness in the shooting they had been led to expect; in fact, at a range of 9,000 yards it was uncommonly accurate, and several hits with the six-inch guns were scored on the *Mikasa* and the *Shikishima* in the first few minutes. Togo had by then committed himself to the turn, but as he issued the order he must have felt some alarm. What had happened to Russian gunnery since the fleet actions of the 10th and 14th of August?

The axis of the turn was the danger point, when his twelve ships in succession would swing round at full helm across the same spot. The operation would take some ten minutes to complete, and during that time the Japanese gunners would be helpless, their sights masked by the other ships of the fleet, while the Russian gunners would be presented in turn with sitting targets, all at the same range. 'Part of the Russian fire followed the *Mikasa*,' said Pakenham, 'but the gradually increasing remainder continued to be converged on the Japanese turning point, and it was interesting to watch each ship approach and run through this warm spot, a feat all were lucky enough to accomplish without receiving serious injury'; it was luck, aided by the 'absolute confusion' among the Russian battleships. The battle of Tsu-Shima, and ultimately the Russo-Japanese war, was to be lost by the momentary hesitancy of a tired and wasted Admiral who could not make up his mind, and when he changed it, disregarded the consequences.

By 1.55 p.m. the two opposing fleets faced one another in two columns on similar but slightly converging courses. Every man at every gun was firing as fast as the breeches could be emptied and re-loaded, the Japanese concentrating their fire on the *Suvoroff* and *Oslyabya*, the Russian ships on the *Mikasa*, and it was these three flagships that were struck most frequently at this opening phase. 'This was the scenic part of the battle. . . . Two long lines of ships attacking one another vigorously, formations as yet unbroken, damages still conjectural, and the fate of the day seemed to hang on every shot.'

The conning-tower of the *Suvoroff* was a cramped circular fortress, barely ten feet in diameter and with a low armour-plated mushroom-shaped roof; the only austere officers' accommodation on the ship, and no place for a claustrophobe. Entry was by means of an aperture, protected by a blast-shield, which led out onto the platform communicating with the bridge above and the lower fighting position below, and to the entrance of a narrow steel cylinder, lined with ladder-rungs, which formed the core of the whole fore superstructure. In action this tube could be used as an emergency passage between the upper and lower bridges and the rest of the ship.

All the apparatus and controls required to direct this one ship and the whole fleet in battle were contained in the cramped space of the conning-tower, in which sixteen men were expected to carry out their duties: engine-room telegraph, wheel and compass, speaking-tube, electric controls linked to the gun batteries, duplicated telephones, range-finders, signalling apparatus, a navigator's chart table. This was the fleet's precious brain cell, protected by a seven-feet-deep circular hoop of ten-inch armour.

It was through one of the narrow embrasures cut into the hardened steel wall of his conning-tower that Rozhestvensky watched the last of Admiral Kamimura's armoured cruisers swing round from an opposite course behind the eleven other warships ahead of it, and open fire.

During the first ten minutes, while the enemy fired only a series of sighting shots with smoke shells, the Russian gunners had scored a number of hits, at least a dozen of them on the *Mikasa* with twelve-inch and six-inch shells. One of these struck the flagship's bridge ladder, scattering splinters across the bridge, ripped off the iron cover of the compass and struck Togo in the thigh as he was peering through his telescope. The Admiral took no notice of the slight wound and did not even bother to turn round.

Nebogatoff's third division, firing with commendable accuracy at a greater range, concentrated on the armoured cruisers. Three shells on the *Yakumo's* fore turret knocked it out of action, the *Asama* suffered a hail of well-placed fire before a twelve-inch shell from one of the *Nicholas I's* two heavy guns disabled her steering and forced her out of line, and a strike by a ten-inch shell on the *Nishin* wounded Admiral Misu. In these first minutes, the Russians had shattered all predictions by damaging three of the enemy's units, hitting several more, and reducing their numbers by 8 per cent.

If Rozhestvensky had given one more order, to alter course to port and slip behind the long Japanese column, pouring a stream of fire into the vulnerable tail end, not only might he have escaped from the trap, but the brief action would have been hailed as a Russian victory. Instead he allowed Togo to push him farther and farther to starboard, until the range had closed to four thousand yards, then to three, and finally to less than a mile; while for the tail of the Russian fleet the range increased and Nebogatoff's gunners found their line of fire more and more obscured by the ships of the first and second divisions.

The whole Japanese line now sparkled from end to end with the muzzle flashes of nearly five hundred guns, half of which appeared to be directing their fire on the *Suvoroff* and the rest on Felkerzam's *Oslyabya* leading the second division. Togo was once more succeeding in crossing the Russian 'T', this time within range of both his medium and heavy armament; and he was manœuvring as he pleased because he had a five-knots advantage in speed over Rozhestvensky, whose maximum was limited to eleven knots by Nebogatoff's third division. So much for Nicholas Klado's strategy of statistics. The 'goloshes'' ten-inch guns had fired with extraordinary accuracy, but within a quarter of an hour they were left with nothing to shoot at.

After getting the range with the sighting shells, the Japanese gunners had opened up with their primary and secondary armament, at first slowly and steadily and then at an increasing rate and with devastating accuracy. A gun here, a gun-crew there, had been destroyed by the Russian broadsides, but the fighting strength of the fleet had not been seriously impaired, and what was far more important, the moral effect of the hits was negligible. With brisk, unemotional efficiency the stretcher crews carried away the wounded, and the dead were cast aside like obstructing litter to be attended to later. In one of the goriest passages of a little book Togo's brother wrote later, he described how buckets of water were thrown across the deck to cleanse it of slippery remnants which might otherwise have impeded the movements of the nearest surviving gun crew, whose rate of fire remained unaffected. Only zealous, highly trained sailors with battle experience could have stood up to that close-range bombardment so calmly; sailors inspired by their Admiral and with the image of the almighty Mikado before them, and with the advantage of the fatalistic courage of their race.

The Russian crews had nothing to sustain their courage when the first instantaneously-fused shells came tearing towards them, clearly visible in the faint misty sunlight, and plunged screaming down on to the decks, blasting open jagged holes in the steelwork, wrinkling the iron-work of deck houses, companionways and boat davits, scorching up or igniting paint and woodwork, filling the air with white-hot splinters and pulverizing all human life in the path of their blasts.

The first hit on the *Suvoroff* landed abreast of the fore funnel and one of the six-inch gun turrets, falling directly on to the dressing station rigged up in this sheltered spot, which served normally as the ship's church. Not one of the medical orderlies survived the explosion; only the doctor remained unharmed beside the Image of Christ with its glass intact, and the candles which still burned in their holders. The next shell struck the side of the ship beneath the centre six-inch gun turret, devastating the captain's and officers' cabins and setting fire to the gangway. Semenoff discovered the firemen standing and staring helplessly at the flames by the main hydrant controls. 'Wake up!' he shouted at them. 'Why don't you turn the water on?'

As the bombardment increased in intensity, as salvo after salvo of twelve-inch 'portmanteaus', eight-inch and six-inch shells raked the flagship from stem to stern, the surviving sailors on deck succumbed to the paralysis of shock, their responses numbed, every emotion but fear stunned by the onslaught. There was no escape from the holocaust of flying metal, nowhere to hide, nowhere to go. The ship's boats, blazing while water sprang in fountains from their splinter-torn hulls, the flames licking across iron plates on all sides—wherever they looked there were grotesque contradictions of everything natural and normal, and even the scattered, distorted corpses bore no resemblance to their living shipmates. The sounds, the smells, the sights, all were overwhelming and beyond human comprehension.

The conning-tower received two direct hits in quick succession, which failed to pierce the armour plate but filled the little steel cell with splinters that screamed round and round like distraught trapped bees, killing and wounding before they at last lost their momentum. The helmsman fell at the wheel, Berseneff, the senior flag gunnery officer, at the rangefinder; Vladimirsky was wounded in the head while peering through one of the embrasures. Both Rozhestvensky and Ignatzius were wounded slightly, and already their control over the movements of the fleet and the complex mechanism of the ship was being lost as cables were severed and speaking tubes smashed.

The first onslaught of instantaneously-fused shells had succeeded in making a shambles of the upper works of the flagship, demoralizing or wiping out the crews of the unprotected light guns and starting innumerable fires. It had killed many men, but if it failed to destroy the turret guns, it extinguished the thin enthusiasm of the surviving crew above the armoured decks, so that their gunfire was irregular and wildly inaccurate. On the *Mikasa* the fighting enthusiasm had been stimulated by the first explosions; on the *Suvoroff* it succumbed at once, so that after the first half-hour of battle not a Japanese ship received a hit, though the Russian fighting power had hardly been materially affected.

At about 2.20 Togo's ships switched to armour-piercing shells and, at a range of little more than a mile, the results were appalling. Two heavy-calibre hits on the flagship's aft main turret jerked one of the guns up at a drunken angle and killed or wounded all the crew, another struck the hull amidships on the waterline, sending the sea storming in; a fourth crashed through to the packed sickbay on the main deck with horrifying results. The main mast was hurled overboard, one funnel lay sprawled across a bed of tortured ironwork, the other was pock-marked and distorted with flames licking at its base.

At 2.30 a hit in the stern jammed the *Suvoroff's* steering gear hard to starboard, and the great ship swung off course, trailing behind her a streaming cloud of smoke and sparks.

The last means of communication with the fleet had been lost with the destruction of all the signalling halyards, and it was no longer possible to see anything from the conning-tower through the smoke and flames and the constant spouts of cascading water from shell bursts in the sea alongside. In an effort to make out what was happening to his ship, Captain Ignatzius felt his way through the thick smoke, tripping over the bodies scattered on the steel floor, and struggled onto the platform outside. He had lost his hat and there was blood all over his head. For a moment he stood dizzily in the open, clutching the hand-rail for support, swaying to and fro before losing his balance and crashing head first down the ladder to the deck below.

The medical orderlies found their captain lying still beside the lower fighting position and rolled him gently on to a stretcher. Before they could move him away he regained consciousness and tried to sit up and slip off again. 'It's nothing—only a trifle,' Captain Ignatzius murmured with an apologetic smile.

After an hour of battle the Admiral was at last smoked and burnt out of his conning-tower at three o'clock. All the instruments and controls had ceased to function, the smoke made breathing impossible and the flames from a direct twelve-inch shell hit on the stump of the fore funnel were licking up against the outside walls. Rozhestvensky, wounded a dozen times in the head, the back and in his right leg, ordered out the survivors among his staff in search of a new control point. Lieutenant Bogdnoff led the way, pushing aside burning hammocks which, intended to protect the superstructure against splinters, had instead provided excellent fuel, and disappeared into a wall of flame.

Clapier de Colongue took charge of the party then. 'We'll have to go down the hatch,' he shouted, though it was difficult to imagine how the dazed Rozhestvensky, who was barely able to stand, could clamber down the vertical rungs inside the tube. Dragging two dead bodies aside, they managed to lift clear the heavy metal cover, and one by one Rozhestvensky, his Chief of Staff, Semenoff and Filippovsky, von Kursel and the three other survivors from the conning-tower struggled into the narrow aperture, coughing and choking, and felt their way thirty feet down the narrow, dark cylinder to the lower fighting position.

But their new headquarters was already a raging furnace, and now the search was for shelter from the flames and shell fire rather than for a control position from which to direct the battle. Wherever de Colongue led them, treading warily over smouldering fragments, round gaping holes, twisted hose-pipes and empty shell cases, they were always baulked by fires or tangled wreckage.

The eight men, like homeless wanderers in a ruined city, crouching at the shriek of every passing shell, got as far as the centre port six-inch turret and retraced their steps again to the starboard side. They were fighting their way aft along beside the upper gun battery when a sudden explosion hurled them all to the deck.

Everyone managed to struggle to his feet again except Rozhestvensky, who had been struck by a splinter in his left leg. Very carefully Semenoff and de Colongue raised him by his elbows and dragged him through the steel door and into the nearby turret, where they lowered him gently on to a steel case.

The Admiral could not walk, could not be moved any farther. The last splinter had severed the main nerve in his leg and paralysed his foot. But it also appeared to have shocked him out of the dazed, lethargic state into which he had been stunned by the ceaseless noise and violence. Gazing furiously about him at the sodden, blackened gunners who were staring back at their Admiral in wonder, he demanded of Clapier de Colongue, 'Why aren't these guns firing?—fall in the crews and open fire immediately.'

CHAPTER TEN

The Admiral is Transferred

Captain Clapier de Colongue: Sir, we must shorten the distance—they're all being killed—they're on fire.
Vice-Admiral Rozhestvensky: Aren't we all being killed?

TRAILING along with his four old ironclads at the tail of the long, curving Russian column, it was all Admiral Nebogatoff could do to keep up with the first and second divisions. He had long since given up hope of firing his guns at the distant Japanese fleet, which was hidden by the smoke from the funnels and the fires raging on the *Suvoroff* and the vessels behind her, and could remain only a helpless witness to the slaughter taking place ahead of him.

The tall, slab-sided *Oslyabya*, Admiral Felkerzam's flag-ship, was the first to go. She had always appeared awkward and gawky in the water, like a crude child's model hewn from a chunk of wood with bits of piping stuck in hap-hazardly for funnels, and her high, vulnerable sides made a fine target for the Japanese gunners. Kamimura's cruisers had already levelled her decks to a blazing wasteland when the *Asahi* sent into her bows three twelve-inch shells, which peeled off the armour-plating and let the sea come pouring into her hull.

The battleship swung out of line, circling and heeling over like a great maimed animal that has lost its reason. For ten agonizing minutes, with the cruisers pouring a

177

torrent of shells into her, the *Oslyabya* listed over farther and farther, while her captain, clutching the railings outside the conning-tower and with a sodden cigarette between his lips, called to his men to jump. 'We're sinking. Good-bye shipmates,' he shouted. 'Get farther away from the ship, the devil take you! If you don't you'll go down in the suck. Farther away!'

He was still there, a small, dirty figure with a cut across his bald head, shouting furiously at his men as the ship heeled to sixty degrees, revealing her ruddy, weed-encrusted underside.

'She suddenly dipped at the bows and began to turn over slowly,' one of the *Nicholas I's* crew told later. 'The impression produced by the capsizing of a vessel of such a gigantic size was awful. We saw how the men thrown off the deck clutched and clung to the sides, or crawled and fell, or were crushed by falling top-hamper, or swept away by a hail of shells.' A few brave men during those last minutes attempted to release the heavy hatchways over the engine rooms and stokeholds in which more than two hundred stokers and artificers had been locked since the action had opened, but the angle of the deck and the distortions caused by shell bursts made the job hopeless. At the last second, as the *Oslyabya's* stern rose high in the air, they rushed for the scattered cork hammocks and hurled themselves overboard.

She went down at half-past three, the first armoured battleship ever to be sunk by gunfire, with her Admiral's flag flying at the masthead, and with Admiral Felkerzam still aboard in his cabin. But Felkerzam never saw the end of his ship. Since the previous evening he had lain in a strong oak coffin on the floor, attired in full dress uniform for his funeral. Only the captain, the ship's surgeon and two orderlies knew that he had died shortly before sundown, for when Rozhestvensky was informed he had given the strictest instructions that neither the *Oslyabya's* crew nor the rest of the fleet should learn the news, in case it had a depressing effect, until after the battle.

Even Admiral Nebogatoff had not been informed of the death of his immediate senior, so that he entered the battle ignorant of the fact that he was second-in-command of the Russian fleet. In the event it did not matter very much. By the time the *Oslyabya* had gone down and the *Suvoroff* had become a crippled, blazing hulk, there was nothing anyone could have done to prevent the long, straggling column from running the gauntlet of Japanese fire as it circled helplessly beneath the smoke of its own funeral pyre.

The end of the *Oslyabya* and the disablement of the flag-ship signalled the end of the first phase of Tsu-Shima. The second was a decline into confusion and chaos that lasted some thirty minutes; and during that time the battle lost all shape and developed into a series of isolated actions, each brief and sharp, mostly inconclusive and always confused. With the break-up of the Russian line, and the dispersing of vast clouds of smoke across an ever wider area of misty sea, it is no longer possible to record the action with any accuracy. No one will ever know precisely what happened in the Sea of Japan after four o'clock on the 27th of May; the timing and position of each disaster and triumph, of every exchange of gunfire, of every event from individual heroism and act of cowardice, to the sinking of great battleships, was lost in the uncertain grey visibility. All that is left to us are glimpses of shattered men-of-war, of sailors at the limit of their physical and mental resources enduring fearful dangers and fearful suffering, of a great fleet disordered and broken.

Captain Bukhovstoff of the *Alexander III* automatically took over first position from his C.-in-C. in the fearful game of follow-my-leader when the *Suvoroff* swung away, his own ship and the *Borodino* behind receiving the con-

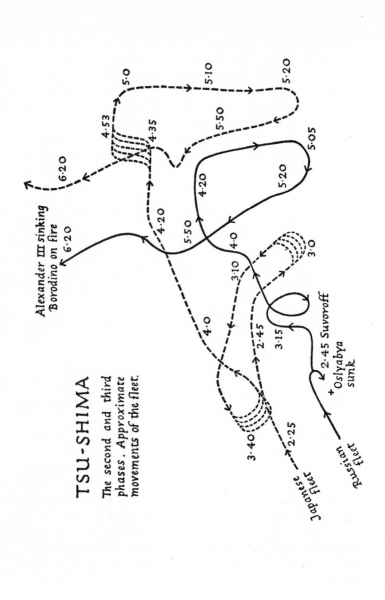

TSU-SHIMA

The second and third phases. Approximate movements of the fleet.

Alexander III sinking
Borodino on fire

+ Oslyabya sunk

2·45 Suvoroff

Japanese fleet

Russian fleet

centration of fire from the Japanese first squadron at a range of one and a half miles. Slowly he completed the full circle, with Togo doubling back on his course in another perfectly executed 180-degree turn to prevent their escape north, and was forced south again into another and wider circle. By these manœuvres, the *Alexander III* brought the fleet no nearer to its goal and no farther from the inevitable reckoning, but the gigantic double wriggle brought with it the confusion that gave the crews brief respites from the Japanese attacks.

In the midst of it all, receiving the spasmodic fire of friend and foe, the unrecognizable burning hulk of the *Suvoroff* drifted slowly east. After some forty minutes of comparative peace, the surviving bluejackets shook themselves out of their state of numb helplessness and were seized with a new spirit of determination to save their ship. Two officers, Bogdnoff, who had somehow survived the flames of the bridgework, and the indestructable von Kursel, acted as cheer-leaders to the firemen, encouraging the men with reports that two Japanese ironclads had been seen to sink. The flames of several of the fires on the main deck were checked with hoses patched with canvas and bound up with wire and by buckets of water passed in relays by men shouting, 'Stick to it! We're beating it!' — and as a stray shell passed over, 'That's only a six-inch, no more portmanteaus.'

These men were joined by the ship's captain, who had insisted on leaving the sick-bay after having his head dressed, bringing up with him a dozen or so lightly wounded men. As always, his enthusiasm was irrepressible and infectious. 'Follow me, lads,' he called to the men behind him. 'To the fire! We've only got to get it under.' But Captain Ignatzius never reached the blaze. A shell struck a hatchway above his head, and when the smoke cleared there was only a gaping hole in the steel deck where he had been running.

At 4.15 a pair of torpedo-boats chanced on the flagship when the fight against the fires was at its height. She looked a helpless sitting target and they closed confidently on to her stern, only to be met with a rapid and accurate hail of fire from the only intact gun left on the ship, a 75 mm. of the stern lower battery, and they were forced to break off to seek help.

Semenoff, on his way to his cabin to try to find some cigarettes, met von Kursel shortly after this cheering incident, and found him in the highest spirits.

'Well, how are you passing the time?' von Kursel asked.

'Badly,' Semenoff told him.

Von Kursel was the only officer to escape from the conning-tower without a scratch. 'They don't seem to be able to hit me yet, but I see you've been wounded,' he added in concern. 'Where are you off to?'

Von Kursel grinned when Semenoff told him. 'To your cabin? I've just come from there. I'll go with you.' And he led the bruised and bewildered Semenoff in and out of the labyrinth of piled wreckage and down twisted ladders until they reached the gaping hole in the battleship's side where the officers' cabins had once been. Semenoff felt unable to enjoy the joke and stumped away in a huff, followed by von Kursel, still hooting with laughter as he offered him one of his cigars. After suffering months of banter in the wardroom, the Courlandian had acquired his own peculiar brand of practical humour.

On the second of its loose, awkward circular movements the rest of the fleet again passed west of the *Suvoroff* in a straggling, smoking line, as if intent on flaunting its battle wounds before its Admiral. The *Alexander III* was listing heavily from a gash in the bows that reached to below the fore turret, and had lost both her funnels. The *Borodino*, now in the lead, was emitting flames from a dozen fires, and the *Oryol* behind her was in little better shape. On the *Suvoroff's* port beam, Togo sailed in to re-open the engagement, caught sight of the stationary battleship between the two lines, and gave orders for the guns to aim at the flagship at one thousand yards' range.

The *Suvoroff* suffered her death agony nobly. 'Her condition seemed infinitely deplorable,' Pakenham wrote in his dispatch. 'Smoke curling round the stern was rolling horizontally away on the wind. If the absence of funnels contributed much to her air of distress, the now extensive conflagration raging amidships showed its reality. Less than half the ship can have been habitable; yet she fought on. . . .'

Again and again at this point-blank range the shells struck home, tearing even wider her gaping wounds. One twelve-inch shell burst in the between-decks, close to the after six-inch gun turret. 'The explosion was accompanied by a backrush of flame that must have been projected fifty feet from her side, and then through the enormous rent thus made could be seen the glow of the newly ignited interior. . . . It was thought that the end must have come at last; but though only the tip of the stern and the ragged end of a stunted mast protruded from the enveloping cloud, the *Suvoroff* still maintained the unequal contest. . . . With unquenchable audacity, solitary but indomitable, she occasionally fired unaccepted challenge to the renewal of combat. Indistinctly outlined in the misty air, and seeming to mingle with the waves that washed over them, one or two divisions of destroyers were making their stealthy way towards her.'

The destroyers were led by Captain-Lieutenant Fudzi-motos; the privilege of giving the flagship the *coup de grâce* was to be his. But not yet. While Togo sailed past in pursuit of the main force and the fire from his guns died, the *Suvoroff's* solitary quick firer, manned by von Kursel, opened up again, and again the hounds sheered away in alarm.

Their place was taken fifteen minutes later by the Russian destroyer *Buiny*, which had bravely left the ironclads to see if she could be of assistance to her tortured flagship.

There had been doubts among some of the *Suvoroff's* crew as to how the Chief of Staff would stand up to the rigours of battle. He was remote and cold with his subordinates, and his position as spokesman, intermediary and apologist for Rozhestvensky had always been a difficult one. But aside from any personal feelings they felt towards him, it did seem possible that this tall, correct, impeccably dressed officer might crumple at the first shot. Instead de Colongue withstood the agony of the flagship's ordeal calmly, his bravery matched only by the animal-like courage of Werner von Kursel.

After settling Rozhestvensky in the turret, de Colongue darted about the ship organizing rescue, repair and fire parties, obtaining reports on the state of the engines and steering gear, and generally trying to retrieve the vessel from its state of confusion. With the death of Ignatzius and incapacitation of the Admiral, de Colongue was in nominal command of the *Suvoroff*, and it was he who ordered an officer to stand on an embrasure and semaphore with his hands to the destroyer *Buiny* to come and take off the Commander-in-Chief.

Rozhestvensky still lay sprawled on the case in the disabled six-inch gun turret, his back resting against a steel wall, his head, wrapped round and round with a blood-stained towel, nodding on his chest. His uniform was torn and covered with soot and filth, his beard half-singed off, his injured foot wrapped in a table napkin. From time to time he raised his head and asked in a low voice how the battle was going. It was difficult to tell in the dim candle light whether his eyes were open or closed when he spoke.

When Semenoff came in through the jammed, distorted door of the turret and crouched down beside the Admiral to tell him that he was being transferred to a destroyer, Rozhestvensky shook his head slowly. All he would say was that he wanted Colonel Filippovsky; he seemed weakly insistent on this point, his fuddled brain perhaps suggesting to him that the Flag Navigating Officer could somehow steer them out of these troubled waters.

'He'll be here in a minute; they've gone for him,' Semenoff told him; and Rozhestvensky shook his head in disbelief. 'Call Filippovsky,' he kept repeating in a dead voice, and at length, when the colonel arrived, shook his head again, saying, 'I don't want to go, no.'

'Come on, sir,' de Colongue implored. 'We haven't much time. There are some cruisers coming up.' Then to the half-dozen sailors standing by: 'Lift him gently, he's very bad.'

Rozhestvensky groaned slightly when they picked him up, but made no other protest as they carried him towards the steel door. 'Go carefully through here, there isn't much room,' de Colongue ordered. It was impossible to edge his big body through without wrenching his limbs, and his jacket was ripped when it caught against a jagged edge of metal. But it was easier when he lost consciousness and went limp in their arms, and they were able to hurry along a cleared path through the narrow gangway between the turrets and the side of the upper battery to the bow embrasure.

Up at the bows a little group of curious bluejackets, hanging about like idle spectators at an accident, had gathered to see off their Admiral—all with blackened hands and faces and torn uniforms, and many with small undressed wounds.

'What are you staring at?' von Kursel shouted angrily, and ordered them to grab mattresses, lengths of rope, anything that could be hung over the side to act as a fender for the closing destroyer. Von Kursel had constructed, and at once cast aside as too dangerous, a rough raft of half-burned hammocks on which he had intended to float the Admiral across to the little ship. Now he was directing the *Buiny* round from the lee side, where the flames shot out dangerously at the frail vessel, and close to the exposed side, shouting instructions to the captain through a megaphone.

It was a dreadfully hazardous operation. The seas were still running high; the sides of the *Suvoroff* were a mass of jagged ripped iron plates, smashed gun barrels and broken torpedo net booms; and the first shells were already falling from Kamimura's armoured cruisers which had become detached from Togo and were coming up from the east.

Somehow the *Buiny* was made fast without suffering serious damage, rolling up and down with the battleship like a miniature outrigger, and von Kursel ordered a group of men to climb down over the side, holding on to whatever projections they could find, and by flattening themselves against the ship's plates, to form a human chute down which Rozhestvensky could be rolled.

The operation had to be timed to a split second. Standing on the embrasure above, with his legs wide apart and the megaphone at his lips, von Kursel waited until the moment before the destroyer began to rise up towards the *Suvoroff* on the roll. 'Not yet, steady, here she comes,' he shouted above the screeching of iron hull against hull. . . . 'Now—let him go!'

At once the waiting sailors released their Admiral over the side, and his long limp body tumbled away, half-falling, half-rolling over the bluejackets' backs into the waiting arms on the *Buiny*.

The destroyer was already packed tight with two hundred survivors from the *Oslyabya* she had picked up two hours before, and there was no question of her being able to take off any of the *Suvoroff*'s crew. Only Semenoff, de Colongue, Leontieff and Filippovsky—together with a dozen or more sailors who leapt aboard in the confusion

—were on board before the ropes securing her to the flag-ship were slashed and the *Buiny* broke free.

'Aren't you coming with us?' de Colongue shouted up through cupped hands to von Kursel who still stood on the embrasure, the megaphone in one hand, waving his cap triumphantly with the other.

'No, sir,' he called back. 'I shall stay by the ship.' He was the only unwounded officer aboard: one midshipman in command of a hundred or so bluejackets and one 75 mm. gun.

The Japanese cruisers were coming up fast in the dusk, flanked by Fudzimoto's destroyers, and a shell splinter killed a man in the bows of the *Buiny* even as she pulled clear. Werner von Kursel was last seen heading towards the quick-firer with a pair of gunners at his heels, and the first shots rang out before the flagship was swallowed up in the smoke from her fires and the thickening mist.

The *Suvoroff* went down at seven that evening, blasted apart by four torpedoes that struck her simultaneously. No one escaped. A few minutes later, the *Kamchatka*, which had strayed by chance to within a mile or two of her flagship during her last minutes, exploded and followed her to the bottom.

CHAPTER ELEVEN

The Admiral Reaches Harbour

There was no single hope, nor any chance of
safety. Two thousand men waited from my lips
the decision of their fate.

Rear-Admiral Nebogatoff

PERHAPS it can be said that the Sea of Japan saw in the
twenty-four hours from the mid-day of the 27th of May,
1905, more human agony and suffering, bravery and
cowardice, more noble acts of self-sacrifice and naked self-
preservation, than any of the oceans have known since
man first took his quarrels to this element. The activities
of the Japanese fleet and its sailors provide fruit only for
the jingoist and the naval historian; if any crew member
fought other than with a fearless devotion to duty, no
one has recorded it. It is the Russians, from admirals to
bluejackets, whose conflicting emotions and divided
loyalties provide the contrasting responses, the wild extremes in human behaviour that make those hours so
memorable, and Tsu-Shima in human terms the most
dramatic naval battle ever fought. If it was a picture only
of foundering men-of-war and death with or without
heroics, it might be too harrowing to be worth recording
again after half a century. But Tsu-Shima was far from
being the annihilation it was popularly imagined to have
been, and certainly not even that blood-stained strip of
water, the Mediterranean, from Salamis to Taranto ever
witnessed scenes as extraordinary as those which took
place on the second day of battle, after a terrible night of
close-range torpedo-boat attack.

188

The *Alexander III* had gone down soon after the flag-ship, the *Borodino* just as a blood red sun touched the horizon, a last shot from one of the *Fuji's* fore twelve-inch guns before she turned away 'producing the sensation of the day. Entering the upper part near the foremost broad-side turret,' ran Pakenham's report, 'it burst, and an immense column of smoke, ruddied on its underside by the glare from the explosion and from the fire abaft, spurted to the height of her funnel tops', leaving only 'a dense cloud that brooded over the place she had occupied.'

Early in the engagement, Rear-Admiral Enkvist's nerves succumbed to the shattering noise and the bewildering sights of the sea battle. He was quite overwhelmed by it all. His fast light cruisers were supposed to be looking after the transports at the rear of the column, but at one stage when the Japanese opened desultory long-range fire, Enkvist's ships were disposed in tight, huddled formation surrounded by a screen of the vessels they were supposed to be protecting. They received more damage from one another than from Japanese shells. The *Ural* rammed the stern of the *Zhemchug*, the *Anadyr* rammed and sank the little *Rousse*. If the enemy had left them to their own devices, perhaps none would have been left afloat the next morning.

For the cruiser squadron the end was to have none of the grandeur and gallantry of some of the battleships'. To Enkvist, the mist was 'a fog', the opposing columns 'a weird confusion', and with the coming of darkness it seemed that every Japanese torpedo-boat and destroyer was bent only on the destruction of his ships. 'I several times attempted to break through the line of battleships and cruisers barring the way north'—long after the Japanese armoured vessels had left the area of battle and handed over to their torpedo craft. 'I decided therefore to make for Manila . . .' continued Enkvist's report blandly.

They were disturbed only once on their long voyage

south, when five units of the United States Navy came out
to meet them, and caused great alarm because they were at
first identified as Kamimura's armoured-cruiser squadron.
A few hours later the *Aurora*, *Zhemchung* and *Oleg* slipped
quietly into peaceful internment. 'The conduct in battle of
all ranks', reported Enkvist to Tsar Nicholas, 'was beyond
all praise', and later answered his Emperor's message of
commiseration: 'The kind words of your Imperial Majesty
have found a joyful echo in the hearts of all ranks in the
division, and will enable us to bear the heavy fate which
has overtaken us.'

One of the ships abandoned by Enkvist was the slow old
Dmitri Donskoy, which had misbehaved herself in the past
so often that she had become the fleet's black sheep. She
covered herself in glory by beating off and seriously
damaging four Japanese light cruisers, sinking two torpedo-boats and damaging a third when they took over the
attack, and finally succeeded in dragging her shattered
hull, with not an unwounded man aboard, into the shelter
of an island cove where she sank in a hundred fathoms.

Of the ironclads that were damaged in the fierce night
torpedo attacks, the *Monomakh* and *Sisoy Veliky* surrendered
at dawn without firing a shot, while the *Oushakoff* was
fought to a blazing wreck. Captains who had been regarded
as weak and ineffectual by their men went down firing
their ship's last workable gun, crews with good records,
who had given the C.-in-C. little trouble on the voyage,
crumpled at the first broadside 'and concealed themselves
to avoid duty on the upper deck'. One of the Japanese commanders discovered to his astonishment only twenty dead
and some forty wounded on a battleship with a complement of nine hundred, the decks of which were a shambles
of twisted ironwork.

Nebogatoff found himself at first light leading the
Oryol, two of his old coast-defence ships and the *Izumrud*
in a grey, choppy sea. It had been a wild and harrowing

night, during which more than fifty Japanese torpedo-boats had swarmed in again and again, pressing home their attacks to a point-blank range, so close that some of the ironclads' guns could not be depressed sufficiently to bear on them.[1] For five hours, with hardly a break, the muzzle blasts of the defending guns had flashed in the darkness to the incessant cries of warning from the lookouts and orders from the gunnery officers. One after another the battleships of the second division were struck and limped out of line; only Nebogatoff's own ships, and the *Oryol* which had no searchlights left to operate, were saved by the accuracy and speed of their fire and because they had been trained to fight at night without searchlights.

It was a cold, dour morning. The men were dead tired, the maximum speed of the ships was seven knots, and the shelter of Vladivostock harbour was still more than three hundred miles away. At 5 a.m. the horizon to port became smudged with distant smoke, revealed momentarily the fighting tops and funnels of five cruisers, and cleared again. When they reappeared an hour later their number had increased to seven, and seven more larger shapes dotted the skyline astern. Others came up to starboard, more and more of them, until by nine o'clock the Russians were entirely surrounded: Togo's first battleship squadron, Kamimura's armoured-cruisers, two or three dozen destroyers and torpedo-boats—the whole Japanese Navy, intact and showing no signs of battle damage, had assembled in impeccable formation for the final killing.

From the bridge of the *Nicholas I* Admiral Nebogatoff, 'in tightly fitting white tunic, which showed off his

---

[1] 'We ought to be able to close in to within twenty yards of the target before she is sunk,' wrote a Japanese torpedo-boat lieutenant to a friend. 'If we are hit, we shall go down with the Russians; if we are hit, the Russians shall come down with us, for the last man alive will steer the spare torpedo into the water. What is life but a dream of summer's night?'

obesity, and wearing very loose black trousers', surveyed the huge ring of steel that encompassed him. Already the call to action stations had been given, the weary gunners were standing by their weapons, and the targets (there were eight or nine for each Russian ship to chose from) had been selected.

'What is the enemy's range?' Nebogatoff asked the Flag Gunnery Officer standing beside him. Already the first Japanese shells were falling, sending up tall fountains in the sea alongside.

'Twelve thousand yards, sir.' There was not a Russian gun left that could shoot above eleven thousand yards. It was clear that the Japanese, with a long day before them, could continue to fire on them at leisure and in complete security. Turning to the duty messenger, Nebogatoff told him to fetch the ship's captain, who lay wounded below, and the rest of the Staff. By the time they all arrived and were assembled about their Admiral in the conning-tower, a dozen hits had already been registered, and a shell in the *Nicholas I's* bows had sent her anchor symbolically clattering into the sea.

To each of his officers in turn Nebogatoff put the question 'What are we to do?'

A twelve-inch shell exploded with tremendous force in the water amidships; the old battleship shivered from stem to stern as another crashed on the deck aft.

It was hard for the first officers to answer. What could they say? The Flag Gunnery Officer confirmed that there was still no Japanese ship within range of their guns, and the enemy showed no signs of closing. Captain Smirnoff, who had lain all night in the sick-bay with a head wound, was the last to give an opinion.

'Yesterday we did our duty, sir,' he told Nebogatoff. 'Today we are no longer in a condition to fight. There is nothing for it but surrender.'

It was the first time the word had been spoken, and it

was succeeded by the crash of more detonations close alongside the *Nicholas I*.

There was a moment's silence before Nebogatoff looked up at the faces about him. 'Gentlemen,' he said in an almost inaudible voice, 'I propose to surrender, as the only means of saving our crews from destruction. Please give orders to run up the white flag.' The officers dispersed, Smirnoff returning to the sick-bay complaining of an aching head.

It took some time to find a large enough table-cloth, and even when this was raised the Japanese gunners scored more hits and killed a number of men before the fire ceased.

Nebogatoff looked like a bent old bearded dwarf when he came to the bridge rail and stood looking down at the assembled ship's company below. In another ten minutes the Japanese men-of-war would be alongside, would be sending over armed boarding parties to take over the *Nicholas I* and the other ironclads, and they would all be prisoners. Already the Japanese flag flew at the masthead below the fluttering white tablecloth.

'Comrades,' the Admiral told his men, 'this is a sad day for Russia, for the Imperial Navy, and for all of us who have survived this terrible battle. But I have decided to capitulate to the enemy because otherwise we should have been annihilated to no purpose. I do so with a heavy heart but in the knowledge that no more human suffering can alter our fate or the fate of our fatherland. I am getting on in years, and my life is of trifling importance,' he ended. 'Let the shame of this action rest on me alone. I am ready to be tried by court martial and prepared for the extreme sentence. I accept the entire responsibility for this surrender. . . .'

Only the *Izumrud* refused to capitulate. Little damaged and still capable of her twenty-four knots, she darted through the closing ring of Japanese warships and the concentrated barrage of fire poured out at her, outstripped her pursuers and disappeared to the north.

The Japanese had seen the white cloth and then their own Rising Sun hoisted on the Russian flagship clearly enough, for visibility was perfect that morning, but they had at first taken it as a ruse. They could not understand why four enemy ships, three of which appeared to be in fighting trim, should give up without firing a shot. For them the act of surrender did not exist; there was no word for it in their service. 'It was utterly beyond our expectations,' Togo wrote later. 'We had opened fire with the strongest determination to annihilate them at once, but all in vain. It really was the strangest occurrence, and we were astonished and somewhat disappointed.'

They closed in slowly and cautiously, still expecting a trap, every gun loaded and trained on the stationary vessels. At closer range the Japanese could see with their naked eyes the shell holes and blast scars on the low, tall-funnelled, faintly comical coast-defence ironclads, the more serious damage on the big *Oryol*, and Russian crews in their dirty uniforms lined up on deck in ragged rows, like herds of tired grey sheep calmly awaiting their fate.

Rozhestvensky spent a feverish, restless night on the destroyer *Buiny*, lying in a hammock slung in the commander's cabin. Surgeon Peter Kudinoff had examined and dressed his wounds immediately he had been brought below, diagnosing a fractured skull and injury to his brain where a sliver of bone had entered it. 'The slightest shock or jolt may prove fatal,' he pronounced. 'He must be disturbed in no way,' a difficult instruction to comply with in this jam-packed little cockleshell with a great naval battle raging all round.

The Admiral's Staff could not have been more solicitous; either de Colongue or Semenoff, Leontieff or Filippovsky hovered by his side all through the night, tendering glasses of water from time to time, asking anxiously if they could do anything to make him more comfortable. At one moment of consciousness, Semenoff asked him gently, 'Are you strong enough to remain in command, sir?' Not unreasonably, Rozhestvensky murmured, 'No, where am I? You can see—command—Nebogatoff,' then in a clear voice, as if his injured brain had momentarily cleared, 'Keep on for Vladivostock—course north twenty-three east.'

Somehow the *Buiny's* captain managed to drive his way northward in the darkness through the swarming Japanese torpedo-boats without a collision and without once being attacked, and by extraordinarily good fortune at dawn, just as his engines were faltering and his fuel running low, he chanced on three of the few Russian ships left afloat. They were the cruiser *Donskoy* and the destroyers *Groznyi* and *Bedovyi*, making their way north at full speed.

The captain went below to his cabin, and finding Rozhestvensky much improved in strength and spirit, asked him to which of the vessels he wished his flag to be transferred. The Admiral chose the *Bedovyi*, which was undamaged and had sufficient coal to carry her to Vladivostock. Carefully Rozhestvensky was carried up the narrow iron ladders to the *Buinyi's* deck on a stretcher and lowered over the side into a boat from the *Donskoy*, while a pinnace from the cruiser shuttled to and fro to relieve the destroyer of her two hundred survivors from the *Oslyabya*.

Sitting upright on his stretcher on the rolling deck of the *Bedovyi*, with his Staff and the ship's officers gathered beside him, Rozhestvensky surveyed the pathetic fragments of his armada—an ancient cruiser, already damaged and burdened with a surplus complement, and three swift little destroyers, one of which was *hors de combat*. He did not know that just beyond the south-west horizon four of his ironclads were hauling down their colours, without firing a shot, under the orders of his second-in-command.

There was no doubt in his mind that these vessels were all that were left to him.

'What are your orders, sir?' How many times had Clapier de Colongue tendered that question to his C.-in-C. over the past eight months?

Rozhestvensky turned his head painfully, and in the curt, sharp tone he had always answered him gave orders for the detachment to proceed north at best economical cruising speed. 'The *Donskoy* is to escort the *Buinyi*, the *Groznyi* and *Bedovyi* to steam together. Course north twenty-three east—for Vladivostock.'

It was the Admiral's last command. Before he could be carried below to have his wounds dressed again, he once more declined into a coma.

The Battle of Tsu-Shima was formally concluded two hours later. The last moments of the final scene before the curtain came down were described in the combat report of the commander of the *Groznyi*, who remained close to the minute flagship until the last possible moment. 'At a little after three o'clock, near the island of Dazhelet,' he wrote to Grand Admiral Alexis, 'we saw two vessels coming from the Straits of Korea, evidently torpedo vessels, which rapidly overtook us. At close distance the vessels were seen to be Japanese, one a two-funnelled destroyer, and the other a four-funnelled one. Approaching the *Bedovyi*, I asked by semaphore what we should do, and received for reply, "How much speed can you make?" I replied, "Twenty-two knots." In reply to the order "Go to Vladivostock", I asked "Why go away and not join battle?" To that I received no reply; but seeing that the *Bedovyi* did not increase speed, and not desiring to leave her by herself, I decreased speed, and kept near her until I saw her display the flags for parley and hoist the Red Cross. Then I gave orders for full speed ahead. . . .'

The *Bedovyi* was as fast a vessel as the *Groznyi*; she too could have outstripped her pursuers and, by burning every inch of her wooden fittings as the *Groznyi* did, could have avoided the humiliation of surrender. It was Clapier de Colongue's loyal devotion to his C.-in-C., for which he was to pay so dearly, that decided otherwise. What had Rozhestvensky left to lose? His fleet had been utterly defeated; he had left his flagship (against his will, perhaps, but who would distinguish that nicety?) and his men to drown in her. His honour and his career were destroyed; only his life was left, and this de Colongue was determined to preserve. The vibration of the little destroyer at full speed would be certain to kill him, if the enemy did not succeed in doing so, but at Masampo and Sasebo the Japanese would have skilled surgeons who might still save the Admiral's life.

Clapier de Colongue had as much difficulty as Nebogatoff in persuading the enemy that the fight was over. At extreme range the leading destroyer opened fire as she tore excitedly through the water, throwing up a great bow wave before her, and continued lobbing shells at the *Bedovyi*, while her companion turned aside in pursuit of the fleeing *Groznyi*, which was returning an accurate fire and was clearly not surrendering. The St. Andrew's flag at the stern had to be hauled down, and the sirens set to send out a continuous high-pitched wail of distress before the Japanese gunners at last ceased fire.

From the one narrow slip of a vessel to the other a boat manned by Japanese bluejackets was rowed at top speed, the destroyer's commander, Lieutenant Ayiba, standing erect at the stern. He had his sword unsheathed when he leapt on board the *Bedovyi*, and for one moment the crew lined up on deck feared the worst. But the lieutenant was concerned only with the wireless aerial; with quick slashes he tore it down, and then turned to de Colongue. 'Are you the captain?' he asked in English. 'I am now in command of the ship.'

Semenoff, the only one among the Staff with a knowledge of Japanese, explained that among his prisoners there was an admiral, the Commander-in-Chief of the Russian force, but in spite of his excellent knowledge of the language it was a moment before the lieutenant could be made to understand. Vice-Admiral Rozhestvensky his prisoner? In this insignificant little vessel? Lieutenant Ayiba's oriental calm was utterly shattered. 'Where is your Admiral?' he demanded.

'In the commander's cabin aft,' Semenoff told him. 'But the surgeon says he must on no account be disturbed.'

'I won't disturb him, gentlemen,' the lieutenant assured the anxious Staff officers, 'but at least I must have a look at him.' Having satisfied himself, Lieutenant Ayiba left a guard on the door and returned to his own ship with de Colongue and the rest of the Staff. The whole operation was carried out with speed, efficiency and the utmost correctness.

On the morning of May 30th the *Bedovyi*, with Rozhestvensky still aboard, was towed into Sasebo harbour. Nebogatoff's ironclads were already there, tied up against the harbour wall, each with the Japanese flag flying at the masthead, dockyard workers already clearing the rubble from their decks. But Rozhestvensky did not see them; he was still lying unconscious below decks.

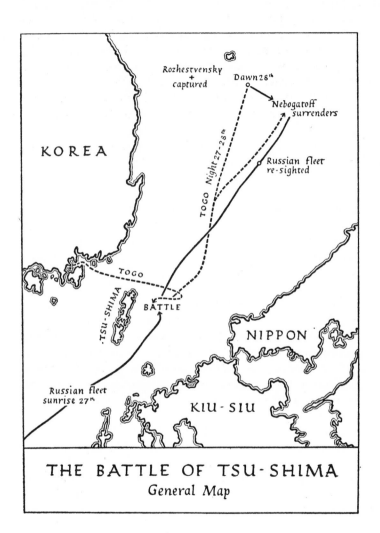

KOREA

Rozhestvensky
+
captured

Dawn 28ᵗʰ

Nebogatoff
surrenders

TOGO Night 27-28ᵗʰ

Russian fleet
re-sighted

TOGO

TSU-SHIMA

BATTLE

NIPPON

Russian fleet
sunrise 27ᵗʰ

KIU-SIU

THE BATTLE OF TSU-SHIMA
General Map

CHAPTER TWELVE

The Admiral Returns Home

A LARGE, expectant and only faintly uneasy crowd collected on the quayside at Vladivostock on the morning of May the 30th, drawn there to meet and welcome the Russian fleet after its long journey and the battle it was believed to have fought somewhere south in the Sea of Japan. How much longer would it be delayed? Had it succeeded in striking a victorious blow against Togo since it passed through the Straits of Tsu-Shima? The newspapers had confidently prophesied victory; surely even Togo could not break that vast armada of Rozhestvensky's.

Rumours circulating about the town told of the Japanese fleet's destruction, the death of Togo; and certainly there had been a great battle, for fishermen returning to harbour had brought back tales of flashes on the southern horizon and the continuous thunder of distant guns. The naval hospital was ready to receive casualties, and surgeons and first-aid men were standing by. Whatever the outcome, there would be damaged men-of-war in harbour that night, with wounded men aboard.

Anxiety increased as the day wore on, with the only news from a Russian cruiser radioing for coal many miles short of her destination. A collier went out to refuel her, and before dusk the two vessels returned together. The *Almaz* could tell little of the battle, her captain reported, because her task had been to escort the transports, but before she had been driven off by an overwhelming force of Japanese cruisers, she had seen one of the Russian ironclads go down, and three others were blazing and battered.

Later the little destroyers *Bravyi* and *Groznyi* followed her in, and the news they brought—of shattered ironclads, of seas spotted with drowning sailors, of a desperately wounded C.-in-C. driven off his flagship—confirmed beyond doubt that the Russians must have met with utter disaster. No more survivors of a battle fleet of some forty men-of-war arrived. These were all: a second-class cruiser—a mere converted yacht—and two little destroyers of 350 tons each.

For several days after he was carried ashore at Sasebo, Rozhestvensky lay half-conscious and in pain in a private ward in the naval hospital. As soon as he was off the danger list, surgeons operated on him, removing the sliver of bone from his broken skull, and by the end of the first week in June it was clear that his sturdy constitution had won and that he would soon be convalescent.

For a vanquished Commander-in-Chief who had, in the eyes of the world, fled his ship and cast away his country's last chance of avoiding defeat, he was treated with uncommon generosity. On June 8th, the Tsar telegraphed his condolences: 'I heartily thank you and all the members of your squadron who have loyally fulfilled your duty in battle for your service to Russia and myself. It was God's will not to give you success, but the country is proud of your courage. I wish you a speedy recovery. May God console all of us.'

A few days later Admiral Togo called on him to apologize for the somewhat spartan conditions in the hospital and 'the absence of comforts due to such a distinguished patient'. Sitting at Rozhestvensky's bedside, the dignified little man—now more than ever the object of adulation in his country—attempted also to console him. 'There is no need for a warrior to associate an honourable defeat with shame,' he told him. 'We fighting men suffer either way, win or lose. The only question is whether or not we do our duty. During the battle your men fought most gallantly and I admire them all and you in particular. You performed your great task heroically until you were incapacitated. I pay you my highest respects.'

In spite of the sympathy, in spite of the cheering visits from Clapier de Colongue and Semenoff, the memory of those terrible hours, of the five thousand men who had died so uselessly, hung like a bitter black cloud in that airless ward. Certainly Nicholas Klado's dramatic account of the battle, related in *Novoe Vremya*, which he read in bed, contained no comfort for him. Written in the neat yet dignified and authoritative journalese of which Klado was a master, it was compiled from wildly inaccurate agency reports, originating mainly from American sources. Klado added his own touches, castigating mercilessly his old enemy, accusing him of entering the arena prepared for defeat rather than victory, of instilling a defeatist spirit among his commanders, and of ignoring the important reinforcements provided for him which could well have given him victory.

Rozhestvensky wisely refrained from replying to these attacks, and the tone of the statements he gave to foreign newspaper correspondents was straightforward and factual. 'During the first half-hour our men fought well,' he told a French reporter. 'In this half-hour the Japanese suffered the whole of the injuries they received. Our men, however, suddenly became demoralized by the terrifying effects of the Japanese fire, and all was then over. . . . The greatest enemy of the battleships was the rain of fire (*nappe de feu*) caused by the incessant explosions of shells. Everything began to burn and even in the conning-tower I was literally enveloped in flames. In all parts of the ship, and especially in the turrets, the heat in consequence was stifling.' There was no attempt at self-justification, there were no excuses.

On the 28th of August Rozhestvensky left hospital and was carried in a rickshaw to the quayside in Sasebo harbour, where he embarked on a Japanese steamer for Osaka. A month later he sailed for home on the Russian merchantman *Veroneye*, 'looking vigorous', an observer reported, 'though he has grown thin from hardships and worries. But the doctor says that is a trifle; his nerves are of iron, and they will sustain him so that he will outlive us all.'

The long journey back to St. Petersburg was cold and comfortless. The country was afire with the spirit of revolt now that the war was over. Even on the voyage to Vladivostock, returning prisoners rioting on the *Veroneye* broke into Rozhestvensky's cabin demanding vodka and threatening 'the man who spilt our blood'. Vladivostock itself was in a state of uproar, and along the route of the trans-Siberian railway many of the towns were paralysed by strikes and local upheavals. If Rozhestvensky had been a victorious returning commander, there would have been little interest in his progress among a people now engrossed in their own struggle against hardship and injustice.

Only at the little town of Tulun was he given any sort of a reception. There a crowd of soldiers and workmen turned out in the bitter cold to welcome him from the station platform. Rozhestvensky hobbled out from his compartment, supported by a stick and with his head still bandaged. A thin cheer met him, the first since he had welcomed Nebogatoff on board the *Suvoroff*.

'Did Nebogatoff's division keep out of the fight?' he was asked. 'Did he duck away astern out of danger?' 'Was it treachery that defeated you?'

'No, there was no treason,' Rozhestvensky told them. 'We just weren't strong enough—and God gave us no luck.'

They waved and cheered again as the train drew out,

calling, 'God grant you good health!' It was a crumb of comfort that someone still cared.

It required only a single call at the Admiralty to make clear to him his future role. It was as he expected. He was to be the scapegoat, a scapegoat to be treated gently, bearing in mind his rank—and the wide knowledge he possessed of the working of the Higher Naval Board. There were enough explosions taking place in St. Petersburg without letting off fireworks in the nation's defence councils. Rozhestvensky was quietly retired on a generous pension, and it was hoped that no more would be heard from him after the two private courts of inquiry—into the surrender of the *Bedovyi* with himself on board, and Nebogatoff's capitulation—had been heard. But at the courts martial of his second-in-command, the captains of the captured ironclads, and his own Staff, that resulted from these investigations, Rozhestvensky insisted on appearing, first as a witness, and then as one of the accused.

In a brief but highly dramatic hearing, Rozhestvensky stood loyally by his subordinates, accepting full responsibility for everything that had occurred at Tsu-Shima. 'I was in full possession of my senses,' he claimed when the prosecuting counsel attempted to pass the blame on to his Staff. 'The witnesses who have declared that I was delirious are mistaken.'

But in spite of all his efforts, it was he who was acquitted, while Nebogatoff and Clapier de Colongue, who behaved throughout with dignity, were sentenced to be shot. Leontieff, Filippovsky and the *Bedovyi's* captain were also ordered to be executed, and though the Tsar interceded to prevent these sentences from being carried out, all served long terms in prison.

Zinovi Petrovitch Rozhestvensky survived for a further four years in retirement, acknowledged by the service to which he had given his life on only one whimsical occasion. On July 19th, 1908, a telegram from the Admiralty arrived at the hotel at which he was staying, giving details of the requiem services to be held in his memory at St. Petersburg. The premature news of his death, announced in every leading European newspaper, the flood of messages of commiseration for his wife and the obituaries which he read with relish, provided him with a much-needed fillip, for he had been in poor health for some time. 'I am still alive,' he reassured callers. 'You mustn't kill me off before my time.'

His time came six months later, on January 14th, 1909.

EPILOGUE

Even before the needless tragedy of Tsushima, moves to end the war were well under way. Japan was virtually bankrupt. As two Russian army corps headed east, she could barely scrape together one and a half new divisions. Peace was a necessity. It was under American auspices – an America newly suspicious of Japanese expansionism – that the peace conference was to be held. The Russian delegation was led by the wiley Count Witte, who, in a very real sense, salvaged much of the Russian position from the ensuing negotiations. The *New York Times* wrote: 'A nation hopelessly beaten in every battle of the war, one army captured and the other overwhelmingly routed, with a navy swept from the seas, dictated her own terms to the victory.'

Japan erupted in fury, not least against the United States she felt had betrayed her. It was a defining moment in the emergence of both countries on the world stage. More and more Japan became seen as the leader of Asia and more and more the European powers began to fear what seemed like her unbridled expansionism. As Japanese strength grew, so it seemed that once again she could obtain the great victory she needed by a massive surprise attack in a war that would be won by a great battlefleet. Her next conflict was to be fought with the shades of the Russo-Japanese war hanging heavy over her and with the crucial lesson forgotten – that, for all her victories, for all the élan of her ships and men, the superior resources of Russia would inevitably have crushed her given time. Japan failed to see that her victory was in many ways an astonishing and never-to-be-repeated achievement, a mirage that would blind her to the cold realities of power and resources.

Hugh Andrew
July 2000

THE SURRENDER AT TSUSHIMA

by Rear-Admiral Nebogatoff
Second in Command of the Baltic Fleet
at the Battle of Tsushima

from *Jane's Fighting Ships 1904–7*

In the present article it is far from my thoughts to give a full account of the naval battle of Tsushima. I take from this catastrophe only several parts to defend myself from the heavy accusations brought against me by many critics.

After the Tsushima battle, I was condemned to the most disgraceful punishment. In ordinary life, the guilty person has the offence of which he is accused made known to him, he is listened to and tried. With me they have acted differently. I was deprived of all judicial guarantees. The judges, unknown to me, did not think it necessary to ask for an explanation from me.

In the present article, I wish to prove that my conduct as commander of the third squadron during the battle gives no occasion for any accusations. Everything that was laid upon me to do, I performed accurately. The catastrophe at Tsushima and the surrender of the ships happened through no fault of mine.

The battle began at half-past one in the day. I began the battle the ninth from the leading ship in the rear column, and in an hour I was already the fifth, as the second division drew out of the line, the battleship *Oslabia* having gone out of the ranks, and my division following me, took up the space between the first and second divisions and about five o'clock in the afternoon I was third in the column, as *Kniaz Suvarof* and *Imperator Alexander III* left the line. During the battle we saw how the ships – coming in the first and second divisions – began to burn one after the other. It was doubtless the wood that was burning, which had not been taken away from the upper deck, also the coal and smokeless gunpowder, which burned like fire. I saw myself how the battleship *Borodino* first heeled, then straightened herself and slowly bent to the right side, and in a minute-and-a-half sank into the water with the bottom upwards, on which crawled seven or eight men. I saw all these horrors, that have scarcely any prototype in history.

The battleship *Suvaroff,* having both her funnels knocked down and being in flames all over, left the ranks. The enemy's protected cruisers rushed upon her, I immediately took my course towards her, and fired on the enemy's cruisers, My manoeuvre, undertaken to defend the battleship *Suvaroff,* gave her the possibility to recover to a certain degree. During my attacks on the enemy's cruisers I succeeded, as has been confirmed by Admiral Togo, in damaging several of them, and the flagship of Rear-Admiral Dewa, the cruiser *Kasagi,* received such a serious hole that it was forced to go to the bay of Aburaya, and did not take part in the further actions. About five o'clock in the afternoon, a shell of about six- or eight-inch calibre, got into the turret of the 12-inch guns of my battleship *Nicolai,* the splinters killing Lieutenant Baron Mirbach, who was standing at the time in the turret. Part of the splinters flew into the conning tower, through the observation slit and wounded the right temple of post captain Smirnoff, who was led away immediately to have his wound dressed, after which I took upon myself the commanding of the ship. During the time of this battle from half-past one till six o'clock in the evening, I received no directions or orders from the commander of the squadron.

At five o'clock in the evening, finding that further manoeuvring in this place was dangerous owing to the setting of the sun, after which the enemy could undoubtedly begin torpedo attacks and throwing floating mines in our way with his numerous torpedo boats, I took the course N 23, E, pointed out to me before the battle, the way leading to Vladivostok. About this time on the transport *Anadir*, a signal was made 'Does Admiral Nebogatoff know . . .' No continuation of this signal appeared. At six o'clock in the evening the torpedo boat *Blestiashi* passed the right side of the battleship *Nicolai*, delivering with voice and semaphore, the following words 'Admiral Rojestvensky has ordered you to go to Vladivostok'. After which I made the signal 'Follow me,' and continued to go to Vladivostok. The battleships *Apraksin, Seniavin, Oushakoff, Orel*, cruiser *Izumrud*, and some other ships followed me. All this was about seven o'clock in the evening. The sun began to set and with it ended the day battle. At this time - the battleship *Borodino*, the stern of which was burning quickly, bent on the right side, and in a minute-and-a-half turned over.

The night battle consisted of ceaseless attacks by torpedo boats, the number of which reached to fifty. The ships of my division successfully avoided these attacks. I explain it in this manner that the captains of my ships were trained by me long before the battle, how to defend themselves from night torpedo attacks, by being used to manoeuvring in the dark without light. The illustration of the success of these tactics is shown by the case of the battleship *Nicolai I*, which was attacked by the, enemy's torpedo boats from a distance of one cable's length. A torpedo boat fired a torpedo at my battleship, but thanks to our being in complete darkness, and turning the helm in time, according to my personal order, the torpedo passed under the stern without touching the ship. During this attack, the torpedo boats fired their guns, and with one of their shots wounded two of my men. I think if the battleships *Navarin, Sisoi, Veliki* and *Nakhimoff*, had kept to my tactics, they would have avoided being hit. It is to be greatly regretted that, in this night battle, these ships made such dreadful lights with their projectors, and so betrayed their exact positions to the enemy. To repulse the attack of the torpedo boats was particularly difficult, owing to the artillery on the *Orel* being utterly unable to act, and the guns of *Nicolai I, Sisai Veliki, Navarin* and *Yakhimoff,* being of old pattern, firing only one shot a minute, instead of 4 to 6 shots as the new guns do. To complete all; the division of cruisers, commanded by Admiral Enkqist, left us and went to Alanila, and the cruiser *Almaz* went to Vladivostok. In one word all the cruiser division with the exception of the cruiser *Izumrud,* dispersed. Our torpedo boats did not help me either.

At dawn, the position of my ships was as follows: in front was the battleship *Nicolai I,* having on the left beam the cruiser *Izumrud,* then followed in the wake the battleships *Orel, Apraksin* and *Seniavin.* No other ships of ours were seen. Between five and six o'clock in the morning, I saw on the left beam five funnels smoking, and was soon convinced that it was the division of the enemy's cruisers of the *Matsushima* type, to which two other cruisers soon joined. I immediately made the signal, 'Prepare for battle,' and ordered all to turn eight points to port, having the intention of attacking the enemy from the front. But as soon as my manoeuvre was noticed by the enemy, the cruisers turned their sterns to us and began quickly to go away.

Seeing that the enemy avoided a battle, and having no possibility of overtaking them, as the speed of my ships was less than the enemy's, I again took the course to Vladivostok.

Between seven and eight in the morning, behind the port beam we saw seven large funnels smoking. I immediately sent the cruiser *Izumrud* to meet them. When the cruiser returned, she reported that it was the division of the enemy's cruisers before us, and at the same time by means of signal asked my permission to go to Vladivostok separately, which she could reach easily, thanks to her speed. I answered by a refusal, as I had not yet lost hope of repulsing the enemy's cruisers, thinking the difference in force, not yet hopeless for us.

Towards ten o'clock, appeared on the horizon, six large Japanese ships and two cruisers, *Nisshin* and *Kasuga* in the direction of the port beam. After some time, more enemy's ships and torpedo boats were seen coming from the east, so that between nine and ten o'clock in the morning, we were surrounded by all the Japanese fleet, in number 27 war ships, not counting torpedo boats. All these ships, as far as we could see, seemed to be, according to their external look, in full order. Coming up to us at a distance of 56 cable lengths, the enemy's ships opened fire and firing rapidly, began to reach *Nicolai*. Several of the shells damaged the side in the water-line forward, the water rushed through the hole in the forward dynamo room. The electric light went out. It was impossible to get at the magazine of this division. To my order to open fire, the gunnery officer reported to me, that firing would be quite useless as the distance between us and the enemy was 56 cable lengths, and our guns could only reach 50. We were perishing without any doubt. There was no hope, no chance of being saved. Two thousand men were waiting to hear their fate from me.

Holding the position of commander of the squadron and guarding the dignity of the Russian flag, I could not yield to the first impression, but had to consider the condition of our ships maturely and honestly, without any thought as to in own career, and after reflecting about our condition amidst the shots of the enemy, I came to the following conclusion:

1. The 12-inch guns of the battleship *Nicolai I* were damaged the day before by the fragments of the enemy's shells. The 12-inch explosive projectiles were all used up in the battle. The remaining ammunition could not do the enemy any serious damage.

2. I have in my command four battleships and one cruiser *Izumrud*. I am surrounded by 27 big ships and a great number of torpedo boats.

3. The range of our guns is 50 cable lengths. The enemy stands at a distance not nearer than 55 cable lengths. When we try to approach him nearer, his ships, having more speed, go further away from us, not lessening the distance. In this manner we represent a target which is very easy to shoot through, and which is not able to respond to the enemy.

4. The crew of the battleship which had behaved with energy, that was above praise in the day and night battles of the day before, understood its position.

5. The enemy was firing continually, killing the men and destroying the helpless ships. A few minutes more we would perish.

Under these conditions I was fully persuaded that a battle was impossible and that further delay under the enemy's fire would bring the officers and the crew to aimless destruction. In view of all that has been stated, the moment had come when the commander of the squadron must use all his exertions to save the officers, the crew and the ships.

Were there any means in my power to save the ships and the crew?

a. We found ourselves in the open sea, having no shore near us or any ships belonging to a friendly nation.

b. Most of the rowing boats were broken, and to launch those that were undamaged was impossible under the fire of the enemy.

Beyond the rowing boats there was a total absence of life-saving means, as the hammocks had been used for arranging tile protection and defence of the most vulnerable parts of the ship.

c. The total absence of time for taking any kind of measures, as the enemy's guns were devastating us.

d. The loss of physical strength from the battle that had lasted a day and a night.

There was no doubt that, in sinking or blowing up the ship, all the officers and sailors would perish. Had I the right to do so according to the law or to my conscience?

The 354th article of the Navy Regulation says:

> During the battle the commander shows the example of courage and continues the battle as long as possible. To avoid useless bloodshedding, he is allowed − but not without general agreement of all the officers − to surrender the ship, if all the cartridges and the ammunition are used up, the artillery destroyed, and all means of defence exhausted, and if there is no possibility of destroying the ship and the crew cannot find a way of saving themselves on the shore or in the boats.

Being persuaded of the impossibility of fighting and also of destroying the ship and at the same time saving the lives of the crew, I, before expressing my own opinion, proposed to Post Captain Smirnoff, and to the other officers that they should express their opinions. Captain Smirnoff, whose bravery and devotion to his duty no one can doubt, declared at once that he personally did not see any means of harming the enemy and saving the ship and the people in it. The rest of the commanders and officer came to the same conclusion. It is known already, that there was not one capable of forgetting the honour of a sailor. In this unanimity there was nothing wonderful, the picture was too clear to allow of any different interpretation. We were in the ocean, under the fire of a numerous squadron, threatened with death in the sea, without hope of any success. All felt and understood the same, and all saw with horror that the time had come, which is pointed out in the 354th article of the Navy Regulation. I well understood, that the claims of the law do not always coincide with all the arguments of morals, and that is why I am ready to defend myself in this affair, in compliance with every moral order. I only beg to have in view, that in deciding the question of surrendering the ships I did not participate for one second in the selfish feeling of saving my own life. In the day and night battles of 17 May, I risked my life sufficiently to be absolved of any reproach of cowardice. If I had been afraid of losing my life, I could have found sufficient excuses for not meeting Admiral Rojestvensky, and with this could have finished my expedition. If I had cared so much for my life, I could have accorded my actions with the exact sense of the 109th article of the Navy Regulation. This article says:

> If the Admiral's ship is very badly damaged, and is not in condition to continue the battle, or is in danger of being in the power of the enemy, the Admiral may go on to another ship according to his own judgment.

In this manner nothing hindered me; on the contrary, according to law I could have removed on to the fast cruiser *Izumrud*, and therefore had the full possibility to escape to Vladivostok. If I had had the care of my life in view, I could have made for the shore, or I could have gone to Manila, as others did. All these means were at my disposal, but I did not think of them, I went forward in the midst of the enemy's ships, with the one idea: to get to Vladivostok, as I had been ordered.

In judging my actions, it is necessary to examine the events of the past time. In contemplating the military naval actions, we always see that our foe was superior to us. I affirm that on 27 and 28 May, in the waters of the Pacific Ocean, it was not two equal enemies who fought, it was not a naval battle, but a definite destruction at sea, without any hope of success.

The first cause of the defeat at the island of Tsushima, was the deficiency of our ships and their bad manning. The second cause which brought us to defeat were the actions of the commander of the fleet, Admiral Rojestvensky. I will note down a few of his actions.

1. Before my joining with the Admiral Rojestvensky, I was struck with the indifference shown by him, with regard to my squadron. The Admiral was bound before leaving Noey Bey or Madagascar, to send to Djiboutly, an officer, with instructions and directions for finding me on the sea. As it is known, Admiral Rojestvensky gave no directions of this kind. I had to seek the Admiral Rojestvensky without any help from him.

2. According to the general order of things, the commander of the fleet arranges several conferences with the Admiral and Captains of ships, at which he explains the substance of the undertaking and general plan. If such conferences had taken place, those under his command would have been imbued with the plans of the Admiral and during the battle would have been active assistants. And here? I, the junior flag officer directly after Admiral Rojestvensky, the substitute of the commander of the fleet, during the whole time of our cruise, saw the Admiral only once, and was not admitted to a conference of coming events, or even to any conversation with regard to them. I received directions every day, where to go or what course to take, and these were the only things made known to me. Wishing to understand Admiral Rojestvensky's plans, I studied his orders, and they consisted chiefly of loading coal, court martial sentences, reprimands and remarks with regard to incorrect manoeuvring of the ships during evolutions and nothing else. Wishing to make these plans clear, I asked my officers to speak with the officers of the Admiral, but still could not find out anything. In this mariner, I knew only one thing, that during the battle we were to follow the leading ship, replacing those which went out of the ranks, and in case the battleship *Suvaroff* went out, to follow the battleship *Alexander III*; and at the beginning of the battle, I did not even know that

Admiral Folkergam had died on 25 May, and that I was direct substitute of Admiral Rojestvensky. Such secrecy and uncommunicativeness of a commander of a fleet has no example in the history of the fleet.

It is possible that the Admiral did not understand that, owing to accidents in the battle, he could be one of the first victims, and that it would be my duty to continue his plans.

3. One of the chief faults which brought about the destruction of the squadron is, without any doubt, the choosing of the strait of Tsushima to get through to Vladivostok. At the disposition of the Admiral there were three ways, through three straits: Tsushima, Tsugaru and La Perouse. The length of the way from these straits to Vladivostok is nearly the same, namely about 450 miles, but in a geographical position the signification of these ways is quite different. At a very near distance from Tsushima Strait is the chief military port, Sasebo. In this manner, forcing our way through the Tsushima Strait, the Japanese fleet leaned on its chief base.

Expecting our forcing the way through the Tsushima Strait, the Japanese fleet could quietly lie at anchor near Sasebo; they could quietly prepare themselves for the coming battle, put their ships in a more advantageous condition for battle, leaving all the extra and harmful articles in the port. Thanks to their anchoring place near their base, the ships of the Japanese fleet at the time of their battle could have all their machinery and boilers in full order and cleanliness. Being near the base the Japanese were able to concentrate themselves and have in readiness a complete number of torpedo boats. At our forcing the way through the Tsushima Strait, the Japanese had the full possibility of watching the movement of our fleet at its approaching the strait, not in the least showing their presence or the place where they were stationed, or the number of their chief forces. Besides, the Japanese had the following advantage, which ought to have been foreseen: the north Chinese sea, extending to the north, is bordered from the east by a group of islands. Tivu-Kiou, then by the islands of which Japan is formed, from the west, by the island Quelpart, by the islands of the Korea archipelago and by the continent of the peninsula of Korea. Such a position of the Japanese permitted them to arrange on these islands many stations of observation, provided with wireless telegraphy. Cruisers and commercial steamers could continually communicate to the chief Japanese forces all the movements of our squadron. The enemy knew exactly the hour our squadron would appear, and he had only to choose the most convenient place and time for beginning the battle. To all these advantages which the Japanese fleet acquired, through our forcing the way through the Tsushima Strait, it is necessary to add several others. For example, the nearness of the base allowed the Japanese to have their crew not fatigued, and to take away the sick.

The Russian squadrons would have found themselves in another position, if they had chosen the way through La Perouse Straits, at a distance of 500 miles from the chief base of the Japanese. Here on this coast, there are no fleets, either military or commercial, and no port. In this manner of the Russians forcing their way through La Perouse Straits, both the fleets would have been in a more or less equal condition. In the month of May, in La Perouse Straits, along the coast of Tartar Strait and near Vladivostok, there are very thick fogs, which would have given us the opportunity to go to Vladivostok, even without meeting the Japanese.

At our moving through La Perouse Straits, the Japanese would have had to spend a great deal of energy and materials to defend their ships from attacks of our torpedo boats, which could come out from Vladivostok and hide in one of the numerous bays on our coast, waiting for a convenient opportunity for attacking. Without doubt coming out of La Perouse Strait, we should not have met those fresh and well-formed forces, which appeared before us in the Korea Strait. On approaching the Korea Strait, we had no news of the enemy, whereas Saghalin gave as the full possibility of organising there several watch posts, from which by means of steam cutters, sloops and coasters, we could have instituted the delivery of news of the enemy in different places, fixed upon beforehand, along the east and west coasts of Saghalin.

If the Admiral of the fleet had effected a conference with me, or some other person, he would no doubt have met with many indications of the utter impossibility of going through Tsushima Straits. I think that Admiral Rojestvensky had no moral right to use his absolute and individual power to undertake such an important decision. Placing us in the position of blind instruments of his will, he forced many to sacrifice their lives for the Tsushima battle, and others left living, like myself, destined to heavier torments.

4. Entering the Korea Strait, Admiral Rojestvensky, sent his reconnoitring ships before him, and therefore took no precautions against any unexpected meetings with the enemy; and no measures were taken to hinder the enemy from communicating to each other by telegraph. The 26 May, just before the battle, he forced us to drill the sailors twice, which fatigued the crew quite uselessly before the battle.

5. Overloading of ships. All the ships of the squadron, by the direction of Admiral Rojestvensky, were surcharged to the highest degree. We took in coal in such great quantities that the armour on the water-line was sunk about two feet in the water. In view of such loading, the ships were armoured on the water-line only verbally.

In reality this most important part was as undefended against the enemy's ships as any merchant ship or transport. The coal was not only in the bunkers and stokers' mess deck and passages, but also in the raised floors of the crew on deck, in the officers' cabins and on the upper deck. In the small armoured ships, coal was loaded even in the captains' cabins. The battleship *Apraksin,* on 28 May, in the morning after the battle and after the attacks of the torpedo boats during the night, still had coal 20 per cent more than the normal quantity appointed for her. It is clear that such overloading of the ships in connection with the weed-grown parts under water hindered the ships from going their proper speeds. For instance, the battleship *Nicolai I,* with the highest pressure of the boilers and machinery, could not go more than 12 knots an hour. This is the sad condition that our ships were in during the battle. The question arises involuntary – what incited Admiral Rojestvensky always to load the ships with coal? According to our calculation – beginning the battle – we had coal for 3,000 miles, whereas the way through Tsushima Strait is less than 900 miles. What sense was there in such loading, and does it not appear a shocking mistake?

6. Fires. In considering the breaking out of fires, I find that I am right in saying that the commander of the fleet took no precaution to overcome fires. I affirm that before the squadron began the battle, it was necessary to remove all the wooden parts of the interior furnishing of the ship, all the structures and superstructions, leaving only the necessary quantity for making up holes. All the rest of the woodwork ought to have been taken to pieces and transferred to the transport. Was this done by Admiral Rojestvensky? No, it was not! Only the ships of my division executed this, according to my order, and, of the other battleships, only *Orel* was cleared from inflammable materials by the initiative of her captain, not by the directions of Admiral Rojestvensky. The result of his attention to his work we see before us.

On the ships of my division there were no fires at all, or they were so trifling that they were extinguished immediately with water, with which all the compartments of my ships were plentifully provided. Quite the contrary happened with the other battleships. Very soon after the beginning of the battle, *Kniaz Suvaroff, Sisoi Veliki, Borodino, Alexander III* took fire. Especially the fire on *Kniaz Suvaroff* was great. I saw this fire personally. It began from the fore charthouse, which burned like a wooden hut. Fiery tongues rushed out of the windows. Soon the fire began to spread aft. The wooden boats, stern cabins, and woodwork gave plentiful food for the fires – a little more and all the battleship was in flames. It is difficult to imagine what destruction a fire brings to a ship. How many people perished in the flames? From the fire all the artillery of the battleships was spoiled. Is it not clear that on the eve of the battle, Admiral Rojestvensky ought to have given orders to remove all the wood from the ships?

7. Capsizing of ships. I have had already the honour to explain that during the battle one ship after another heeled and sank into the water, turning bottom upwards. Thousands of men perished at once without having time to harm the enemy. I am sure that our ships perished on account of their being overloaded with coal, and also, according to the directions of the commander of the fleet, there were too many machines and capstans, and it is owing to this that our ships had no stability.

Besides this, to extinguish the fires, they poured water; and the absence of the scuppers gave no possibility for the water to disappear. Gradually a heavy weight formed above the waterline, and the ships turned over.

8. Only between five and six in the evening, when I was already going to Vladivostok, I received the confirmation of my decision. How must one designate this kind of commanding? Before the battle no one was acquainted with the plan; during the battle no one gave any directions. Not one conference with us before the battle. Choosing the way to Vladivostok through the Tsushima Strait without warning us about it, even on the eve of the battle. Not

one order about the battle, neither on the eve of the war operation, nor during it. The overloading of the ships, the wood not taken away, the fires, the turning over of the ships, the overburdening by the transports, the division of the cruisers and torpedo-boats wasted uselessly.

Having pointed out the actions of Rojestvensky, I shall say a few words about Admiral Enkqist, who had the duty of guarding the transports. Where did Enkqist disappear during the battle? Did he take part in it, did he help us during the night attacks against the Japanese torpedo-boats?

Reading the reports of Admiral Enkqist, we see that according to his words he tried several times to break through the line of the enemy's battleships and cruisers, to pass to the north but had to reject this object 'on account of the continual attacks'.

In this manner, Admiral Enkqist 'on account of the continual attacks', went away to Manila. The question is, what battleships and cruisers of the enemy stopped his way to the north?

Now it is certain that at sunset the enemy's battleships and cruisers went to the east, to the Japanese coasts, and did not hinder our ships from sailing further to the north, the best proof is the moving thither of my division. We know that during the night battle we were attacked only by torpedo boats. During such a battle the cruiser division would have been especially desirable, as the cruisers possess great speed and a quantity of quick-firing artillery. If the cruisers of Admiral Enkqist's divisions had defended the end of the rear column following me, we should not have lost so many ships in the night attack. Nothing, in my opinion, hindered Admiral Enkqist from remaining with me, like the cruiser *Izumrud*. As he was under my command from six o'clock in the evening, he had no right, according to military law, to leave me and go away to Manila without my permission.

The picture of the battle, described by me, is less than the reality, less than the horrors seen by me.

All that I have stated above has been represented by me not with the object of making anybody's position worse, but to prove and establish the fact that, at dawn of 28 May, I found myself in a most fearful position through no heedlessness of mine, but by will of others and reasons independent of me. From the time I joined Admiral Rojestvensky, I was his subordinate. He placed me in the position of a blind instrument, and only in the character of a blind instrument I can be answerable before society and before the world. I declare and confess with pride that while I was independent I did not err in any way against my duty as a sailor. Leaving Libau, I safely bore with the squadron all the difficulties of sailing to the tropical sea. I avoided all complications that I met on my way. Moving towards Admiral Rojestvensky, I made the passage from Libau to Kamarahn in the shortest time, not losing one extra day. I brought my squadron to Admiral Rojestvensky in proper order. Foreseeing the torpedo attack, I taught my squadron to defend themselves from them by moving in darkness. Foreseeing the possibility of fires, I had all the wood taken off from the ships before the battle. By continual drilling and military education I brought the collected crew to know their duty as sailors. Other ships burned, turned over, perished from torpedo attacks: mine did not. Meeting the enemy 27 May, I made him bear a considerable loss. Not receiving any directions on 27 May, I did not rush towards the coast to go on shore, neither did I go to Manila. I obeyed the one order of Admiral Rojestvensky to go forward to Vladivostok and was going there without stopping

The cruisers and torpedo boats left me and I moved alone. At dawn of May 28 all Admiral Rojestvensky's squadron, that was under his command was dispersed, destroyed, and I remained alone at my post. If there had been fogs, if the Japanese ships had had less speed, if I had had at my disposal proper sea-going warships and not coast-ships overloaded with coal, I could have gone to Vladivostok. If I had had better guns, even equal to the Japanese gnus, I could have begun the battle, and my officers and crew would have known how to die in a battle together with me. Unhappily circumstances were different. A curse lay on us for other people's guilt.

From the point of view of my judges, who have sentenced me to a disgraceful punishment, I ought to have blown up the ships in the open sea, and turned 2,000 sailors into bloody pieces. I ought to have opened the Kingstons and drowned 2,000 men in a few minutes. In the name of what? In honour of the Andrew flag?

But this flag represents the symbol of that Russia, which, imbued with the sense of the duty of a great nation, preserves the dignity and life of her sons, but does not send them to their death in old ships in order to hide and drown in the sea moral bankruptcy and plunder, incapable service, errors, mental blindness and dark ignorance of the elementary principles of the naval art. For the representatives of such a Russia I had no right to drown 2,000 men.

THE BALTIC FLEET AS SEEN
BY ITS AUXILIARIES

by Henry Reuterdahl

Associate United States Naval Institute

from *Jane's Fighting Ships 1904–7*

As very few details regarding the personnel of Rojestvensky's
ill-fated fleet are to be found published, it may be very
interesting to have recorded the impressions of some of
those Germans and Dutch who served on board the sea
going tug-boats, *Russ* and *Sviet*, from Libau to the very
last, the debacle at Tsushima. Last fall I had the luck
to come across these men and to hear their experiences.
What I have got together here is not the mere yarn of
one man, but a carefully verified version of what they all
had to say about their unique experiences as onlookers in
the strangest drama ever witnessed. All were agreed on the
main details here recorded. To them, at least, Tsushima was
no surprise.

During the eight months' journey they had very full
opportunities to witness and observe the motley collection
of Russian seamen, and the incapacity from admiral to
stoker, never before perhaps observed in the whole world,
unless in the Turkish Navy. For from the time the fleet left
Libau, these two tug-boats were in constant attendance,
pulling the destroyers, and at other times the big ships,
which often were 'lame ducks' from engine room defects.
This indeed was little to be wondered at, seeing that the
engineers were from factories and railroads, of whom some
had never before been to sea, and others not much. The
sailors also were conscripts from inland towns, and of these
also, to many, the sight of the sea had been previously
unknown. Of the officers it may be said that they were

always phlegmatic and calm when they were sober, but excited when drunk.

The *Russ*, on leaving Port Alexander III, Libau, went to Kiel for provisions, thus separating from the main fleet, and going through the Kiel canal rejoined the Russian main fleet off Brest. From there on it was a crawl towards the south, the tugs towing the torpedo craft most of the time.

During all this journey to Madagascar there was never any attempt to practise with the guns, the only practice being with tube cannon. And, during the whole of the cruise from Libau to Tsushima, not once was there fired one medium or heavy gun in target practice, indeed none of the new ships had fired their guns at all sinoe their gunnery trials.

It was during the stay at Madagascar, that the revolutionaries first appeared strongly in the fleet, several court martials being held, but the statement that they were hanged is incorrect, because the custom was to send them back to the Black Sea naval prisons. On board the flagship there was hanged one white man, who it was reported had been found to be in the pay of the Japanese and sending information to them.

The discipline here was very lax indeed, the men answering back to their officers and always very sullen, especially so when drunk. Drink was always to be obtained in abundance it seemed from the German colliers, where the market price was fifteen marks per bottle. The officers were always armed with revolvers, which they flourished conspicuously at the least sign of insubordination. The clothes of the men were in miserable condition, having no kind of uniformity, some nearly in rags. Their shoes were all worn out, and at Madagascar they obtained sandals from the natives.

For convenience of the officers there were kept on board the ship many cows and sheep with which the men herded, adding much to the dirty condition of the ships, which were in places like farmyards as much as ships.

While the fleet was here, there was a few times practice with the small quick-firers at targets, but no firing of big guns, or sign of war, except that at night when the fleet was anchored a patrol was kept with two cruisers using searchlights.

At Madagascar, the coal was transhipped from the colliers to the German liners which accompanied the fleet, and all the battleships took very large deck loads of coal, both on the upper decks and between decks in every possible place in sacks.

From Madagascar, course was shaped to the Indian Ocean, and of that there is little to say, except that the big ships could not keep station, and in bad weather were continually leaking.

The speed of the fleet in ordinary weather was about ten knots and, in spite of this slow speed, the ships of the *Alexander* class could with difficulty keep station, and continually were falling behind. The stoking was always bad, most of the stokers being conscript landsmen, quite untrained. In fact the entire engine room force was poor throughout the fleet, and at Madagascar, the German engineers of the colliers and transports were continually called for consultation, while repairs were being made, without which assistance some of the ships would never have got any further.

Sometimes in the Indian Ocean the transports would stop and the destroyers go alongside them to coal, when the big ship would proceed alone, leaving the cruisers and auxiliaries to crawl after them. In this way the fleet was often much scattered.

At Cameron Bay, Nebogatoff joined with his old ships of the third squadron, generally in a better state, so far as was noticed, than the first and second squadrons. Of the stay there is nothing else fresh to say, except that here the revolutionaries became more ugly tempered than before, growing daily more openly mutinous, without however, the officers exercising more control than before, except by showing revolvers more freely.

The best story of the battle was given me verbatim as follows:

It was on Saturday, the 27th of May, that we first saw the Japanese. There was a strong breeze and heavy sea, rising almost to a gale, and on the starboard bow was a Japanese cruiser which stayed there observing until eleven o'clock, when it was joined by three other cruisers, which also observed us, closing in. Our fleet then opened fire for the first time, which the Japanese answered, doing no harm to the Russian ships or receiving any damage themselves that I could see.

We shaped course for Tsushima, the twelve armoured ships in two columns ahead, followed by the transports, and on each beam the cruisers succeeded by destroyers and the tugs.

At 2.30 the Japanese were firing, and the Russian battleships answered. Before three o'clock the *Osliabia* and *Suvaroff* were burning, and our lines broken.

The Japanese were quick to notice the helpless position of the cruisers and auxiliaries, and at once detached their armoured cruiser squadron to cut us off. Shot began to fall all around us, the transports being the sole target for the detached squadron.

Till now the battle bad been well ahead of us, but when the detached squadron attacked us the battle fleet turned about and came down back to us, the heavy ships forming a circle all around the transports so as to protect these auxiliaries. Before, however, this formation could be completed the Japanese with incredible speed changed also, and formed a great outer circle round the entire Russian forces. So here were we, going round and round, outside in the fog the Japanese ships, hardly to be perceived and sometimes not to he perceived at all; inside the next circle our battleships steaming round and round, firing back at the flashes in the fog, themselves in bright light; inside again the cruisers also in a circle; inside again the transports, and behind them the destroyers and tugs, all driven together like sheep inside a fold and no ship making any attempt to got out.

On all the Russians the sun was shining brightly, but the fog completely hid the Japanese, going round and round outside, firing very heavily, mainly at the four battleships, *Suvaroff, Borodino, Orel* and *Alexander*, and on the Nebogatoff battleship of the third fleet. The *Osliabia* steamed about without any masts or funnels, a quite bare hull burning fiercely, but still firing till she was torpedoed and sank with all hands. Then near us a Russian torpedo boat suddenly sank without a soul being saved. Right before my eyes I saw a Japanese cruiser and also a Japanese armoured cruiser sink.[1] This has been stated and denied, but at times the small Japanese cruisers came up quite close to the Russian battleships firing, their flags plainly visible, and I distinctly watched two sink. No Japanese battleships were ever visible from the *Russ*.

About four o'clock the *Russ* was hit and began to sink, and all the crew abandoned ship in the boat, and we were later picked up by the *Sviet*.

Now the Japanese formed a circle round the entire Russian fleet, firing front every point of the compass into the mass. The Russians tried to break through but failed, for at dusk it was still the same, the Russians bunched in a heap, without much order, and several ships on fire; it was only darkness that helped the Russian transports and cruisers to escape. We could then see nothing more of

---

1 Suggested sinking Russians which had hoisted Japanese flag. All the men stuck to this story.

the main fleet, and we knew nothing of it till we came to Shanghai, for the smoke after four o'clock became too thick to see anything in it. The *Ural* (ex-liner *Maria Theresa)* was badly shelled at half-past four, and her crew took to the boats leaving behind the wounded, but all the holy *ikons* were carefully put into the captain's boat.

The tug *Sviet,* the transports *Anadir, Belgia, Irkitok* and *Corea,* escaped to the south, conveyed at first by Enkqist's cruisers (which later went to Manila) and reached Shanghai.

The battle in my opinion was lost for various reasons, of which the following are some: because they had no scouts out, the ships were not honestly built, the crews were landsmen, they had no big gun practice, and none ever seemed to realise, that they were going to battle. They were all a most hopelessly incompetent lot, with no idea about anything whatever except praying, of which they did an enormous amount at the least sign of bad weather.

COMMENTS ON TSUSHIMA

by Admiral Sir J. O. Hopkins, G.C.B

from *Jane's Fighting Ships 1904-7*

It is fairly easy from the various accounts to gather the principles underlying Togo's attack, and once more we see history repeating itself, by the, victor on this occasion throwing the weight of his attack upon a portion of the enemy's van, whilst threatening the rear with his lighter vessels.

And apparently Togo followed out in respect to Rojestvensky the ancient instructions of the King of Syria, to his captains, 'Fight, neither with small or great, save only with the King of Israel,' by seeking out the Russian Admiral at the head of his column, and concentrating his guns on the leading ships, to their ultimate destruction.

The second day's disaster to the Russians – for their night losses by torpedo-boats and destroyers do not appear heavy – was the result of the able manner whereby the Japanese kept touch of their enemy and appearing next morning in force at the psychological moment, had them at their mercy, when dictates of humanity counselled surrender by the Russian Admiral.

Rear Admiral Nebogatoff's narrative of the battle of Tsushima throws a new sidelight on that action, and it must be acknowledged that from his point of view the final bloodless surrender was actuated by the noble motive of not uselessly sacrificing life by a prolonged and unprofitable struggle which could only have ended in useless bloodshedding, and his moral courage in so acting will doubtless be borne out by the verdict of posterity.

Once again we gather from this article that the head of Admiral Rojestvensky's column was the enemy's objective, and that Nebogatoff's ships (which occupied a rear position) were little damaged in the earlier stages of the action.

From Nebogatoff's showing, the 'comradeship' which is so great a factor in the efficiency of fleets was conspicuous by its absence, and Rojestvensky's want of this accessory quality, his faulty dispositions, the absence of any tactical skill and his mania for carrying in the fighting units of his fleet inordinate loads of coal helped to produce the fiasco which overtook him.

Of tactics generally there is little mention, but it is clear that the Japanese took up the positions that best suited them, were not pushed from them, and pounded their opponents as they best pleased; important factors in the case being superior speed, superior marksmanship, and better ranging guns, and further may be pointed out the enormous advantage of fighting with well-trained veterans united to the sea by the experiences of years, versus recently raised conscripts with but little experience of blue water and lacking the *esprit de corps* and cohesion of long service.

The general lessons to be deduced from the two days' fighting have been ably told by various writers, but it may be beneficial to discuss once more a few of the salient features of the combat, and particularly those which affect the devolution of the battleship in respect to armament and speed.

With reference to the former, the *Dreadnought* is undoubtedly the outcome of the school of thought which foresees the battle of the future being fought at very long ranges, and consequently aims its ship to deliver crushing and armour-piercing blows from all its weapons at extreme ranges, and if all naval battles are in the future to be fought outside 7,000 yards, this armament of 12-inch guns seems common sense.

But who can guarantee this, and may not future admirals close in – as Togo is said to have done – to 4,000 yards when a quicker firing and more numerous armament of lighter guns, such as the 9.2 in the *Lord Nelson* class and carried as an auxiliary to the four 12 inch, may prove more effective.

And if we accept *Dreadnought*'s tonnage for future *Lord Nelsons* they can probably be armed with six 12-inch and ten 9.2-inch, the latter a most formidable weapon, equal in range and accuracy to the 12-inch and capable of piercing at 5,000 yards 10 inches of Krupp armour, or in other words, one inch more than the penetration of the 13.5-inch guns at that range.

Then in regard to speed, though certain naval writers infer that Togo did not benefit in this respect, can we ignore the fact that his superiority in this gave him the option of choosing his position, and must have added largely to the moral force which the 'weather gauge' affords to every combatant who possesses it, and a large section of the Naval world will rejoice in the fact of *Dreadnought*'s 20 or 21 knots as another proof of an up-to-date design.

It only remains to add a few words in recognition of the organization, patriotism, and 'do or die' methods of the Japanese, which, with their sea experiences, made for special qualifications in the business of warfare, but what served them best of all was their undoubted superiority in shooting, especially at long ranges Doubtless, too, their fire control was excellent, and the concentration at will of their guns upon any particular unit was irresistible.

Then Togo, without under-valuing his opponents, apparently, realized their limitations, and, like Nelson, took full advantage of his intuitive grasp of affairs.

It is by no means clear that the smaller guns in the Japanese fleet did not materially advance the fortunes of the day, as their 12-inch guns were not numerous, and, in point of fact, numerically inferior to those of the Russian squadron, which should with better marksmanship have made a more equal fight of it.

THE FATE OF THE RUSSIAN SHIPS AT TSUSHIMA

Monsieur I. Bertin

Late Chief Constructor, French Navy

from *Jane's Fighting Ships 1904–7*

I feel very sorry to answer so unsatisfactorily the request of *Fighting Ships*. It is the lack of sure and precise information concerning the loading (*chargement*) of the unfortunate Russian ships engaged at Tsushima, as well as knowledge as to the exact nature of the damages their hulls had suffered before they capsized, which prevents my writing fully.

It is really impossible for me to determine up to what point the catastrophe has confirmed those fears which I have always expressed, especially during the last fifteen years, as to the security of this type of 'fighting ship'. I can only say that the facts seem to have confirmed my fears.

I am completely ignorant as to how much of the conception of the *Tsesarevitch* was of Russian origin, and how much belongs to French constructive ideas, and I do not think that this last ship served particularly as prototype to the other Russian battleships of the *Borodino* class which perished at Tsushima. These battleships, in substance, represented a type common to nearly all navies up to a very recent date.

Models like the *Lord Nelson* and *République* are in each case exempt from the unhappy defects contained in the units of Rojestvensky's fleet. But do not conclude from that any advantage of priority in favour of the *République*. The improvement of English models goes back so far as the laying down of the *Majestic* after the plans of Sir William White.

AFTERWORD

One evening, I was pacing slowly to and fro athwart the station platform at Irkutsk, thinking regretfully, yet philosophically, of the thousands of gallant dead upon the Plains of Liaoyang, when a woman's quick sob at my elbow pulled me out of my smug meditation into the reality of death and suffering. She was a poor woman, decently dressed in black, with a puling infant, swaddled in a shawl, close-huddled to her bosom. I followed her along the creaking platform, watching her as she passed through the glare from the windows of the buffet into the blackness of the intervening shadows. Creeping into the station hall she paused for a moment irresolute, with wide-open, dumb, imploring eyes, seeking for comfort yet expecting none. Seeing me she tendered a card she had carried in her tight-clenched mother's hand. It was a postcard with a gaudy representation in blue, and red, and yellow, of a giant Russian guardsman bayoneting a wizened Japanese. Beneath it were scrawled a few words in Russian. To me she murmured something in the language of the people, and I, for the thousandth time, murmured my stock phrase in reply: 'I do not understand Russian.'

There was a friend of mine, a long-coated captain of artillery, clanking impatiently up and down the room. I led her to him and explained my inability to assist her in her trouble. He was a big, loud-voiced man, newly back from the bluster and brutality of battle. He glared for a moment at the woman who dared to interrupt his musing, but out of courtesy to me took the card and studied it. The heavy figures of peasants stretched upon the floor watched wonderingly. A railway official hurried about his business.

The officer shifted uneasily, cleared his throat, re-arranged his swordbelt. The woman stood patiently waiting. His voice had grown strangely soft when he answered in Russian that even I could understand: 'Your husband was killed at Tashichiao on July the eleventh.' The salt despair was welling out of the woman's eyes as he spoke. 'Yes, my child – he has done his duty – to his Tsar.'

The officer crossed himself, and a broken figure in rusty black went tottering blindly down the steps and into the fog and darkness of Irkutsk.

My captain of artillery sought his sleeve cuff for his handkerchief, speaking angrily as though someone had insulted him: 'She could not read. God! Sir, it is like sentencing a man to be hanged to answer such a question. God help the woman and her children!'

And he too, strode into the darkness.

The Campaign with Kuropatkin,
Douglas Story

BIBLIOGRAPHY

Vladimir Semenoff: Rasplata: The Reckoning (1909).
   The Battle of Tsu-Shima (1906).
   The Price of Blood (1910).

A. Novikoff-Priboy: Tsu-Shima (1936).

E. S. Poliofsky: From Libau to Tsu-Shima (1906).

Nicholas Klado: The Battle of the Sea of Japan (1906).
   The Russian Navy in the Russo-Japanese War (1905).

Fred T. Jane: Heresies of Sea Power (1906).
   The Imperial Russian Navy (1909).
   Jane's Fighting Ships (1903-7).
   The Imperial Japanese Navy (1904).

Various Authors: Cassell's History of the Russo-Japanese War
   (1905-6).

G. A. Falk: Togo and the Rise of Japanese Sea Power (1906).

R. V. C. Bodley: Admiral Togo; the authorised Life of Admiral
   of the Fleet, Marquis Heihachiro Togo, O.M. (1936).

H. W. Wilson: Battleships in Action (1926).

Admiral Sir Reginald Custance: The Ship of the Line in Battle
   (1912).

Admiral of the Fleet Lord Fisher: Memories and Records
   (1919).

E. Sharpe Grew: War in the Far East (1906).

F. Green and H. Frost: Some Famous Sea Fights (1927).

J. Cresswell: Naval Warfare: an introductory study (1936).

Committee of Imperial Defence: Official History of the Russo-
   Japanese War (1910).

David Divine: The Story of Sea Warfare (1957).

J. R. Hale: Famous Sea Fights from Salamis to Tsu-Shima
   (1911).

A. P. Steer: The 'Novik' and the Part she Played in the Russo-
   Japanese War (1913).

G. A. Ballard: The Influence of the Sea on the Political
  History of Japan (1921).
  Cambridge Modern History.

H. C. S. Wright: The Life of Togo (1907).
  With Togo (1905).

Captain Kichitaro Togo: The Naval Battles of the Russo-
  Japanese War.

George Blond: Admiral Togo (New York 1960)

R. C. Hargreaves: Red Sun Rising: Siege of Port Arthur
  (London 1962)

Shumpei Okamoto: The Japanese Oligarchy and the Russo-
  Japanese War (New York 1970)

A. D. Walder: The Short Victorious War: The Russo-Japanese
  Conflict 1904-5 (London 1973)

Newspapers, Periodicals, Papers, etc.

The Times.

The Illustrated London News.

The Sphere.

The Morning Post.

Blackwoods Magazine.

Journal of the Royal United Services Institution.

The Natal Mercury.

United States Naval Institute Proceedings.

Nauticus.

Royal United Service Journal.

Royal Naval Attachés' reports on the Battle of Tsu-Shima.

Papers captured from the Russians by the Japanese and
  re-translated from the Japanese by G. V. Rayment.

Fleet Orders of Rear-Admiral Z. P. Rozhestvensky.

Pages from the diary of an officer of the battleship *Sisoy Veliky*.